U.N. Universal Declaration of Human Rights and Criminal Justice

(The Total Revision)

About the Author

Dr. James Vadackumchery, Ph.D. is a noted author of more than 58 authentic and research books in the special areas of crime, police and justice and thus his name is in the Limca Book of Records-2006. He is the recipient of the Distinguished International Scholar Award for Lifetime Achievements (2003) of the American Society of Criminology. He has, to his credit, 1000 articles—both professional and popular—published. He is honoured for his insightful writings by the University of Calcutta with Suprabha Deb Gold Medal in 2007. He is a telecaster and broadcaster in Indian and international TV network. He has been a researcher throughout his professional life as criminologist (Professor) at the State Police Training College and during his research career, he has done noteworthy researches—both doctrinal and empirical—to develop a better system of justice administration. Dr. Vadackumchery has been the Member, Board of Studies in Universities, examiner for civil service and University examinations, public speaker, human rights activist, Member, State Prison Review Committee, teacher, Member, State Advisory Board on Correctional Administration, visiting professor in universities, police and judicial academies, banks including the Reserve Bank of India, institutes of higher education and training, public undertakings, consultant to police commissions and above all an iconoclast in every sense of the word.

U.N. Universal Declaration of Human Rights and Criminal Justice

(The Total Revision)

Dr. James Vadackumchery

CONCEPT PUBLISHING COMPANY PVT. LTD.
NEW DELHI-110059

ISBN-13: 978-81-8069-912-2

First Published 2012

Published and Printed by

Concept
Since 1974

Concept Publishing Company Pvt. Ltd.
A/15-16, Commercial Block, Mohan Garden
New Delhi-110059 (India)
T: 25351460, 25351794, *F*: 091-11-25357109
E: publishing@conceptpub.com, W: www.conceptpub.com
Editorial Office: H-13, Bali Nagar, New Delhi-110 015, India.

Cataloging in Publication Data--*Courtesy:* D.K. Agencies (P) Ltd. <docinfo@dkagencies.com>

Vadackumchery, James.
U.N. Universal Declaration of Human Rights and criminal justice : the total revision/ James Vadackumchery.
p. cm.
Includes bibliographical references (p.) and index.
ISBN 9788180699122

1. Human rights. 2. Criminal justice, Administration of. 3. United Nations. General Assembly. Universal Declaration of Human Rights. I. Title.

DDC 341.48 23

To

Anna, Maria and George

Preface

I had been to New York, U.S.A. in 1986 and visited the U.N. Headquarters. Indeed, a beautiful building !, and a huge structure when viewed it from outside. I entered the building and found that the building was not as beautiful as it was when viewed it from outside. I had a different impression about the 'inside' of the U.N. Headquarters and it was, in one way, formed from what I read and heard about the U.N. and its activities. Almost like that, I have a feeling about the Universal Declaration of Human Rights. On 10th, December, 1948, the UDHR was simply wonderful pregnant with ideals and concepts for a beautiful world ! How far or how much of those ideals and concepts was implemented or enforced in various parts of the world is a question of dispute! The Declaration, just like the U.N. Headquarters, was really beautiful once upon a time, but its implementation in reality was, as I saw the inside of the U.N. building, not as beautiful as it was thought of. Why? Take for example, the Protection of Human Rights Act enacted in 1993 in India. The oft-alleged criticism against it is that the Act has no teeth. Anybody can become a member of the Human Rights Commission if he has the needed political patronage and godfathering. Countries which talk loudly about the worth and value of human rights violate them purposefully and continuously and many nations in the world show a near total indifference to their activities and violations of human rights. Even the United Nations are viewed with suspicion as to the sincerity of their manifold activities for the enforcement of human rights(?) The operative part of the Declaration reads that all peoples and all nations, every individual and every organ of the society, should strive by teaching and education to promote respect for those rights and freedoms and by progressive measures, national and international, to secure their universal and effective recognition and observance, both among the peoples of Member States themselves and among the peoples of territories under their jurisdiction. Fantastic and fine indeed! When one views the advertisement, in the internet, for appointment of Human Rights Officers in various parts of the world where the UN has responsibility, he may be very much pleased to see the heavy demand for the services of human rights officers. In spite of their services, human rights violations take place lavishly. The mighty and the affluent nations violate human rights in plenty and people around them sing "HOSANA" for achieving their parochial interests actualised. Likewise, within a particular nation, human rights violations do occur and people clamour for the enforcement of human rights. Their cry in the wilderness is unattended and more often than not, the full enforcement of human rights has become a costly luxury or better, an unattainable task.

In the special and specific area of criminal justice administration, one observes a variety of human rights violations. Many are seen to be taking a tolerant attitude to the violations of human rights in the field of criminal justice administration. Why? Is it because the articles contained in the UDHR are sterile and ineffective for their meaningful implementation? Nearly sixty long years are now over since the UDHR has come into operation, nevertheless human rights violations are a recurring reality. The violators are not afraid of anybody - are accountable to nobody! The violators justify their otherwise illegal and many a time, immoral acts on flimsy grounds and ununderstandable principles. The Articles in the UDHR say many things which the enforcers at the operational level do not know, or better do not understand or care. Some of the Articles have very old and often rejected theories of jurisprudence behind them and that takes matters from bad to worse. It has become a fashion today to talk highly about human rights outwardly and mock at them inwardly.

Human rights are for human beings and many a time the human rights violators treat people as sub-human/less than human beings. These lesser mortals want iron hands to establish their rights. My attempt has been to help them to achieve their end. In my pursuit, I see the immediate need to revise and amend the UDHR so that matters must improve to the better.

About some 30 years ago, an engineering college student was butchered by a group of police officials who were making programmes to annihilate the Naxalite movement in Kerala State. No doubt, it was a human right violation and the UDHR was well in existence at that time. Some say that the body of the murdered was burnt to ashes by using petrol; others think that the corpse of the murdered was thrown into waters for disposal . . . and thus a dozen explanations are in vogue even now. Today (10-6-2006), I find a reputed Malayalam Daily bringing out several articles in a serialised manner and the investigative journalists ask the question: "What did you do with the body of the murdered?" According to them and their religious beliefs, they need to do some religious rites and *karmas* if the soul of the dead to get salvation. The father of the murdered engineering student asked: "Why do you still keep the dead body of my murdered son in the rain"? No Human Rights Commissions, no courts of law, no laws, no authorities seem to open their mouth to speak out the hidden truth. Human right to life is butchered and the victims of the abuse of power/ misuse of authority are kept still in darkness even after 30 long years of deep or purposeful silence. This may not be an isolated instance of human rights violations in the area of criminal justice administration. In spite of the UDHR in its glamour and grandeur, there take place informal arrests, illegal detention, unfair trials, false prosecutions, undue delay in trials, death in custody, torture and degrading treatment, prejudiced court actions, unjustified convictions, less justice administration, miscarriage of justice, indifferent acquittals, corporal punishments in correctional institutions, refusal to pay reasonable wages in prisons, etc., and the list of human rights violations is indeed long. What to do and how to go about to prevent human rights violations or at least to curtail their extent and intensity? In fact, this painful situation has prompted and motivated me to make suggestions for amendments and recommendations for the revision of the UDHR for the twenty-first century. The twentieth century UDHR has limited scope for the new century.

I have many dictionaries with me, but I find that the meanings, explanations and illustrations given in the Random House Colllege Dictionary are the best for the purpose of this book. I have consulted the same wherever necessary and all the meanings for the expressions/words in the UN documents have been explained in this book by the help of that dictionary only.

I must thank my wife who offered me abundant encouragement to think along with her for a better tomorrow. I thank Abhilash Varghese Koikara, Neethu, Martin Joseph Madathiparambil, Neethie, Anna, George and Maria for their appreciation in my work to create a new world order. When *Limca Book of Records* put my name in their 2006 edition, all of us together said "Hallelujah" to God. My name is in the Book of Record for authoring and publishing the most number of authentic and research titles in the special areas of crime, police and justice. *Ad Majorem Dei Gloria*. In 2007, the University of Calcutta honoured me with Suprabha Deb Gold Medal for the insightful writing.

Thiruvananthapuram,
November 20, 2011

Dr. James Vadackumchery,
Criminologist & Advocate

Contents

1

The Old may be Gold; But the Old is always Old

In 1948 when the United Nations brought out the Universal Declaration of Human Rights, it was felt to be a new thing and the novelty continued for some days, months, years and decades. All or many of the framers of the Declaration have already died and those who are alive today desire seriously to have a revision or at least to make some amendments to the existing UDHR which was resolved by the General Assembly of the United Nations on 10th, December, 1948. Who must do it? Or, what must be done ?

The Universal Declaration of Human Rights survived for more than 60 years means that it will survive for some years more. No doubt, it has withstood the test of time and people need it with amendments or revision so that it satisfies their aspirations. Mrs. Roosevelt, while the Universal Declaration came for deliberations in the General Assembly of the United Nations stated that the Declaration was "the first and foremost a declaration of the basic principles to serve as a common standard for all nations. It might well become the Magna Carta of all mankind". She stated further that its proclamation by the General Assembly "would be at importance comparable to the 1789 proclamation of the Declaration of Independence of the United States of America, and similar Declarations made in other countries". It may be remembered that the Magna Carta of 1215, the Bill of Rights of 1689, the Habeas Corpus Act and the strong determination that "To none will we sell, deny or delay the right or justice"—all those, though sublime and lofty at that time and even now, have become part of history. The French Declaration of the Rights of Man and Citizens of 1789 and the American Bill of Rights of 1789—became historically important documents today. Yes, they are gold but old.

"The aim of all political association is the conservation of the natural and inalienable rights of man. These rights are: *liberty, property, security and resistance to oppression*. One sees so in the French Declaration along with a number of other rights for the people and they include (*i*) all men are born and remain free and equal in their rights, (2) all men are equal before the law, (3) all men should have the freedom from arrest, and (4) all men are innocent until they are proved guilty, etc. No doubt, they are forerunners or precursors of the presently upheld human rights. As time got elapsed, the concepts and ideas too got changed. For example, even today, the accusatorial system of justice presumes that all men are innocent until proved guilty. I have my strong objection to such a presumption. Being innocent and proving guilty–both are two different things. Suppose, one is not able to prove the guilt of the other, it does not mean that the other is innocent or not guilty. Hence, I may say that the presumption is faulty, however sweet it may be to hear. The presumption should be certainly different from what the United Nations hold today. This will be further discussed elaborately later in this book.

The Americans, as early as in 1774 said that the colonies had derived their rights from the immutable laws of nature. They further stated: "We hold these truths to be self-evident that, all men are created equal, that they are endowed by their creator with certain inalienable rights, that these are life, liberty and pursuit of happiness". The concepts of *creation and creatorship*, etc. are points of dispute today and in the Universal Declaration of Human Rights, the world community did make an honest attempt to make it more perfect. Certainly, it needs further perfection and still further perfection and the process of perfecting the Universal Declaration of Human Rights should and will continue until man lives in this world. The American Declaration made their rights clear and they were the rights to life, liberty and pursuit of happiness and asserted that "to secure these rights, Governments are instituted among men, deriving their just powers from the consent of the governed; that whenever any form of Government becomes destructive of these ends, it is the right of the people to alter or abolish it...". The American Declaration did not say specifically anything about the dignity of man, but today the human rights laws give great importance to the dignity of man just like they give it to the right to life, equality and liberty. Every man is born with dignity and such a birth should be honoured.

The Universal Declaration of Human Rights-1948 must undergo revision and must be amended to include more rights/ to delete the unwanted ones. The Constitution of India which came into existence in 1950 [i.e., two years after UDHR] claimed to be one of the best in the world when it was enacted. Nevertheless, it was amended several times in an honest pursuit to make it perfect—to suit to the aspirations of more than one hundred crore of people in India. Even today, amendments are thought of, suggested, discussed and enforced and all are for the better. There are interested people to do so in every country. Frustratingly enough, such amendments do not take place in the case of Universal Declaration of Human Rights. In seminars and symposia, people speak about the INFALLIBILITY of the UDHR. What is infallibility? It means "exempt from liability to error, as persons, their judgment, pronouncements, etc.". I, for one, do not think that the Articles (rules) contained in the UDHR are infallible ones. Catholic Church speaks of the infallibility of the Pope, i.e., immune from fallacy or error in expounding matters of faith or morals. That is altogether a different thing and the UDHR is not dealing with a matter of faith or morals as the Catholic Church does. Whatever that be, the UDHR needs a thorough revision and in this book I am especially interested to make honest suggestions for a **Total Revision: The U.N.'s International Criminal Laws on Human Rights**. There may be—no, are—many areas with which the UN is concerned in the UDHR; but, as a criminologist committed to the cause of administering holistic justice—equal justice to the crime-doers, victims of crime/victims of the abuse of power and misuse of authority, to the society, and to the justice system, I am enthusiastically interested in making some suggestions for the international community to ponder over and discuss in the days to come. I do not find many thinking in this direction and that is the sole reason why I take up the initiative hoping that the world moves to the better always. We must reach the OMEGA.

I notice 30 Articles in the UDHR and some of them are directly concerned with the administration of criminal justice while some others are indirectly concerned with the administration of criminal justice. The chapters that follow discuss them in detail, but as a prelude to such discussions, I may say that the criminal justice is not something in itself, rather is a part of the whole, the whole being administration of all types of justices with very many descriptions. Human rights laws must take into account the victim justice, juvenile justice, gender justice, administrative justice, social justice, equal justice, distributive justice, justice to women, to the handicapped, to the old and infirm, to the coloured, to the caste-ridden and so on when criminal justice is administered. I have my own doubts whether or not the UDHR-1948 had kept in mind these truths when it was drafted during the latter half of the 1940s. Perhaps, these new concepts are of recent origin and, therefore, the framers of the UDHR-1948 did not think seriously the ramifications, effects and impact of the Articles in the UDHR-1948 on various types of justices during criminal justice administration. The old concepts on which the criminal justice jurisprudence has been constructed need immediate alterations, additions, deletions and amendments. The museum piece Articles, if any in the UDHR-1948, must be deleted and new concepts in administration of criminal justice must be added. Perhaps, the suggestions may make the Articles more in number and I am certain that some individuals may express protests and show their resistance. Does not matter, yet they must be amended. An idea changes or can change the whole world and brings out a newer world order. An idea destroys the world, defeats many ideas of sublime thinkers, damages the whole edifice of human rights concepts. Hence, let us think together whether or not the old ideas are to be changed or polished or put in new bottles for the generations to enjoy in the new century in the new millennium.

2

Recognition: Difference from Acceptance and Acting Upon

"And, thus the Universal Declaration of Human Rights are adopted and proclaimed by the General Assembly [Resolution 217 A(III) of 10th December, 1948]"—I wrote so in my book titled *Human Rights and The Police* in India published in 1996. It was in 1993, India enacted the protection of Human Rights Act. More than six decades have elapsed since the Universal Declaration of Human Rights was proclaimed; nevertheless there has taken place no revision or amendments of the Articles in UDHR. Why? I do not know the reasons and at the same time, many people want the entire text to be revised *in toto*. According to them, "the old may be gold; but the old is always old". They need timely repairs. The law is dynamic and if so, the human rights laws too are dynamic. They need changes and amendments.

PREAMBLE simply means "an introductory part of a statute, deed or the like, stating the reasons and the intent of what follows" and the UDHR has a PREAMBLE. Yes, it reads–

> "Whereas recognition of the inherent dignity and of equal and inalienable rights of all members of the human family is the foundation of freedom, justice and peace in the world".

The many meanings given in the Random House College Dictionary for the word "recognize" are—

(i) to identify as something or someone previously seen, known, etc.
(ii) to identify from knowledge of appearance or characteristics.
(iii) to perceive as existing or true; realize.
(iv) to acknowledge as the person entitled to speak at a particular time.
(v) to acknowledge formally as entitled to treatment as a political entity.
(vi) to acknowledge or accept formally.
(vii) to acknowledge or treat as valid: to recognize a claim.
(viii) to acknowledge acquaintance with (someone that one meets).
(ix) to show appreciation of (achievement, service, merit, etc.), as by some reward, public honour, or the like.
(x) Law to acknowledge (an illegitimate child) as one's own.

Accordingly, the many meanings given to RECOGNITION in the same dictionary are–

1. the act of recognizing someone or something.
2. the state of being recognized.
3. the perception or acknowledgment of something as true or valid.
4. appreciation of achievements, merits, services, etc., or an expression of this.
5. formal acknowledgment of a person's right to speak at a particular time.
6. International Law. an official act by which one state acknowledges the existence of another state or government, or by belligerency or insurgency.

A microscopic reading of all meanings given in the dictionary may show many things, but the fact remains that RECOGNITION is different from ACCEPTANCE. ACCEPT in the same dictionary means–

1. to take or receive (something offered)
2. to agree, consent, or accede to; to accept an apology.
3. to respond or answer affirmatively to: to accept an invitation.

4. to undertake the duties, honours, etc., of: to accept the office of treasurer.
5. to receive or admit formally, as to membership.
6. to accommodate or reconcile oneself to: to accept a situation.
7. to regard as true or valid: believe.
8. to regard as normal, suitable, or usual.
9. to understand as having a meaning, etc.

The PREAMBLE states only about RECOGNITION and not ACCEPTANCE AND ACTING UPON. People may recognize many things, but need not necessarily accept them and act upon them. For example, a police officer may recognize the fact that everyone is equal before law, but will not accept it in his words and resultingly will not act upon it accordingly. What is the earthly use or benefit if one recognizes certain truth, but not prepared to accept and act upon it? Hence, I may emphatically say that the PREAMBLE of the Universal Declaration of Human Rights is not full or total. It must be—

> "Whereas recognition of the inherent dignity and of equal and inalienable rights of all members of the human society is the foundation of freedom, justice and peace; acceptance and acting upon it are essential for ensuring human happiness and social welfare in the world".

Does the recognition of the *inherent dignity and of equal and inalienable rights* of all members of the human society become the foundation of freedom, justice and peace? I do not think so. Why? Foundation means: "(1) that on which something is founded, (2) the basis or groundwork of anything: a moral foundation of society, (3) the natural or prepared ground or base on which some structure rests, (4) the lowest division of a building, wall or the like, usually of masonry and partly or wholly below the surface of the ground, (5) the act of founding, setting up, establishing, etc..." And *found* simply means to set up or establish on a firm basis or for enduring existence. No doubt, the foundation of freedom, justice and peace can be or should be many and, therefore, it should not be limited or restricted to the recognition of the inherent dignity and of equal and inalienable rights of all members of the society.

Of course, the recognition of the inherent dignity and of equal and inalienable rights of all members of human society is very essential, inevitable and necessary so much so that I will say that it is a *conditio-sine-qua-non* for establishing freedom, justice and peace in the world–that is all. Mere recognition is not enough and as I forcefully stated earlier, there should be the "acceptance and acting upon" too.

The expressions freedom, justice and peace are not couched in clarity. What do the United Nations think about the freedoms they talk about? Freedom means a lot and if the simple dictionary meaning of freedom is taken, then it will be:

1. state of being at liberty rather than in confinement or undue physical restraint.
2. exemption from external control, interference, regulation, etc.
3. power of determining one's or its own action.
4. (Philos) the power to make one's own choices or decisions without constraint from within or without; autonomy; self-determination.
5. civil liberty, as opposed to subjection to an arbitrary or despotic government.
6. political or national independence.
7. a particular privilege enjoyed, as by a city or corporation: freedom to levy taxes.
8. personal liberty, as opposed to slavery.
9. absence of or release from ties, obligations, etc.
10. exemption or immunity from the presence of anything specified (usually followed by *from*).
11. erase or facility of movement or action.
12. frankness of manner or speech.
13. absence of ceremony or reserve.
14. a liberty taken.
15. the right of enjoying all the privileges or special rights of citizenship, membership, etc.
16. the right to frequent, enjoy or use at will.

The Random House College Dictionary says further that "FREEDOM, INDEPENDENCE, LIBERTY refer to an absence of undue restrictions and an opportunity to exercise one's rights and powers. FREEDOM emphasizes the opportunity given for the exercise of one's rights, powers, desires or the like: freedom of speech or conscience; freedom of movement. Independence implies not only lack of restrictions but also the ability to stand alone, understand by anything else: Independence of thought promotes invention. LIBERTY, though most often interchanged with freedom, is also used to imply undue exercise of freedom. He took liberties with the text. Thus, going through the many and various meanings given in a single dictionary, I am totally confused about the freedoms spoken by the United Nations in the UDHR. The Constitution of India guarantees many fundamental freedoms to her citizens. Similarly, all Constitutions in all nations will be ensuring fundamental freedoms to their citizenry. There may be differences in the freedoms thus guaranteed by various Constitutions. When the United Nations (UDHR) speak about the "foundation of freedom", what do they mean by it? Do they mean all the "freedoms" given in a dictionary and enjoyed by people or denied to the people? Do they mean 'liberty' or 'independence'? One needs clarity and specificity to understand and appreciate the *freedoms* expressed in the UDHR-1948.

Justice is a nebulous term. I have brought out the vagueness/ confusion about justice in my books already published. The cloudy or cloudlike, indistinct, hazy, nebular (resembling a nebula or nebulae) nature of justice makes the PREAMBLE of the UDHR-1948 ununderstandable. Do the United Nations mean justice of all descriptions and every type? In other words, do they mean criminal justice, victim justice, economic justice, juvenile justice, political justice, administrative justice, total justice, equal justice, holistic justice, domestic justice, justice to women, to the old, to the infirm, to the handicapped, to the members of the Scheduled Castes and Scheduled Tribes, to the mentally handicapped or differentially abled? The litany of justices is very long and the recognition of the inherent dignity and of equal and inalienable rights of all members of the human society guarantees all these justices of various descriptions? If the UDHR means so, then it would say "justice of all types, nature and descriptions". It does not say so in the PREAMBLE and what is to be presumed by the man on the street?

Is justice a myth or reality? Some people including I say that it is only a myth. If that is true, then are we going forward to this myth?—i.e., a belief or a subject of belief whose truth or reality is accepted uncritically? A court of law convicts a person and an appeal court acquits him. Both have done justice (?). A country punishes the offenders by retributive theory while another country does the same thing by applying the philosophy of correction, reformation, rehabilitation, resocialization and reintegration to society. What is just here? What is considered as just today may be treated as unjust tomorrow. Likewise, what was treated as unjust yesterday is considered as just today and may be unjust tomorrow. What is justice then? A nation attacks another nation and it is justice for them and the history proves such just/ unjust attacks and aggression. Does the recognition of the inherent dignity and of equal and inalienable rights of all members of the human society ensure justice to people? If so, then the questions arise "(i) What is inherent human dignity?, (ii) What are the equal and inalienable human rights of all members of the human society?".

PEACE means a state of harmony among people or groups. It also means, (1) the freedom from disorder normal in a community, (2) cessation of or freedom from any strife or dissention, (3) freedom of the mind from annoyance, distraction, etc., (4) a state or condition conducive to proceeding from, or characterized by tranquillity, (5) silence; stillness. The first meaning given in the dictionary is: "the normal, nonwarring condition of a nation, a group of nations, of the world". United Nations have peacekeeping operations. They are nothing but "the maintenance of international peace and security through military force, as by operations in a particular area by the UN. Whatever that be, there is no doubt that the recognition, acceptance and acting upon the lofty and of equal and inalienable sublime principles by virtue of which the inherent human dignity and human rights are honoured will lead the people and nations to live in harmony and human co-existence. Putting everything together, why cannot the Preamble be revised or amended to read:

> "WHEREAS recognition of the inherent dignity and of equal and inalienable rights of all members of the human society is an absolute condition for establishing total and equal justice; visible acceptance and positive acting upon it are essential for ensuring human happiness, coexistence and social welfare in the world".

Why do I suggest so for the international community to discuss and deliberate? *Total and Equal* justice means holistic justice which includes human freedom, freedom of conscience, freedom of movement, peace, harmony, fairness, equity and what not? The philosophy and thinking when the UDHR-1948 has been drafted have changed a lot during the last six decades and precisely, therefore, it is time now to redraft/redefine the PREAMBLE of the UDHR-1948.

3

Failure, Refusal and Disregard to Honour Human Rights

BARBAROUS, OUTRAGE and CONSCIENCE OF MANKIND–they need to be understood, explained and appreciated if one wants to honour human dignity, person in the individual and human rights. In the PREAMBLE of the Universal Declaration of Human Rights, one sees the use of the words stated above. According to the PREAMBLE, "disregard and contempt for human rights have resulted in barbarous acts which have outraged the conscience of mankind". Disregard means "to pay no attention to; leave out of consideration; lack of regard or, attention; neglect, inattention, oversight, indifference, etc". Contempt means "(i) the feeling with which a person regards anything considered mean, vile, or worthless; disdain; scorn, (2) the state of being despised; dishonour; disgrace, (3) law: wilful disobedience to or open disrespect for the rules or orders of a court or legislative body". The Random House College Dictionary continues: "contempt, disdain, scorn imply strong feelings of disapproval combined with disgust or derision. Contempt is disapproval tinged with disgust for what seems mean, base or worthless. Disdain is a feeling that something is beneath the level of one's own dignity or is unworthy of one's notice or acceptance . . . Scorn denotes derisive, open or undisguised contempt, as for a thing thought unworthy of considerable treatment".

There can be wilful disregard or innocent disregard. Many people show disregard to human rights without knowing that they are violating human rights. How many people in various nations know the concept of human rights? My studies prove that many have little or no information about human rights. With such people, regard or no regard, disregard or respect to human rights makes no difference. There are people who want their human rights to be disregarded and they consider such disregarding necessary for human coexistence and social welfare. A contempt is a contempt only if and if only the person at the receiving end feels so; otherwise it ceases to be a contempt. It is true that disregard and contempt for human rights have resulted in barbarous acts. They have also resulted in better human coexistence and social welfare. It is a fact to be reckoned with that certain barbarous acts for a particular nation need not necessarily be so in another nation. The nature of a barbarous act is often decided by the culture/ sub-culture prevailing there.

Barbarous means uncivilized, savage or crude. It also means savagely cruel or harsh. Further it means "not conforming to classical standards or accepted usage". An eye for an eye and a tooth for a tooth principle of administration of justice was not barbarous or uncivilized once upon a time in many developed countries today—it is not barbarous even today in certain countries which claim to be very civilized. Hence, barbarous acts are limited by time and space, nationality and culture; customs and traditions, etc. The framers of the UDHR-1948 had certain concepts about barbarous acts and the conscience of mankind. CONSCIENCE means "(1) the sense of what is right or wrong in one's conduct or motives, impelling one toward right action, (2) the ethical and moral principles that control or inhibit the actions or thoughts of an individual, (3) conscientiousness, etc." The issue here is: "Is there something called the conscience of mankind?" So long as mankind is not a human individual, the conscience of mankind is a concept which is understandable. There may be psychologists who speak about universal conscience or universal consciousness. Certainly, their concept is not the concept called the conscience of mankind as seen in the PREAMBLE of UDHR-1948. It is vague and there is darkness in the very concept itself. The conscience of a man has a developmental period and there exists a number of theories for the development of human conscience in the upright direction. Mankind is a faceless mass and such a mass cannot have a conscience. Hence, the PREAMBLE needs amendment or revision.

Contempt is an undesirable expression and people everywhere in the world and in all cultures, from time antiquity, have shown respect to human rights though they did not use the expression called 'human rights'. I find that the people honoured human rights from time immemorial and we have evidence to show that the people respected human rights from *vedic* period, from Mose's time and earlier. Even in Hamurabi's Code, one observes provisions to respect human rights. 'Outrage' means "an act of wanton violence; any gross violation of law and decency, fury or insolence", etc. So long as there exists no conscience of mankind in reality, no question of outraging the conscience of mankind arises. Precisely, therefore, that expression 'outraging the conscience of mankind' should be deleted from the PREAMBLE. Hence, I suggest the following amendment or revision for the beginning of the second paragraph in the PREAMBLE, i.e., "whereas a failure or refusal to recognize and respect human rights or disregard shown to human rights are found to have been instrumental for human unhappiness, difficulties or hinderances to harmonious coexistence and social welfare . . .".

The PREAMBLE again says that the disregard and contempt for human rights have resulted . . . in the advent of a world in which human beings shall enjoy freedom of speech and belief and freedom from fear and want has been proclaimed as the highest aspiration of the common people. How can the United Nations assert that the highest aspiration of the common people is the enjoyment of the freedom of speech, etc. ? No. The observation is not factually true as the freedom of speech and belief and freedom from fear and want, etc., are some of the strong aspirations of the people in general. The expression 'common people' is not acceptable as they are the aspirations of all people of the humanity irrespective of colour, creed, community and caste. The aspirations of the people should not be limited to the specific areas of "freedom of speech and belief and freedom from fear and want". When human rights mean the rights of the people to life, to liberty, to equality and to dignity, the freedom of the people must cover all those areas and the expression should be "freedom to enjoy human rights relating to life, liberty, equality and dignity". These rights include (i) freedom from torture and inhuman treatment, (ii) right to liberty and security, (iii) right of detained persons to be treated with humanity, (iv) right to fair trial, (v) right to recognition as a person before law, (vi) right to privacy, (vii) freedom of opinion and of expression, (viii) right to assembly, (ix) freedom of association, (x) equality before law and above all, (xi) the right to life. Ofcourse, the UDHR in its articles specify them, but that is not enough. What is to be stated in the PREAMBLE should be stated there itself. The rights enumerated above from (i) to (xi) are respectively stated in the articles. 5, 3, 5, 10, 6, 12, 19, 20, 20, 7 and 3 of the UDHR. The same rights are stated clearly in many Constitutions throughout the world. For example, the rights enumerated above (i) to (xi) are stated under articles 21, 21, 21, 21 and 22, 14, 21, 19, 19, 19, 14, and 21 respectively in the Constitution of India.

Putting everything together, the PREAMBLE of the UDHR-1948 may be amended to read:

> "Whereas a failure or refusal to recognize and respect human rights or disregard shown to them are found to have been instrumental for human unhappiness, difficulties or hindrances to harmonious coexistence and social welfare disabling the people to enjoy their human rights to life, equality, liberty and dignity with freedom from fear and want which are proclaimed as very genuine and legitimate aspirations of the people of the world and humanity."

All people should feel free from fear and want. Fear is "a distressing emotion aroused by an impending pain, danger, evil, etc. or by the illusion of such". There is an anxiety associated with fear, i.e., something of which one is afraid or that causes fright or apprehension. The meaning given to fear in the Random House College Dictionary is further strengthened by various theories and explanations given by psychologists of many schools of thought. The UDHR-1948 is primarily intended for removing the fear caused by the failure, refusal to respect human rights/or disregard shown to the enjoyment of human rights by the members of the humanity. There should not be any scope for 'fear' in the enjoyment of human rights. Fear mentioned here is not irrational rather it is real. It does not rise within the individuals, more or less, from any instinctual source; rather is very much associated with some real situations denying the enjoyment of human rights. Hence, it is a "reality fear". What about the "want" stated in the UDHR? "Want" means a "feeling of a need or desire for". There is a craving for it. For example, the suspects in a criminal case crave for a human treatment. They do not want any torture, cruel or degrading treatment or punishment. It is a real desire, a demand, a wish. They are in a state of need. They feel a "lack of or absent, as a part or thing necessary for completeness." Hence, I insist that the same expressions must be there in the Preamble of the UDHR.

The third paragraph in the PREAMBLE of the UDHR is about the necessity for protecting human rights. It is in accordance to what is stated in the Charter of United Nations. It is written: 'We, the people of the United Nations, determined . . . to reaffirm faith in the fundamental human rights, in the dignity and worth of the human person, in the equal rights of men and women and of nations large and small . . . have resolved to combine our efforts to accomplish these aims". The chapter that follows analyses the third paragraph of the PREAMBLE of the UDHR-1948 with those sublime and lofty principles in mind.

4

From Tyranny to Rule of Law and Justice

'To tyrannize' means "(1) to exercise absolute power, especially, cruelly or oppressively, (2) to govern despotically, cruelly or oppressively, (3) to govern as a tyrant, (4) to govern tyrannically" Tyranny, therefore, means arbitrary or unrestrained exercise of power, despotic abuse of authority; oppressive Government on the part of any ruler; undue severity or harshness, etc. A tyrant, accordingly, means a kind of ruler who uses his power oppressively or unjustly, any despotic person, an absolute ruler and so on.

'To oppress' means (1) to be as a heavy burden to, (2) to subject to a burdensome or harsh exercise of authority or power, (3) to weigh down, to put down, to subdue or suppress, etc. 'Oppression', accordingly means "the burdensome, unjust exercise of authority or power". As a synonym to oppression, the Random House College Dictionary gives tyranny along with despotism, persecution. It may mean further that tyranny and oppression are one and the same in many ways. Whatever that be, the third paragraph in the PREAMBLE to UDHR-1948 contains both TYRANNY and OPPRESSION. I do not know whether or not they were put together to convey any special message and meanings or to give some real beauty when the paragraph is read or heard. The paragraph reads :

> "Whereas it is essential, if man is not to be compelled to have recourse, as a last resort, to rebellion against tyranny and oppression, the human rights to be protected by the rule of law".

The PREAMBLE presumes that the man will be forced to have recourse to rebellion if human rights are not protected. Rebellion means "(i) an open, armed resistance to ones Government or ruler, (2) a resistance to or defiance of any authority, control or tradition". The synonym for rebellion is mutiny, sedition, etc. It may further mean a revolt, insubordination, disobedience, etc.

The issue here is: "How can the human rights be protected by law when the ruler himself is despotic?—if he is exercising absolute power?—when he administers everything in an oppressive way?—in a cruel manner?—when he misuses power and abuses authority?—showing undue severity or harshness in administration?" Who will guard the guardians? In Latin, the dictum is: *Quis Custodiet Ipsos Custodes*? If the ruling despot himself is the problem, the problem can be resolved not by the rule of law but by rebellion against the tyrannical rule. History proves it well. According to Hon'ble Justice Mukherji: "Tyranny whether of a state of nature before the advent of any state, followed by tyranny of tribal leaders and tribal chiefs, tyranny of kings and monarchs, subsequent tyranny by nobility and aristocracy and later tyranny by diversified monopolies of caste, colour, creed, physical might and wealth, and of power and influence, organizational or otherwise crystallised fear in the ordinary individual impelling him to protect his minimum liberty in exchange of the benefits of the state. The memories of the revolutions at Runnymade leading to Magna Carta reducing the irresponsible power of monarchy, the French Revolution leading to the fall of the French monarchy, the American Revolution and the declaration of American independence destroying colonialism and imperialism and the Russian Revolution leading to the overthrow of Czar left bitter memories in the mind of the individuals. It is these memories and experiences which make them today seek the protection of fundamental rights in the modern political constitutions". [Mukherji, 1968]. Since the protection of human rights by the law is difficult, if not impossible, against a despotic ruler, rebellion will be the only option. Of course, protection of human rights by the rule of law is possible if the ruler has a commitment to recognize and honour human rights. Therefore, I suggest splitting of third paragraph in the Preamble to UDHR-1948 as :

> "Whereas it is essential, if man is not to be compelled to have recourse, as a last resort, to rebellion against tyranny

> and oppression by a despotic ruler, the human rights should be respected and honoured."
>
> "Whereas, it is essential, if man is not to be compelled to have recourse, as a last resort, to rebellion against tyranny and oppression by administrators under a ruler who has commitment to respect human rights, the human rights should be protected by the rule of law and effective supervision."

In the first part in the above PREAMBLE, I may suggest to delete the expression "as a last resort" and put "as an inevitable and necessary strategy". For, the expression "as a last resort" implies that there exists no other options. When the expression "as an inevitable and necessary strategy" is used, it means that the people do not have any other stratagems or methods or maneuvers for reaching or obtaining a specific goal or result. The stratagems employed need not necessarily be the last, but at the same time are inevitable and necessary for the purpose of achieving the goal or result.

In the second part of the PREAMBLE to the UDHR above, I may wish to add by the rule of law and justice. Why do I want to add "justice"? The prime reason, I find, is that sometimes, the rule of law does not ensure holistic justice or total justice. The law itself may be questionable and such a law, if at all there is the rule of law, cannot and does not administer holistic, equal and total justice. For example, the law may be to award a retributive punishment to a person committing a human right violation. When the rule of law comes into being, he may have to suffer very humiliating and degrading punishment. It will be affecting adversely the 'dignity of man' which is a human right law. Hence, the human rights should be protected by the rule of law coupled with rule of justice.

Again, in the first part of the PREAMBLE, I find the need to insist that the ruler, if at all he is despotic, should respect and honour human rights. Why? Normally, it is not possible to protect human rights of the people by rule of law if he is despotic. With him, one can pray that he should at least show respect and honour to human rights. If he is not prepared to do so, then he will have to face the direct consequences of showing disrespect and dishonour to human rights. In such situations, rebellion may be resulted and at the end, he may be either defeated or destroyed.

In order to avoid such a painful situation, the UDHR must insist that he should respect and honour human rights. When we go through the mystical writings of Indian *ṛsis* and sages, we read :

> "Let every hand give comfort to all living beings..." (Rg *Veda,* 10 + 137-7).

"They who neglect their social duties for their individual life fall in darkness and those who sacrifice their individuality for social popularity fall into greater darkness" (*Isha Upanishad*). Let the despotic ruler realise the meanings and inner meanings of these revealed truths. They are old mystical revolutions and they are gold for the people today. Nevertheless, people want more and more ideas, concepts and thoughts to develop upon the old thinkings of great men down the millennia.

NOTE

1. Mukherji, P.B., Civil Liberties: Ramananda Lectures of the Calcutta University, N.M. Tripathi Pvt. LTd., Bombay, 1968.

5

Human Rights Oriented and Centred Relations between Nations

The fourth paragraph in the PREAMBLE to the present Universal Declaration of Human Rights reads: "Whereas it is essential to promote the development of friendly relations between nations" and the PREAMBLE continues further. Why does the United Nations restrict the scope of the U.D.H.R. and limit only to the promotion of the development of 'friendly relations' alone between the nations? I do not know the reasons for it. FRIEND means "(1) a person attached to another by feelings of affection or personal regard, (2) a person who is on good terms with another; not hostile, etc. FRIENDLY, therefore, means "(1) characteristic of or befitting a friend; (2) like a friend; kind, helpful, (3) favourably disposed; inclined to approve, help or support, (4) not hostile or at variance; amicable, etc. Whatever may be the meanings, inner meanings, vague meanings, beyond or beside meanings, shadow meanings or side-meanings of the expression FRIENDLY and its ramifications in maintaining good and healthy relations between nations, I, for one, think that the expression does not convey the full ambit of human rights in national or international relations. Because, a mere friendly relationship between nations is not enough for the protection of human rights. The relationship can be many and various, i.e., (1) between parents, (2) between siblings, (3) between parents and children, (4) between friends, (5) between neighbours, (6) man and woman, (7) between man and man, (8) between woman and woman, (9) between the young and the old, (10) between the rich and the poor, (11) between the haves and have nots,

(12) between the leader and the followers, (13) between the mother and the child and thus goes the endless list of human relations. If so, why or what is the special importance and significance in developing only FRIENDLY relations between nations. The relationship can be economical, trade and business, financial, cultural, political, commercial, etc. Therefore, the narrow way of looking at the development of relations between nations and limiting or restricting them only to "FRIENDLY" does not mean much and does not expose the very purpose of UDHR.

I have a suggestion to amend the said PREAMBLE as :

"Whereas it is essential to establish and/ or promote positively human rights oriented and centred relations between nations" and why do I want to put "establish" in the PREAMBLE? "To promote the development of friendly relationship between nations" presumes that already there exists friendly relations between nations and the sole or prime purpose of the UDHR is only to promote the already existing friendly relations. This is not true always, rather is misleading in some cases and nations. Hence, it is good to bring *establish and/ or* in the PREAMBLE. If the relationship is not established, let the UDHR establish it and then promote it. On the other hand, if there exists already a healthy, good or fine relationship, let the UDHR further develop it. In any case the relationship ought to be human rights centred and human rights oriented. If the countries recognize human rights, then the relationship will be smooth and enviable; if not it will be undesirable and unhealthy. For, human rights have no boundaries. There should be faithful allegiance, i.e., loyalty, to the Articles contained in the UDHR.

I have used the expressions (1) Human Rights Oriented and (2) Human Rights Centred in the proposed amendment. Why? Oriented here means to turn toward the protection and promotion of human rights. It means mutual recognition of human beings as human beings or as it is written in *Rig Veda* 50.60.5. "There is none high or low amidst you. You are all brethren and therefore, strive all together to attain prosperity". A human rights oriented relationship between nations ensures and guarantees peace, harmony, human coexistence, justness, fairness, equality, freedom, prosperity, dignity and what not? After all, this earth is the common property of all, but has been divided into parts by the people. The partition does not mean much if the people are prepared to recognize, accept and respect the human rights of the people who live under the same sun which provides heat to all irrespective of caste, colour, creed, territory, language, views and opinions alike. The sun is at the centre and all the universe revolves around it. Likewise, the relationship between the nations must be human rights centred. Let the Human Rights be at the centre of the universe and the nations must centre around it. Human rights must be the pivot or the kingpin of relations between the nations. An idea may, as stated earlier, change the world and certainly, this idea will change the world to establish a new world order in which people will respect the human rights of the people everywhere. Nevertheless, I find the people failing or refusing to recognize, accept and respect human rights. That is the reason why I want to retain the expression "Whereas it is essential . . ." used in the UDHR-1948 in the newly proposed UDHR too. The word ESSENTIAL is not a mere desirability, but an inevitable necessity in the new UDHR. "Essential" here means "absolutely necessary and inevitable" without which the idea cannot be expressed meaningfully.

"Between nations" means a lot. The relationship here is between two nations. The expression BETWEEN suggests a relationship that is not necessarily physical. It can be in many or various ways and in all descriptions. Precise users of English use *between* chiefly when only two persons or things are involved. I have no difficulty to accept this usage when two nations are involved and have again no difficulty to accept this usage "between" in the UDHR as one sees more than two nations (many nations) involved in their individual or reciprocal relationship as far as human rights are concerned. The relationship is between all nations in the world and, therefore, the expression "Between nations" may be taken in that sense too.

The nations in the world are different in many ways. Some are developed, some are under development and others are undeveloped. The relationship among the developed, developing and undeveloped ones are indeed difficult if they are not prepared to recognize and respect human rights in spirit and letters of the international law. If they do not do so, what to do and how to go about is a real problem aching the well-meaning international community.

6

Peoples of the United Nations and Human Rights

"Whereas the peoples of the United Nations have in the Charter reaffirmed their faith in the fundamental human rights, in the dignity and worth of human person and in the equal rights of men and women and have determined to promote social progress and better standards of life in larger freedom". This is what is seen in the PREAMBLE and I do not understand the meaning and relevance of the usage FAITH in the said PREAMBLE. It is not a matter of FAITH, rather is a matter of TRUST.

Faith, of course, has the meaning "confidence or trust in a person or thing", but more often than not, it is used to mean a "belief that is not based on proof". In religion, it means a "belief in God, in the doctrines or teachings of religion". In Christian Theology, "faith means the trust in God and in His promises as made through Christ and the scriptures by which man is justified or saved." Of course, the word faith may mean many things such as (1) belief in anything, (2) occurrence of a future event, (3) the obligation of loyalty or fidelity to a person, etc. All said and done, I, for one, do not like to use the word FAITH (which is often seen in theology or scriptures or religious literature) in the newly proposed U.D.H.R.

Firstly, I thought why cannot the word allegiance be substituted for faith? Allegiance means, *inter alia,* loyalty or devotion to some person, group, cause, or the like and as such it is 100 per cent better and more fitting than FAITH. UDHR-1948 is a man-made Declaration and, therefore, there is no need or necessity to bring the contents contained in faith in such a document. The Charter of the United Nations too is not different from the UDHR-1948 as far as it also is a man-made document. Since they are man-made, let us not bring *Divinity* and the expression signifying divinity. 'Faith' is thus rejected. Why not Trust be brought in the place of faith and that was my second thinking. Trust means (1) belief in and reliance on the integrity, strength, ability, surety, etc., of a person or thing, (2) confident expectation of something; hope, etc. The peoples of the United Nations should have TRUST (instead of faith) in the fundamental human rights . . . and, therefore, I propose an amendment to put TRUST instead of FAITH in the PREAMBLE.

There in that portion of the PREAMBLE, one sees too many unnecessary words or wordings and, it appears to me that they have been used without any purpose. The first part can be rewritten as "Whereas the peoples of the United Nations have in the Charter reaffirmed their trust in human rights . . . ". Why do I propose a shorter version? The reasons are :

1. The use of "fundamental" is unnecessary. For, the concept of human rights contain the word "fundamental" in it. For, human rights are the basic-fundamental-inalienable-universal birth rights of human beings and if so, why should the PREAMBLE retain "fundamental" to human rights? I may even say that the use of the fundamental before human right is nothing but a tautology, i.e., needless repetition of an idea in different words as in 'widow woman'. It is better to avoid such tautologizing in the newly proposed UDHR. Again, why should the expression in the dignity and worth of human person be put in the PREAMBLE here? Human Rights to Dignity means and includes everything contained in the above expression. I do not understand the exact meaning of the expression "worth of human person". If it is the existence of man, then there will not be any worth for a mentally retarded [retarded at profound or severe levels] or a lunatic or a person who has only a vegetative existence. In my view, as said earlier, human rights to dignity recognizes and respects the ESSENCE of man and not the EXISTENCE of man. A human being is a human being whatever may be his earthly worth as a human being. The mentally retarded people are not called morons, imbeciles and idiots today. They are known as people who are differentially abled. This is the human rights view. Again, there exist no destitutes

today in orphanages. All of them are the children (people) who need special care and protection. The "essence of man" is something that exists in him, especially spiritual or immaterial entity. When the essence is gone, he is dead. In Malayalam language, there is an expression, saying, *chattupoyi* which means "expired or dead". The essence in Malayalam is "*satha*" and when people say that the "*satha* is gone", it means "*satha poyi*", i.e., the essence is gone. Essence is gone which was earlier said to be "*satha poyi*", has now become "*chattupoyi*" in due course of time. It means that the "essence" of man is the "worth of the person". Right to Dignity means the Right to live with the essence of man. Dignity continues even after death. The dignity of the dead—the dead body—is always respected. Any disrespect shown to a dead body is a punishable act in many countries. As the expression 'worth of human person' is found to be unnecessary, it can be deleted from the original text of the UDHR-1948.

Human right to equality means equal right to men and women. Why should a discrimination based on sex be brought into the PREAMBLE without any need, necessity, justification and rationale? If such a discrimination is brought in the UDHR-1948, then it becomes necessary to make such discriminations and distinctions applicable to the literate and to the illiterate (on the basis of education), to the haves and have nots (on the basis of affluence), to the crime-doers and victims of crime (on the basis of the commission of crime and its impact), and so on. I find it necessary to delete the entire portion, i.e., in the equal rights of men and women from the original test of the UDHR-1948.

Instead of making the PREAMBLE simple and plain, I take note of the fact that it has been made complex and complicated by the use of unnecessary words, expressions and concepts which are tautological, irrelevant and conveying no special meaning/s. What about the second portion in the above paragraph? It reads :

> "...have determined to promote social progress and better standards of life in larger freedom".

The issues are :

1. What is meant by social progress?
2. What is the meaning of better standards of life?
3. What is said to be the larger freedom?

How is the first portion and the second portion in the above said paragraph related? Does the reaffirmation of the faith of the peoples of the United Nations in the Charter in the fundamental human rights have anything to do with their determination to promote social progress and better standard of life in larger freedom? I am yet to understand the full meanings of social progress, better standards of life and larger freedom. When the PREAMBLE in full is read carefully, I find many words/ concepts like freedom, justice and peace, freedom of speech, freedom from fear and want, development of friendly relations between nations, etc. Naturally, the social progress, better standard of life, larger freedom, etc., are there in those words/ concepts. Freedom from fear and want contains social progress; justice, peace, friendly relations contain better standard of life; freedom, freedom of speech, freedom from fear and want, etc., contain larger freedom. The UDHR-1948, it seems to me, in its PREAMBLE puts one and the same words/ concepts repeatedly signifying little or nothing. Hence my suggestion to rewrite the same will be :

> "Whereas the peoples of the United Nations have in the Charter reaffirmed their trust in human rights have determined to establish and promote human happiness, freedom and social welfare".

Here social welfare means everything including social progress and better standard of living, etc.

Peoples of the United Nations mean the Member States and the following paragraph is about the pledge they have taken to achieve their goal. It is discussed in the chapter that follows.

7

Pledge and Human Rights

> "Whereas Member-States have pledged themselves to achieve in co-operation with United Nations, the promotion of universal respect for and observance of human rights and fundamental freedoms."
>
> (*Preamble to U.D.H.R. 1948*)

Pledge means "a solemn promise or agreement to do or refrain from doing something". Beautiful and nice to hear the wordings in the PREAMBLE of the U.D.H.R 1948. As the pledge has been made by the Member-States of the United Nations, it is more beautiful and nicer to hear it. The question here is: "Are the Member-States serious in their solemn promise"? This is a point of dispute throughout the world. I was in police service and was on the Faculty of the Police Training College, Thiruvananthapuram. We have a PLEDGE that every trainee makes the pledge on the day of their passing out parade and it is done in the presence of the senior police officials including the Director General of Police, press and public and they do it keeping the National Flag and the Police Flag to witness the solemn oath. The oath contains wordings to protect the human rights and dignity of people. I read often in the media and press that the police violates the human rights of people in many ways and in different manners. I used to ask the police trainees who come to the police training college to attend in-service training courses to recollect the wordings in the PLEDGE which they loudly made on the day of their passing out parade. Frustratingly enough, none so far could told me any wordings in the pledge. I have done it not less than 100 times in my career and invariably, I read out the PLEDGE once again to remind them what they promised or agreed to do or refrain from doing on the day of their passing out parade. Their answer to my question used to be always: "Sir, we forgot it." It means that the PLEDGE becomes a ritualistic formality on the day of their passing out. I have quoted my experience just to say that the PLEDGE in the PREAMBLE of the U.D.H.R. 1948 too is nothing but a ritualistic formality that may be seen in all declarations or documents of like nature. Once again, I raise the question: "Are the Member-States of the United Nations serious when they make the PLEDGE" or is it only an empty formality signifying nothing Amnesty International, world organisations, National, State or Regional NGOs bring out instances of human rights violations every now and then and many or all of them are from the Member-Nations of the United Nations. All of them have made the SOLEMN PLEDGE in a colourful way. A PLEDGE that is not actualised is no pledge at all.

If the Member-States were serious and sincere in their solemn PLEDGE, then the world would have been altogether different today. Therefore, I suggest to delete the expression PLEDGE and substitute it with another–say, AGREE to read:

> "Whereas the Member-States have agreed themselves to achieve and actualise, in cooperation with the United Nations . . . "

"Promotion of universal respect for . . . " is a good expression. Nevertheless, before promoting something, one needs first the recognition of that thing. Universalization of recognition, acceptance and promotion of human rights is what is required. Recognition of something does not mean necessarily the acceptance of that thing. Hence, acceptance must follow recognition. I have seen many recognising something and then failing or refusing to accept that thing in practice. Once the recognition and acceptance are there, then promotion of the same may follow. Hence, the amended PREAMBLE should be :

> " . . . the universalization of the recognition, acceptance and promotion of respect for . . . "

Human rights means and includes fundamental freedoms as

well. There are no fundamental freedoms beyond, besides and above human rights. Precisely, therefore, the expression "fundamental freedoms" can be deleted from the PREAMBLE to read :

> "Whereas Member-States have agreed themselves to achieve and actualise in cooperation with the United Nations, the universalisation of the recognition, acceptance and promotion and respect for and observance of human rights."

I have put "achieve and actualise"—two expressions which mean almost one and the same thing. "Achieve" means "to bring to a successful end; accomplish" and "Actualise" means "to make actual; realise in action or fact". It is just for giving a double emphasis to the content and thereby to give more meaning to the expression "AGREE" introduced by me instead of "PLEDGE" in the U.D.H.R. 1948. The advantage in bringing the expression *actualise* along with *achieve* is to show that everything must be realised in action or fact when one reaches a successful end.

8

Understanding : An Absolutely Necessary Condition

> "Whereas a common understanding of these rights and freedoms is of the greatest importance in full realisation of this pledge."
>
> (*Preamble to U.D.H.R. 1948*)

"Common" means "(1) belonging equally to or shared alike by two or more or all in question, (2) pertaining or belonging equally to an entire community, nation or culture" and in law, it means" the right or liberty, in common with other persons, to take profit from the land or waters of another". Fine. The expression means a lot. Yet, I, for one, think that it is not full and total. It may be really better if the UDHR. brings out the idea that the common understanding is or ought to be among nations of the world in a universal way. The meaning of the expression "Common" contains the words "belonging equally to or shared alike by two or more or all in question". The "two or more or all" are the nations in the world or the Member-States in the United Nations. The understanding is not simply common, but universal. The universal rights–are about the inalienable rights of all human beings, all over the world, in all cultures at all times everywhere–the birth rights of all irrespective of any distinctions in people. Because of these facts and factors, the understanding becomes necessarily universal and precisely, therefore, that idea too should be brought in the UDHR.

What is this understanding? The expression "understanding"

has many meanings and the one which I think to be most suited is: "promoted by, based on, or demonstrating comprehension, intelligence, discernment, empathy, or the like". No doubt, understanding means simply the "mental process of a person who comprehends". Is it enough to have only a common understanding of these rights? No, I do not think so. I am inclined to say that the common and universal understanding should be coupled with REALIZATION of human rights. Realization means "(1) to grasp or understand clearly; (2) to make real; make reality to (a hope, fear, plan, etc.)". This is what is most needed. There should be the realisation of human rights to all. I, therefore, suggest an alteration in the PREAMBLE as–"Whereas a common and universal understanding and realisation of these rights . . . ".

" . . . and freedoms" is unnecessary because of the obvious reasons shown in the previous chapter. Human rights contains "FREEDOMS" too and, therefore, there is no need to bring "and freedoms" too in the PREAMBLE unnecessarily. Without FREEDOMS, the human rights have no meaning.

I do not think that the expression "of the greatest importance" is the best and the most suited in the PREAMBLE. I must but say that " . . . understanding and realisation of these rights" is a *conditio sine qua non* (i.e., a condition without which) for the full actualisation of the 'pledge' the Member-States of the United Nations have made. *Conditio sine qua non* is otherwise expressed as a "necessary condition", i.e., most inevitable and absolute. Hence, I suggest :

" . . . are an absolutely necessary condition . . . "

I have in my mind three words "(1) Full", (2) "Total" and "holistic" and they respectively mean (1) "containing all that can be held; filled to utmost capacity; complete; entire, maximum (2) constituting or comprising the whole of something; entire; of or pertaining to the whole of something; complete in extent or degree, (3) comprising the full quantity, amount, extent, number, etc., without diminution or exception, entire, full or total. When I analyse the three words and meanings, I prefer "wholistic" (holistic) to "full" and "total". I find that "wholistic" means "full and total". Therefore, my proposal is :

" . . . for the wholistic . . . " and the question is whether or not "realisation" or "actualisation" will be better there? In my view, actualisation will be better there as we have already used that expression in the PREAMBLE and the reasons for the use of the word have been stated in the previous chapter. It follows, therefore, that the amended PREAMBLE should be :

". . . wholistic realisation of . . ." and a further question is: "whether or not one must use PLEDGE or AGREEMENT in the amended PREAMBLE." For reasons explained in the previous chapter, agreement will be better and more acceptable. The agreement here means :

1. The act of agreeing or coming to a mutual arrangement.
2. The state of being in accord.
3. An arrangement that is accepted by all parties to a transaction.
4. A contract or other document delineating such an arrangement.
5. Unanimity of opinion; harmony in feeling.

These meanings given in the Random House College Dictionary are what I too mean in the AGREEMENT in the PREAMBLE. The "agreement ranges in meaning from mutual understanding to binding obligation"–says the Dictionary. Accordingly, the changes in the proposed PREAMBLE will be-

> "Whereas a common and universal understanding and realisation of these rights are an absolutely necessary condition for the wholistic actualisation of this agreement."

This is followed by :

"Now, therefore, the General Assembly" and the next chapter is about the use of such expressions in the PREAMBLE.

9

Resolution, Proclamation and Operation

> "Now, therefore, the General Assembly Proclaims this Universal Declaration of Human Rights as a common standard of achievement for all people and all nations, to the end that every individual and every organ of society, keeping this Declaration constantly in mind, shall strive by teaching and education to promote respect for these rights and freedoms and by progressive measures, national and international, to secure their universal and effective recognition and observance, both among the people of the Member-States themselves and among the peoples of territories under their jurisdiction."

This is a Universal Declaration and as such, the proclamation of the same must be done by the people of the Member-States and not by the General Assembly of the United Nations. Hence, in my considered view, the wordings should be :

"Now, therefore, we, the people of the Member States of the United Nations . . . .

"proclaim" means "(1) to announce or declare in an official or formal manner; (2) to announce or declare in an open or ostentatious way; (3) to indicate or make known publicly or openly", etc. Before proclaiming the Universal Declaration, it is necessary to take a resolution which is nothing but "a formal expression of opinion or intention made, usually after voting, by a formal organization, a legislature, a club or other group". Without a resolution by the people of the Member-States of the United

Nations and territories thereunder, how can a proclamation be made? Hence, in my view, it should be :

"... have solemnly resolved to proclaim ...". Can the General Assembly function as a formal organisation to make a resolution for the people of the member-states? Yes, it can and the reasons are obvious.

"Solemnly" means "seriously or earnestly "or" made in due legal or other express forms".

"... this revised Universal Declaration of Human Rights ..."

"Common standard of achievement" must be rewritten as "a necessary standard of achievement". Why do I suggest *necessary* instead of common? Standard means an "approved model". It also means "(1) anything, as a rule or principle, that is used as a basis for judgment, (2) an average or normal requirement, quality, level, etc. The meanings given to standard indicate that there is "commonness". At the same time, the said or seen commonness may not be found as necessary which means essential, indispensable, or requisite. More than a 'common standard', it must be a necessary standard for the international community to recognize, accept and act upon. Thus, the portion of the PREAMBLE will read :

"... as a necessary standard of achievement..."

Organ of society-what does it mean? Nothing is clear or better, it is not couched in clarity. I may, therefore, suggest to substitute "institution" instead of organ. Institution means :

(1) an organisation or establishment devoted to the promotion of a particular object, especially, one of a public educational, or charitable character;
(2) a place of confinement, as a prison, mental hospital, etc.;
(3) a well established and structured pattern of behaviour or of relationship that is accepted as a fundamental part of culture, as marriage;
(4) any established law, custom, etc.;
(5) any familiar practice or object; and
(6) any establishment or the act of setting up, etc.

In any case, the word institution which is pregnant with many meanings is always better than the expression 'organ'. Hence, the amended portion should be :

> "... for all people and all nations to the end that every individual and every institution of the society, . . .".

The next portion following the above is :

"..., keeping this Declaration constantly in mind . . ." and nothing is said about the "how" of it. How should the declaration be kept constantly in mind? My considered view is to write "... keeping this Declaration constantly alive in mind". Alive means "having life, existing, not dead or lifeless", etc. There are situations in which individuals and institutions keep many things in their mind in a dead way—in an indifferent way or even in a negativistic manner. It should not be there and I insist that the Declaration and its contents must activate in the human mind and the activation should be positive or constructive. Hence it follows :

> "..., keeping this Declaration constantly alive in mind, shall strive positively and constructively..."

The striving is a nice expression and it means "to exert oneself vigorously; try hard; to make strenuous efforts toward any goal". My view is that the striving must be constructive and positive. Why do I say so? Situations are plenty to show that people who keep the Declaration in mind act negatively and destructively. They talk aloud with a long tongue and a wide mouth, but act negatively and to the destruction of others. I have seen such exhortations, talks and activities coming out of the heads of the States and Member-States of the United Nations. Such unscrupulous people claim that they are the ardent advocates of protecting human rights, but behave as violators. It is an agreement and the agreement between the people of the Member-States of the United Nations must be "to strive positively and constructively-and nothing less than that.

Continuing the PREAMBLE further, ". . . . by teaching and education . . ." This is not enough. It must be-

". . . . by teaching, educating and acting upon. . . . " Teaching and educating without acting upon becomes meaningless, ineffective and empty.

". . . . to promote respect for these rights. . . . " Here too, promotion of respect alone will not drive us to the desired destination. Freedoms may not be necessary for reasons already pointed out. In my view, it must be restructured to :

> ". . . . to establish, accept and promote respect for them . . . ."

Further, ". . . . and by progressive measures and strategies, national, international, to secure and cement their universal and meaningfully effective recognition, observance and operating upon, both among the people of the Member-States themselves and among the people of territories under their jurisdiction".

Why do we put strategies along with measures? Measures mean "actions or procedures intended as a means to an end". Strategy means "a plan, method, or series or manoeuvres or stratagems for obtaining a specific goal or result". The measures should have a plan, method or series of manoeuvres or stratagems. They can be or should be for a short term or for a long term or both. Any action or procedures intended as a means to an end without a well planned strategy will not yield the expected result.

The measures and strategies—national and international—should be not only for securing the recognition and observance of human rights, but also for cementing their universal and meaningfully effective recognition, observance and operating upon . . .". Cementing becomes essential as the purpose of the Declaration is to unite together the objectives of the Member-States of the United Nations and territories thereunder. Recognition, observance and operating upon in a united manner and in a meaningfully effective way should be there. Putting everything together, the amended PREAMBLE will be :

Now, therefore,

> We, the people of the Member-States of the United Nations and territories thereunder have solemnly resolved to proclaim this new Universal Declaration of Human Rights as a necessary standard of achievement for all people and all nations to the end that every individual and every institution of the society keeping this Declaration constantly alive in mind shall strive positively and constructively by teaching, educating and acting upon to establish, accept and promote respect for those rights and by progressive measures and strategies, national and

international, to secure and cement their universal and meaningfully effective recognition, observance and operating upon, both among the people of the Member-States themselves and among the peoples of the territories under their jurisdiction". Yes, everything must be meaningfully effective to establish a new world order—a better tomorrow.

10

Equal Rights, Upright Conscience and Brotherhood

"All human beings are BORN FREE EQUAL IN DIGNITY AND RIGHTS. They are endowed with REASON AND CONSCIENCE and should act in toward one another in a spirit of BROTHERHOOD". This is the first Article in the existing Universal Declaration of Human Rights. This is certainly a wishful thinking and not at all a reality and it has, perhaps, little or no application in the administration of criminal justice in a human rights friendly way. Great thinkers have said that "man is born free, but chained everywhere". In my view, a man is born into a family as the son/ daughter of parents living in a country, state, district, taluka, panchayat, culture, sub-culture, religion, caste, sub-caste, colour, race, language, ethnic origin, economic and financial status, social milieu, occupational/professional background, customs, traditions, faith and thus the list is surely endless. All of them without exemption put restrictions on the freedom of the new born. No man is born free and as far as crime and criminal behaviour may be considered, the presumption that a man is born free cannot be accepted and acted upon. Cessare Lombruso spoke about born criminals in which case a man is destined or better condemned to become a criminal. Born free or not born free, he cannot but become a criminal. Anyway, later researches disproved his theory of born criminality, but at the same time, the researchers advanced many theories including the multiple causation approach. Whatever that be, the criminal laws today have linkages with the classical school of criminology.

Bentham and Beccaria brought the FREEDOM of WILL and HEDONISM to explain the causes of crime. St. Thomas Acquinas of the Catholic Church said the same thing when he explained the causes of sin which was nothing but the violation of a religious law which again was a form of crime as it is understood today.

If man is born free, then there is no harm in punishing him when he commits an offence. It is so because he has misused/abused his freedom and precisely, therefore, he must suffer the punishment. Today, sociologists, psychologists, victiomologists and criminologists advance many theories which explain why people commit crimes. In their explanations and theories, the freedom of man is not discussed. Instead, they speak about compelling, facilitating, provoking, instigating, prompting circumstances . . . as well as man's weak ego structure, push-pull-ego factors, ego-superego-id factors, personality structures, endocrine influences, interaction of heredity and environment, etc., etc. What is more? the geographers, statisticians, anthropologists, spiritual men, psychiatrists, theologians, philosophers, social workers, criminologists and so on give their explanations about the etiology of crime. In their studies and views, the approach of the classical school of thought about the FREEDOM OF MAN does not figure much, yet the criminal justice system today centres around that thought to a great extent.

Now, the United Nations in the Universal Declaration of Human Rights seem to have accepted the rejected classical school of thought about the FREEDOM OF MAN and formulated the first Article. Any criminal law enacted basing on that approach will certainly and without doubt deny the enjoyment of human rights by crime-doers and so-called criminals.

"All human beings are . . . equal in dignity and rights"–This portion of the Article I of UDHR is acceptable and it has been stated by Swami Ram Tirath-

> "If we look through all the earth men we see have equal birth made in one great brotherhood, equal in the sight of God, the good, food or caste or place of birth cannot alter human worth."

Yes, people have equal birth, great brotherhood, equality in the sight of God and human worth of people and the UDHR reaffirms the equality in dignity and rights.

'Dignity' means "nobility or elevation of character; worthiness". In my view, no man is born equal in dignity. How can the dignity be measured? It can be assessed or measured qualitatively by studying how noble one is or how best is the elevation of character which one possesses. If everyone is born with equal dignity, then he cannot commit crimes. But people do commit crimes and it shows that the criminals express behaviour which does not manifest an elevation of character. Though people are not born with 'equality' in dignity, everybody is born with a potency to develop nobility in him and it is his responsibility to develop his potency and claim 'equality' in dignity. Suppose, one does not develop his potency in the proper way, then he may involve in committing crimes. Here arises a question, i.e., does a person who behaves without dignity is entitled to claim dignity and equality in dignity as a right? Human rights laws may attest to the view that he is entitled to be treated with dignity. Accordingly, he has a right to be treated in a human rights friendly way, i.e., free from cruel, degrading and inhuman way. No one should show an attitude of "a criminal after all" to him. It is not because he is born equal in dignity, but because he is a man after all with the "essence" of a human person. The *person* in him is respected.

Is a man born equal in rights? A *right* means the freedom of doing or possessing something for the infringement of which there is a legal sanction. *Right* again is an interest which is recognised and protected by law. What I have said above are the definitions of *right* given by legal dictionaries/ law literature. Freedom of doing something does not mean the liberty to do anything, i.e., no unrestricted freedom and in that sense all human beings are born equal in rights. Right, as I said above, is an interest which is recognised and protected by law. Law can be many such as social laws, gender laws, religious laws, ethical laws, criminal laws, human rights laws, victiomological laws, etc. I am of the firm view that man is to be protected by all laws available. Nevertheless, that is not possible. Only those interests which are protected by laws and enforceable by the courts of law are now seen in the Article I of UDHR. Whatever that be, my suggestion is to draft anew the Article I of the UDHR as under :

"All human beings are born equal in rights..." I delete "born free" and equal in dignity as nobody is born free and equal in dignity at the time of his/ her birth. At the same time everyone has a right to be treated with dignity irrespective of his caste, colour, creed and community or whatever.

The second part of the Article I of the UDHR is about reason and conscience. ENDOW means "to furnish, as with some gift, faculty, or quality". In other words, the word means "equip". The question is "Is man endowed with reason and conscience"? Philosophers describe man as a rational being which means that he has reason or reasoning power. It means that the specific difference of man from animals is that he has reason or reasoning power. The definition or description of man without this specific difference from the animal world is meaningless and, therefore, is not a definition/description at all. Why should the Article I of the UDHR put reason when the Article itself begins with the words "All human beings . . .". The concept "Human Being" contains "reason" and, therefore, there is no need to put "reason" with human beings. The Article contains two expressions (human being and reason) with the same meaning and is, therefore, a tautology in every sense, content and meaning. Hence, the word REASON should be deleted from the Article.

If all human beings are endowed with reason implies again that the man is endowed with intelligence which means the capacity for reasoning, understanding, comprehension, memorizing and for similar forms of mental activities. Reasoning means a lot and it includes man's mental powers concerned with forming conclusions, judgments, or inferences. Does it mean that a person without the above capacity or faculty is not a human being? In that case, what about the people who suffer from an "unsoundness of mind"?, who suffer from "mental retardation"? who suffer from "severe or profound retardation" or people who are psychotic? (or psychoneurotic as well in some instances). Don't they have a right to enjoy human rights? Power of reason means the capacity for sound judgment, good sense, sanity, etc. United Nations, therefore, may subscribe to the view that the power of reason/ reasoning should not come in the way of people's right for the enjoyment of human rights.

Further, I cannot but disagree with the view of the United Nations. According to the UDHR-1948, "All human beings are endowed . . . with conscience" and many psychologists through their experiments find that man is endowed only with a potency to develop a conscience—this way, that way or anyway. UDHR does not make clear about the nature of the conscience man is endowed with. Mother Theresia (a saintly nun) had a conscience, Mussolini (1883-1945, the Italian Fascist leader), Hitler (1899-1945, Nazi Dictator of Germany), Mahatma Gandhi (1869-1948, Nationalist and Socialist Reformer of India), Martin Luther King, Jr. (1929-68, Civil Rights Leader) had their conscience which is nothing but the superego of Signmund Freud (1856-1939, the Austrian Neurologist and the founder of Psychoanalysis), the DO's and Don'ts of society, the inner voice of man, etc. According to me, there will be the feeling of guilt when someone does an act against his conscience/omits to do an act according to his conscience. This Conscience is formed by an interaction between the hereditary potencies and environment. It is the heredity and environment which make the human conscience this way-that way-anyway. Inadequate formation of the human conscience will make a man to commit crimes without any feeling of guilt. Whatever that be, how can the UDHR-1948 claim that man is endowed with conscience when he is endowed only with a potency or potentiality to develop a conscience. Theologians go to say that one must develop his conscience in the right direction in an upright way. Therefore, my suggestion is to rewrite the entire Article I of UDHR in the following way, i.e.,

> "All human beings are born equal in rights and endowed with a potency to develop a conscience . . .".

The conscience here means an upright conscience rightly formed in the right direction. This is and should be one's human rights. The question here is: "What is an upright conscience rightly formed in the right way?". It is nothing but a conscience which recognises human rights, dignity and the person in the other—the essence of man, etc. The Article I continues:

"... Should act in toward one another in a spirit of brotherhood". Is "in a spirit of brotherhood" and "in brotherhood" one and the same thing? I am inclined to think that they are entirely different. I do not accept a "spirit of brotherhood" which may be a pasted one, annexed one, attached one, etc. There is or will be lack of sincerity/ honesty in "a spirit of brotherhood". The UDHR being an international declaration, "a spirit" would mean "the true or basic meaning or intent of a statement, document, etc. (opposed to letter)". O.K., Why should the United Nations demand such a "spirit"? The view can be better framed as "should act toward one another in brotherhood". Brotherhood means "the condition or quality of being a brother or brothers", i.e., the quality of being brotherly. It is to say that all human beings engaged in human rights friendly pursuits should act brotherly toward one another, regardless of differences in race, caste, sub-caste, colour, ethnic origin, creed, nationality, etc. All put together Article I of the UDHR must be redrafted as :

> "All human beings are born equal in rights endowed with a potency to develop an upright conscience rightly formed and should act in toward one another in brotherhood."

Article 1 and Criminal Justice

When the subsystems in criminal justice recognize the human rights in the way stated above, then the consequence will be that the subsystems will ensure equal rights to all guaranteeing equal, total and holistic justice in a distributive manner to the crime-doers, victims of crime, victims of abuse of power/misuse of authority, to the society and to the justice system itself with an upright conscience rightly formed and behaving toward one another in brotherhood.

Do the people act in a spirit of brotherhood? Brotherhood, as said above, means "the condition or quality of being a brother or brothers; the quality of being brotherly; fellowship". Brother means "a male offspring having both parents in common with another offspring; a male sibling". A male offspring having only one parent in common with another offspring is called a Half Brother, i.e., step brother. A half brother also means "a male member among the same kinship group, nationality, profession, etc., as another; a fellow member, a fellow countryman, a fellow man, etc". Evidently, the Article speaks about brotherhood and not about half-brotherhood. What is seen today? One sees terrorism and the terrorists killing innocent people at random. People treat others on the basis of the colour, creed, caste, sub-caste, community, professional status, origin of birth and one observes no I-THOU relationship; rather an I-IT relationship is noticed. Communal riots, religious bigotry, fundamentalist activities, racial conflicts, slavery, slave-trade, subhuman treatment, manslaughter, genocide, sex-discrimination, euthanasia, miscarriage of unborn children, neglect of the old and the infirm, sexual sadism, naxalitism, degrading and cruel treatment, inhuman and animal like behaviour to fellow brethren, adulteration of food, pollution, manufacture of hootch, etc., are seen and thus the list is indeed very long. The expression brotherhood ceases to have any meaning and perhaps an expression like hostility has better relevancy in man-to-man relationship. The conflict between men and women on the basis of gender justice makes a man to look at a woman as hostile to him and *vice versa*. Some women (so-called human rights activists) go even to the extent of saying that the Article 1 of the Universal Declaration of Human Right ought to have been written as "should act in one another in a spirit of sisterhood" instead of brotherhood. Discrimination on the basis of gender in the very Declaration on Human Rights is human rights unfriendly. According to them, the Article would have been written more realistically as "in a spirit of brotherhood/ sisterhood". Correct or incorrect their version or interpretation of the Article 1 in the UDHR-1948, there is a point in what they complain of. Moreover, it shows the attitude of women towards men in transactions. Language experts say that the word "sister" has an informal meaning as well. It is nothing but a "form of address used to a woman or girl, especially jocularly or in contempt". The reality today, according to some, is that the "spirit of brotherhood" now used by people is nothing but a form of address employed to a man/woman, boy/girl jocularly or in contempt. If that is a true version, certainly it is unjust and intolerable. A situation has emerged even in the family where the husband is the enemy of his wife, one parent the enemy of the other parent and grand-parents. There is an increase in the number of disorganised families. The governments in power ignore the family and home values. The schools do not care for domestic values. The religious organizations do not get time to make families the centre of love, brotherhood, sisterhood, etc. What is more? The Article I becomes the hope of the United Nations when the wind is found to be in the opposite direction. If situation is not set right, injustice will be resulted and everything will go beyond the control of the United Nations.

11

Inherited and Acquired Status and Human Rights

"**Everyone** is entitled to the rights and freedoms set forth in this Declaration, without distinction of any kind, such as race, colour, sex, language, religion, political or other opinion, national or social origin, property or other status.

"Furthermore, no distinction shall be made on the basis of the political, jurisdictional for international status of the country or territory to which a person belongs, whether it be independent, trust, non-self-governing or under any other limitation or sovereignty."

Rights in U.D.H.R. means, includes and contains the right to freedoms as well. Rights mean here the "human rights" and human rights mean the right to **Life, Liberty, Equality and Dignity**. *Liberty* in human rights is nothing but *Freedom* and if so, why should the UDHR bring again the "**Freedoms**" set forth in this **Declaration** along with the **Rights** as seen in Article 2 of U.D.H.R.?

The word "**Entitled**" means *"to give (a person or thing) a title, right, or claim to something; furnishing with grounds for laying claim"*. Can the Article 2 be better expressed without "entitled"? In other words, why can't the United Nations declare–

"Everyone has the rights and freedoms set forth in this Declaration . . ." A Declaration which in Article 1 said categorically that "All human beings are born equal in rights . . ." should not have any hesitation to say "Everyone has the rights set forth in this Declaration". If the people have the said rights, certainly they will claim them. There is no need to give any *Claim* for their enjoyment of the rights declared in the Declaration. "Set Forth" means *stated* and therefore, the Article 2 may be redrafted as :

"Everyone has the rights enshrined in this Declaration without distinction of any kind." There is no need to put "race, colour, sex, language, religion, political, or other opinion, national or social origin, property or other status." What does the expression "other" mean here? It means many other things which give *status* to individuals. They may include, caste, sub-caste, economic or financial status, occupational or professional status and in criminal law, the status may mean the standing of a person before the law as the witness, the accused, the suspect, the remanded, the detained, the incarcerated, the punished, the acquitted, the released, the arrested and so on.

The issue is: "Can those who have different status before the law and criminal courts enjoy the rights in an equal way"? The plain answer is "no", because a witness is different from an accused; an accused is different from a suspect, a suspect is different from a convicted, a convicted is different from an acquitted, an acquitted is different from an incarcerated and so on. The expression "other status" causes a lot of confusion and, therefore, it may be a desirable thing to delete such a confusing expression from the UDHR. If needed, more items such as caste, sub-caste, economic, professional, occupational status, etc., should be added to the existing items and thus make the Article clearer and more specific. Do we need it?

'Status' is either inherited or ascribed. The status—such as race, colour, sex, caste, sub-caste etc.—is inherited while the status like professional, occupational, political, economic, financial, educational, etc.–is acquired. As the facts are like this, it is better to redraft the Article 2 as follows :

> "Everyone has the rights without distinction of any kind in status, either inherited or acquired as the case may be."

Whenever a person commits a crime, he acquires the status of a crime-doer. When he is convicted, he acquires the status of a convict. When he is incarcerated, he acquires the status of a prisoner. The international human rights law grants sanction for the enjoyment of human rights for the crime-doers, for the arrestees, for the convicted and so on. All of them must enjoy the right to life, liberty, equality and dignity. Nevertheless, they enjoy only restricted freedom while they are under custody or during incarceration, etc. Precisely, therefore, their rights should be specified in the Declaration itself. Hence, a sub-clause to Article 2 becomes necessary and that is :

> "Provided that those who are involved in the commission of an offence will be entitled to enjoy only those rights sanctioned by the criminal laws which are human rights friendly." Provided further that the infliction of death penalty is considered to be human rights unfriendly as it violates the right to life". Annihilation of one's life for having committed a crime is a human rights violation.

The second portion of the present Article may be retained in the revised UDHR as well.

Article 2 and Criminal Justice

In criminal justice administration, researches indicate that discrimination and differential treatments are often seen and experienced. Distinction is seen between the haves and have-nots, between the affluent and the poor, between the influential and the non-influential, between powerful and the powerless and this distinction leads to discrimination of all kinds or descriptions. Accordingly, differential treatment is provided to those who are handled by all subsystems in justice administration. According to me, there is scope for a new Article here and it must be :

"Everyone subjected to proceedings by the criminal justice system is entitled to rights without any discrimination based on the power-political; affluence-financial; status-social; and are entitled to enjoy the same and similar treatment." Of course, Article 7 of the UDHR says that "All are equal before law and are entitled without any discrimination to equal protection of law." This is not enough. Without discrimination to equal protection under law is one thing and differential treatment is quite another thing. For example, everyone will be detained in police custody and accordingly everyone will get equal protection under law. Some will be kept in police lock-ups while some others will be kept outside the police lock-up in police custody. Some will be provided with food purchased from the local hotel while some others will be provided with food purchased from the star hotel. Some will be given water from the common tap while some others will be given mineral water brought from the cool bars. Instances are reported that the affluent, the powerful and the influential are provided with luxuries while the poor, the downtrodden and less influential are given only creature-comforts in police custodial facility. This is nothing but differential treatment shown by the sub-systems in criminal justice administration. The UDHR does not speak anything about such differential treatments. Remember always that the laws in principle need not necessarily be the laws in practice. In practice, one may see gross violations of human rights when the laws are enforced. The human rights laws should take into account the principles contained in gender justice, juvenile justice, victim justice, social justice, etc., while the laws are enforced. Therefore, the Article should include :

"Provided that while the laws are enforced, the principles contained in gender justice, victim justice, social justice and juvenile justice should be honoured and respected". Human rights to women, to the victims of crime, to the victims of abuse of power/ misuse of authority, to juveniles, to the old and the infirm, to the members of the Scheduled Caste/Tribe, to the socially and economically handicapped, to the powerless and the less influential, and so on will be protected if these concepts too are incorporated in the Article 2 of the UDHR.

Article 2 and Justice

There are countries which do not recognise and respect human rights as declared by the Universal Declaration of Human Rights. There are individuals, groups and institutions in countries which do recognise and respect human rights. There are, as well-countries which loudly accept, recognise and respect human rights not only in the way the Universal Declaration of Human Rights say, but also much more than that; but there are countries which violate rights in many ways and implement them as they want. All these are injustices and, therefore, it is very necessary that they should implement everything they preach in the way it must be. All of them do take part in committing injustice and to do so is a moral sin. It is as well a violation of the basic human right. They do involve in violating human rights and thereby participate in actions or perform activities which are intrinsically incompatible with human dignity–with man's right to life, liberty and equality.

Countries which claim to show respect to human rights do commit crimes in the name of establishing and promoting human rights of people. It is like people living in filth talking against one's life in filth. Those countries are financially affluent and very powerful in their military strength. The countries which are poor look at them for financial assistance and they do not react to the human rights violations committed by them and painfully, reluctantly or with silence but with strong objection to tolerate their tyrannical decisions. Everyone's including that of their conscience rightly rejects those crimes against humanity. Instead of reacting against by those who love human rights in their own country, are helplessly tolerated or defencelessly suffered by the victim nations. The crimes committed by those unscrupulous tyrants are legitimized by vested interests through their political strength and voting power in the international fora. What an injustice indeed !

Why do people in power refuse to recognise and respect human rights? They put a lot of *'ifs' and 'buts'* in order to accept human rights and the *ifs and buts* are in the name of race, colour, sex, language and a variety of other things. What happens as a result? The peace and harmony of the society is shaken. Peace which is not built upon the values of human rights of people will not be peace at all. I remember to have heard the T.V. address of the head of a rich nation to the people and he said that he would establish peace in a particular country by a war and he promised them a "better tomorrow". The country he attacked was destroyed and a civilisation ruined. He did everything with his military supremacy and every other word he uttered in his T.V. telecast was "Human Right" or "human dignity". His words were empty and today (July 22, 2006), I find massacre, mass murders, killings of innocent human beings in the name of establishing eternal peace which, I am sure, will never be there until that country stops the military operations. He must acknowledge, respect and promote values which he can never create, modify or destroy there. Let him remember that he should not permit the killing of innocent human beings in the pretext of establishing peace in that country or world outside. When major powers or powerful countries violate the human rights law, the United Nations will have to adjust their strategy, views and vision in accordance to the tune of their voice. This too is injustice and to be honest, there are people who speak against the United Nations and their endeavour to promote human rights. The United Nations advertise vacancies for the appointment of Human Rights Officers in many parts of the world and do many constructive things for the protection and promotion of human rights among the nations of the world. At the same time, what do the United Nations do to promote human rights to the people living in the countries of the major power and economic affluence? Or, do the United Nations make attempts to promote human rights in those countries which simply refuse to listen to them? Perhaps, some countries are superpowers and above the United Nations. If that is a truth, it too is injustice in every sense.

12

Security of Persons, Slavery, Slave Trade, Servitude, Crime Syndicates, Nexus Crimes and *Mafias*

Everyone has the right to
Life
Liberty and the
Security of person

Article 3 of the UDHR speaks about one's right to life, liberty and security of a person. The question is: "Why is the UDHR silent about the other rights, namely, the "right to equality and freedom?" The above Article could have been better expressed as :

Life
Liberty
Equality and
Dignity

I do not know the *why and how* of putting the *Security of a Person* in Article 3 of the UDHR. Does not "Right to life include the security of person as well"? *Security* means "freedom from danger, risk etc., to the person". "Person" means "(1) a human being, (2) the actual self or individual personality of a human being, (3) the body of a living human being, and in law, it means again a "human being" or "a group of human beings" etc. Whatever that be, the *right to life* means the "the right to the security of person". Therefore, the right to the security of person is unnecessary in the

Article and in effect is nothing but a tautology of what has been stated in "Right to Life".

Again, I do not know the *why and the how* of the UDHR failing or refusing to put "rights of equality and dignity in the Article 3"? If it would have brought those concepts too in the Article 3, readers would have got a comprehensive idea about the "what" of human rights or what were the "human rights" of people at the beginning of the Declaration itself. If everyone has a right to life, it means that the State has no authority to take away one's life. If everyone has a right to life it means that everyone has a right to *life with dignity*. Like capital punishment, mercy killing/euthanasia has no place under human rights law.

Since the Right to Dignity was not declared as a fundamental human rights in Article 3 of the UDHR, the next Article 4 that followed ceased to have any logical sequence. Article 4 reads :

> "No one shall be held in slavery or servitude; slavery and the slave trade shall be prohibited in all their forms."

Slavery or servitude, slavery and slave trade are degrading to human dignity. If the right to dignity were declared in Article 3, then the Article 4 would have been logically followed showing a sequence. Slavery means the "ownership of a person or persons by another or others". Slavery is bondage and it emphasises the idea of complete ownership and control by a master. Bondage shows a state of subjugation or captivity often involving burdensome and degrading labour. Servitude is a compulsory service, often such as is required as a legal penalty. In penology, servitude, i.e., compulsory service or labour was a sort of punishment for criminals. In law, servitude means a right possessed by one person with respect to another's property for a limited purpose. In the history of penal treatment, one sees *slave ship*, i.e., a ship for transporting slaves from their native homes to places of bondage. In US history, one sees slave-state, i.e., any of the states where Negro slavery was legal until the Civil War.

Slavery is a violation of the *Freedom* guaranteed by many Constitutions of the world and so long as the human rights recognise freedom as an inalienable, inherent, fundamental, basic and universal right of human beings, the denial for the enjoyment of such a right by people is certainly a grave violation of human rights. Sometimes, the slaves die of poverty, hard work, malnutrition and lack of care and protection. As far as the criminal laws are concerned, it is inevitable and necessary to make slavery, servitude and slave trade punishable under law.

Worse than slavery is the working of organised criminals, crime syndicates and *Mafias*. They show no respect to human rights–to life, freedom, equality and dignity. Nexus crimes are seen today in plenty. Enforcement crimes are practised and perpetuated everywhere. Terrorism, terror-causing 'isms', insurgency cause violations of human rights in many ways. Therefore, I recommend a new Article to the revised edition of the UDHR.

> "No one shall be made a victim of organised crimes, crime syndicates, Mafia, nexus criminality, enforcement crimes, terrorism', terror causing 'isms' and insurgency. They must be prohibited by laws and made punishable under the criminal laws."

If slavery, servitude and slave trade make the individuals to suffer, the above mentioned crimes victimise many individuals in the society. Innocent people are killed, maimed, exploited and injured and the superior strength of them make human life miserable and enjoyment of human rights very difficult, if not impossible. In 1948 when the UDHR was accepted, the information about Nexus Crimes, *Mafia*, Organised Crimes, Crime Syndicates, Enforcement Criminals, etc., was not available and data on their activities against human rights enjoyment were not in hand. Terrorism has become a global phenomenon and insurgency, likewise, is a threat to human life. Nexus Crimes, *Mafia* Crimes, organised crimes promote gangs, *goondas* and unprincipled men who show no respect to human life, the person in the individual and human dignity. Like slave trade, these criminals involve themselves in flesh trade, hooch trade, manufacture of illicit liquor; frauds, murders, etc., and thus make human life miserable. Hence, they must be prohibited by law in an international level. Today, the society has become *a slave* to many of these nexuses, organised and enforcement criminal activities and injustice.

The question of life comes when people discuss the nature of life. Injustice comes for discussion when the question is about the life in the suites in 5 star or 7 star hotels for some and the same for those who live in slums and subhuman environments. Everybody has the right to life, but how?–like pigs in dirt or like 'gods' on earth? Right to life means the right to live with dignity. People say that the animals kept in the zoo live in comforts whereas the convicts in prisons live in inhuman or subhuman conditions without even enjoying creature-comforts. What about their food, housing, accommodation, clothing, nutrition and healthcare? People die of starvation and the deaths reported of famine, flood, cold wind, coldness, etc., are numerous. Yet, many claim that they recognise and respect the human rights of the people to life. The number of people sleeping on footpaths, inside the water pipe, under the bridge, in railway platforms and in huts run to millions in many countries where the political leaders, bureaucrats, businessmen, religious men, spiritualists, theologians, social workers, human rights activists, traders live in luxuries which only human imagination can conceive of. Is it justice to see people living like pigs, worms and animals in dirt?

Right to liberty is a declared right. Women complain that they live like slaves in a patriarchal system of family life. They are not liberated from men. Convicts in prisons complain that they are denied of freedom under the parole system if they do not have political godfathers. There are prisoners who could not go out from the prison just because they do not have political patronage or administrative goodwill. At the same time, there are prisoners who enjoy freedom both inside and outside the prison. They get permission from the prison authorities or Government to go home under the *ticket to leave system* whenever they want under the pretext of emergency grounds. What type of human rights do the prisoners enjoy? The members of certain religions complain that their freedom to practise religion is taken away by vested interests on grounds which are not religion supported. There are methods of excommunication by virtue of which an ardent believer in a particular religion is prohibited by force from exercising his right to live in a religious society by practising his faith. Excommunication is seen not only in Christian churches, but also in other religions. Castism, racism, untouchability and other customs do not permit people to mix and mingle with people. Their freedom is curtailed and there are religions which do not allow the women to enter the place of worship to adore the gods. What type of freedom is declared by the United Nations if people are not allowed to exercise their freedom on the basis of sex, caste, race, custom, tradition etc. ? Is it not unjust to do so when everyone wants to enjoy human rights equally ?

Right to security is again a declared human right. Are the people safe? It is roughly estimated that nearly 40-45 per cent of the total investment in the construction of a house is spent for the security of people. Children are kidnapped, women are abducted and even the policemen take into custody people on arbitrary grounds. Lock-up deaths are reported from police and judicial custody. Custodial violence is reported from police, prisons, hospitals, college hostels and where people live under custodial care or legal guardianship. Father rapes the daughter and incestuous sex violations are reported from many parts of the world. The old and the infirm are not safe and the governments ought to have ensured the right to security for their citizens, but the governments do not do so. They are not able to provide security for the life and property of the people and what is the meaning of talking about justice *via* human rights administration when the governments in power are helpless to protect human rights ?

13

Treatment and Punishment to Crime-Doers

"No one shall be subjected to torture or to cruel, inhuman or degrading treatment or punishment". What is torture? This has been described in the Convention Against Torture and Other Cruel, Inhuman or Degrading Treatment or Punishment. In this context, I may quote from *Anushasana Parva,* 115, 25 in *Mahabharata* that "Abstention from injury is the highest penance. It is also the highest truth from which all duty proceeds." If so, torture is a human right violation.

According to the Convention Against Torture and Other Cruel, Inhuman or Degrading Treatment or Punishment, torture means "any act by which severe pain or suffering, whether physical or mental, is intentionally inflicted on a person for such purposes as obtaining from him or a third person information or a confession, punishing him for an act he or a third person has committed or is suspected of having committed or intimidating or coercing him or a third person or for any reason based on discrimination of any kind, when such pain or suffering is inflicted by or at the instigation of or with the consent or acquiescence of a public official or other persons acting in an official capacity. It does not include pain or suffering arising only from, inherent in or incidental to lawful sanctions". This is a narrow definition/ description of torture and if this is what UDHR means by the expression Torture in the Declaration, then it must be amended. According to United Nations, "Any act by which . . ." and it means that the international organisation thinks of only "commissions" and not "omissions". If committing an act can cause torture, then it is equally important to note that "omitting to do an act" too can cause severe pain and/or suffering. One can violate human rights by commissions and/or by omissions. More often than not, human rights are violated by omissions rather than commissions.

Article 5 of the UDHR tells about cruel treatment or punishment. What is cruelty? *Cruel* means "wilfully or knowingly causing pain or distress to others." The synonyms of 'cruel' are (1) barbarous, bloodthirsty, merciless, etc. Cruelty implies pitiless, ruthless, brutal or savage type of treatment which contains hard-heartedness and positive refusal to show compassion. It suggests fierceness and brutality, physical violence and unscrupulousness, letting nothing stand in one's way and using any methods necessary. Though the word "CRUEL" is pregnant with a lot of concepts, I am still confused as to what it really means and what constitutes cruelty so that one can say that one violates the human rights of others.

My question is: "What is a cruel treatment?–or a cruel punishment?" What is felt as cruel by one will be treated as *not cruel* by another. For example, the law in one country says that a detainee in police custody must be provided with necessary wearing apparel and the police officials used to keep him in under-clothings, in half-nakedness or in nakedness covered with/without newspapers. Is this a cruel treatment? According to police officials, the nakedness/half-nakedness is a precaution taken against one's commission or attempt to commit suicide. It is not cruelty, rather a sort of protection and care to safeguard his right to life. Here, one's right to life conflicts with his right to dignity.

About cruel punishment, UDHR does not say anything. Is capital punishment based on an eye for an eye, a tooth for a tooth cruel? Is incarceration with hard labour and without paying reasonable/adequate wages cruel? Is overcrowding in prisons cruel? While one recognises the infliction of cruel treatment or punishment as a violation of human rights, no one speaks anything about the scale/criterion to decide the same. Some "nice to hear" words or expressions stating that some lofty and sublime things are done may be fine, but means nothing.

Again, what is this "degrading treatment or punishment"? "Degrade" means

(1) to reduce someone to a lower rank, degree, etc., deprive of office, rank, degree or title, especially as a punishment;
(2) to lower in character or quality; debase, deprave;

(3) to lower in dignity or estimation; bring into contempt", etc., and "degrading" means "that degrades; debasing". Any punishment is degrading and I do not think that there can be a punishment which upgrades a person's status and dignity. How can the United Nations fix degrees in punishment from "upgrading to degrading" or *vice versa*? Any punishment from imposition of fine to infliction of death penalty is degrading and, therefore, the entire Article 5 of the UDHR must be rewritten as :

"No one shall be subjected to torture–physical, mental or both;

"No one shall be subjected to cruel, inhumane or degrading treatment;

"Provided that the criterion to decide the nature of 'cruel, inhumane or degrading treatment' shall be the cultural/sub-cultural laws and majority views of the people put together."

What is *inhuman*? "Inhuman" means "lacking sympathy, pity, warmth, compassion, or the like; cruel; brutal; not human. I may prefer to use the expression "inhumane" instead of "inhuman" in the Article 5 of UDHR. Why? "*Inhumane*" means "not humane", i.e., lacking humanity or kindness. "Humane" means characterised by tenderness, compassion, and sympathy for men and animals. UDHR ought to take human dignity to be of primary importance and as such why not "*humane*" be used instead of "human" in the Article 5 of UDHR ?

Treatment and Punishment must not be clubbed together in one and the same Article. Treatment is one thing and punishment is quite another thing. Treatment does not contain punishment while punishment may contain treatment. Treatment simply means an "action or behaviour towards a person" whereas punishment means infliction of pain—physical, mental or both to a person who is found to have committed an offence under law. As they cannot be put together, a new Article may be introduced to the UDHR as :

> "No one shall be subjected to a punishment which is not intended for the personality development of the punished in nature and content."

It may be remembered that every punishment is only a means to an end—the end being the personality development of the crime doer via correction, reformation, resocialisation and reintegration of the crime-doer back to society. "Corrective" means "tending to correct or rectify; remedial" and correctional is the adjective of correction and it is intended to set or make right; remove the errors or faults from the crime-doers. Therefore, the Article thus added should specify clearly the ultimate objective of punishment (correction) to be personality development through reformation, resocialisation and reintegration of the crime-doer to the society back. Hence, the Article should include :

> "Every punishment shall have its objective to be the development of the personality of the punished via correction, reformation, resocialisation, rehabilitation and reintegration of the crime-doers to society back."

If personality development through correction, reformation, resocialisation and reintegration of crime-doers back to society is recognised by the UDHR; then parole, probation, ticket to leave, after-care services, clinical treatments, etc., get greater importance in prison administration and management. The present Article 5 is silent about the noble and desirable objective of punishment and as such the corrective or correctional nature and content are ignored or visibly neglected. The objective of correction in punishing crime-doers guarantees their human rights to life and dignity. Corporal punishment will not have any scope during incarceration. Capital penalty which annihilates the crime-doer (the person to be corrected and reformed) will not have any place in the list of punishments. No human rights law can tolerate the annihilation of a person to be corrected and reformed. It is a grave violation of the right to life of an individual.

Man judges man or a man makes judgments about another man and his activities. If a man is susceptible to errors, any human judge is no exception to it. In my view, there may be one dozen causes for convicting or acquitting a person in administration of justice. Nevertheless, one or two causes may be stated in the judgments and the rest may be hidden or unconsciously operating in the mind of the judge. Colour, creed, caste, community, race, place of birth, relationship, introductions, contacts, nationality, sex, language, etc., may work as a cause of conviction or acquittal as the case may be.

14

Person before Law with Rights and Duties

"Everyone has the right to recognition everywhere as a person before the law." A person means a *human being*. A human being has the *essence* and *existence*. When the essence is recognised, then the *person* in the other is respected. Consequently, an I-Thou relationship comes into being; otherwise what is seen will be an I-It relationship. In approving the I-Thou relationship, the actual self or individual personality of a human being is accepted and it is done irrespective of his existence in whatever manner. He may have a vegetable existence or may have outlived the utility. Still, he is a person recognised to be so before the law. In law, a person is a human being or a group of human beings recognised by law as having rights and duties. The rights here mean human rights and any person who claims human rights has many *duties* to perform as such person. He himself must recognise and respect human rights of others. The Article 7 is not full as it does not speak anything about his *duties*. Therefore, the Article needs amendment, as :

> "Everyone has the right to recognition everywhere as a person before law and has the duties which follow from the enjoyment of such rights."

What I have seen in my research career is that the people are conscious of their rights and unaware of their duties. Many Constitutions of the democratic world do guarantee fundamental rights (these rights include some of the human rights too) to their citizens to enjoy and correspondingly do not say anything about the fundamental duties. In India, the fundamental duties of the citizens were later added to her Constitution under Part IV-A. When the law recognises an individual as a person, he should have the following duties as well when he enjoys the human rights. These may be the duties :

1. to abide by human rights laws in letter and spirit;
2. to recognise and respect the ideals enshrined in the UDHR, international conventions and covenants and national laws on human rights;
3. to uphold and protect the human rights of all residing in any part of the world irrespective of any considerations;
4. to defend the human rights of others wherever necessary and to protect their interest in the enjoyment of human rights;
5. to render services for the promotion of human rights when called upon or even otherwise;
6. to promote human rights-consciousness among the people so that they live in harmony and human coexistence;
7. to maintain common brotherhood amongst all people of the world transcending religious, ethnic, linguistic, caste, sub-caste, colour, regional, racial, sectional diversities;
8. to renounce practices derogatory to the dignity of man, woman, children, the old and the infirm, the handicapped—socially, economically, politically and culturally;
9. to valuate and preserve the rich heritage of world's pursuit to the enjoyment of human rights; and
10. to strive towards excellence in all spheres of human rights activities so that the peoples of the United Nations/world will rise to highest levels of social progress, better living and enjoyment of larger freedom in letter and spirit.

There can be more duties enlisted and I do not know why the United Nations failed to incorporate the duties while they declared that everyone has a right to recognition everywhere as a person before law. Instances are plenty to show that people who claim their right to recognition before law forget conveniently their duties to be performed before they make such claims. In criminal law enforcement, this neglect, failure or refusal to perform the duties are very visible. Terrorists, Naxalites, Maoists, insurgents and so on are found to be gross human rights violators and they claim this right even when they flatly refuse to perform their duties. Such a situation arises because the UDHR–1948 does not contain the duties to be performed by people who claim human rights for them.

When, more often than not, police are accused of human rights violations, people everywhere raise the point that they were not recognised as "Person" before law. The policemen too make a counter argument that they were not recognised as "Person" before law. Whatever may be the arguments—*pro and contra*—the fact remains that everyone has a right to be recognised as a person before law with duties on the other side. Rights and duties are the two sides of the same coin. The accuser should not be accused as a violator of human rights. Duty means "something that one is expected or required to do by moral or legal obligation". It is a binding and obligatory force of something that is morally or legally right. The governments are bound to offer such environments for a person to perform his duties.

Objections may be there to put *duties* in a Declaration on human rights. The objections cease to have any relevance or validity, because the enjoyment of human rights without performing the obligations attached to the enjoyment is hollow in every sense. The issue here is: "Is a criminal recognised as a person before law"? The obvious explanation is that all criminals—the suspects, the arrestees, the detainees, the accused, and so on have their rights sanctioned by law in many countries. Such rights are :

1. As a person, there is the right against arbitrary or illegal arrest.
2. As a person, there is the right to be released on bail and the right against illegal detention.
3. As a person, there is the right for protection against cruel or inhuman treatment during investigation.
4. As a person, there is the right for benefit of doubt.
5. As a person, there is protection against conviction/ enhanced punishment under *ex post facto* law.
6. As a person, there is the protection against self-incrimination.
7. As a person, there is the right for remedies for enforcement of human rights.

8. As a person, there is the right against arbitrary or unreasonable searches and seizures.
9. As a person, there is the right for the protection of life and equality before law.

Corresponding to their rights, do they have any duties? They have a lot of duties. They have to appear before the courts to defend their case, to co-operate with the investigating machinery during investigation, have to observe the conditions under which the bail has been granted, to abide by the rules during judicial remand or while they are incarcerated. The rights and duties attached to a *person* before law are many and the revised UDHR need to be clear about them in the Article itself. For, the human rights are the sweetest thing man created for man, but he forgot to put a soul into them by enlisting the duties of man along with his enjoyment of rights. Any enjoyment without obligation is no enjoyment at all.

15

Same Laws and Equality before Laws

"All are equal before the law and are entitled without any discrimination to equal protection of the law. All are entitled to equal protection against any discrimination in violation of this Declaration and against any incitement to such discrimination."

[*Article 7, UDHR—1948*]

"All are equal before the law"—no doubt, this is a noble and lofty principle. The problem that I have seen in my studies is that the *law in principle* is found to be different from the *law in practice*. The law can and will take its course if violations of human rights are seen. It may be remembered that it is not the law that takes its course, rather is the individual behind the enforcement of law that decides the course to be taken. In such a situation, there may not be any equality before the law in practical law enforcement and administration of justice. Politicians are different from the ordinary man on the street, the powerful are different from the powerless, the affluent are different from the poor and the down-trodden, the social higher ups are different from the socially handicapped. In such a world, can or will the law treat everyone equal before it? No, it does not and it cannot ! There are any number of research studies to show and prove that there is differential treatment when the law is enforced and the principle of equality before law is only in theory and on paper and not in practice. It is a myth in every sense. The makers, enforcers, protectors and adjudicators of law show preferential treatment to those coming before them not on the basis of any human rights rationale or intelligible differential, but on the basis of the gravity and force of the pressure exerted on them from within or outside or from various quarters, political or otherwise. In this state of affairs, what is the meaning, relevance or implication of the UDHR-1948 insisting or declaring about EQUALITY BEFORE LAW in practical field? Hence, I may suggest an amendment to Article 7 of the UDHR-1948 as-

> "All are equal before the law in theory and the law in practice...".

Here I find a problem. In reality,

> All are equal to all
> Some are equal to some
> None is equal to anyone.

This is a naked truth and as such, the question is "how can all be equal before law?" It being the case, I make another suggestion, i.e.,

"The laws are equal to all in theory and practice" or they ought to be so. In this new approach, equality will mean "sameness" and as such, why not we rewrite the Article 7 as under, i.e.,

"The laws are the same for all in theory and practice". "Sameness" means the "state or quality of being the same; identity; uniformity". "Same" means "being one"—"unchanged in character, condition, nature, etc. *The same* means "in an identical or similar way". Laws can be the same for all, but all cannot be the same for the law. Likewise, laws can be equal for all and all cannot be equal for the law or before the law. The expression "Before the Law" is quite confusing and misleading for the simple reason that the LAW is not an individual, rather is a principle which cannot act by itself. When we say that the laws are the same for all, then it guarantees equality for all.

"Equal protection of the law" is another expression that needs discussion. The UDHR-1948 reads :

"All... are entitled without any discrimination to equal protection of the law". Again, what is meant by *equal protection*? "Protect" means to defend or guard from attack, loss, insult, etc., cover or shield from injury or danger". How can the law offer equal protection to all? "Equal" means "of the same in quantity, degree, merit, etc." In this sense, *equal protection* is quite understandable. Nevertheless, it should not be "of the laws" but must be "under the laws". For, the protection is given by the people enforcing the laws. Individuals can ensure protection under the law or with the authority of law. Hence, I suggest an amendment to Article 7 of UDHR-1948 as :

"All . . . are ensured without discrimination to equal protection under law". The question here is: "Why the expression *entitled* is substituted by *ensured*"? The answer is that the expression "entitled" does not convey the full meaning and implication of what is guaranteed by the UDHR. *Entitle* means "to give (a person or thing) a title, right, or claim to something". "Ensure" means "to secure or guarantee", i.e., making sure or certain or making secure or safe. This is what is required more than giving a right or claim to something. One can make claims to many things, but he needs not necessarily get his claims allowed. One may have a right for something and that right needs not necessarily be a legal right. It can be a moral right. Of course, legal rights can be enforced through a court of law while moral rights cannot be. Why to cause confusion? Why cannot the UDHR give a guarantee and for it, use the expression "ensure" in the Article and that is the reason why I suggested the amendment in the way stated above.

"Any discrimination" is another expression seen in Article 7 of UDHR-1948. "Discriminate" means "to make a distinction in favour of or against a person or thing on a categorical basis rather than according to actual merit". Fine indeed ! The problem that I have seen is that in some instances, there may not be any discrimination, but there will be some distinction made while ensuring protection to people. "Everything being equal", the protection is ensured on the basis of certain distinctions specially made in favour of some or against others. "Distinct" means "distinguished as not being the same; not identical; different in nature or quality; dissimilar, etc. For example, people say that this gun is distinct from that gun when both are guns made in the same factory, with the same metal and with the same specifications. Hence, distinctions are made between people possessing the same qualities, merits and characteristics. I have seen that DISTINCTIONS making graver problems than DISCRIMINATION. Bias, prejudices, favouritism, partiality, self-interest or anything of similar nature will be a factor causing *distinctions* between people. Therefore, the Article 7 may be finally amended as: *"The laws are the same for all in theory and in practice. All are equal before the law and are ensured without discrimination and distinction to equal protection under the law"*.

The second part of the Article 7 of UDHR-1948 too needs a discussion. It reads *"... All are entitled to equal protection against any discrimination in violation of this Declaration and against any incitement to such discrimination"*. This part of the Article 7 makes the people entitled to equal protection against any discrimination as well as against any incitement to such discrimination. I fail to understand the full meaning of the expression "equal protection" in this part of the Article 7. Do the United Nations bring victimological principles here? In other words, do they speak for the victims of discrimination? If victimological compensation, restitution or anything of like nature is what is intended here, I do not find a need for such a special provision for this Article 7 apart from other Articles in the UDHR-1948. The portion can be deleted and a separate Article covering the entire UDHR can be brought into.

Article 7 and Criminal Justice

My research experience proves that the equality before law and equal protection of law—both are not strictly adhered in practical law enforcement, prosecution and adjudication. If and when one visits a prison, he often sees less influential, poor, socially handicapped, moderately educated or illiterate convicts more in number than the affluent, influential, socially higher up people. Why? Does it mean that only the poor, powerless, handicapped and illiterate people commit crimes? No. The equality before law is not properly seen in practical administration of justice. The better lot somehow or other escaped punishment and the principles of 'equality before law and equal protection of law' was not applied strictly. Money, influence, power pressures, etc., have something to do and they are in favour of the crime doers. As such, they purchase more favoured treatments, decisions and judgments and equality before law ceases to have any effect or impact on such situations. The purchaser's market overpowers the sellers' market so much so that equal protection of law becomes an empty provision in the human rights legislations. Do the people arrested, detained, tried and incarcerated enjoy equality before law and equal protection of law in practical administration of criminal justice? Third degree methods are used against some while VIP treatment is offered to others. Inhuman, degrading and cruel treatment is shown to some while most human, highly dignified and human rights friendly attitudes/ approaches are shown to some while the basic creature-comforts are denied to others revealing that the law in theory is not the law in practice. Some die in custody, some commit suicide and some enjoy luxuries and all are done under the same laws which guarantee equality before law and equal protection of laws.

16

Not Fundamental Rights; But Human Rights

"Everyone has the right to an effective remedy by the competent national tribunal for acts violating the fundamental rights granted to him by the Constitution or by law."

(*Article 8, UDHR-1948*)

The rights are fundamental and they are ensured by the Constitution or by law. In such situations, naturally and necessarily there will be effective remedies for acts violating the fundamental rights. In India, for example, Article 32 of the Constitution reads:

(1) The right to move the Supreme Court by appropriate proceedings for the enforcement of the rights conferred by this part is guaranteed.

(2) The Supreme Court shali have power to issue direction or orders or writs, including writs in the nature of *habeas corpus, mandamus, prohibition, quo-warranto* and *certiorari,* whichever may be appropriate, for the enforcement of any of the rights conferred by this part.

(3) Without prejudice to the powers conferred on the Supreme Court by Clauses (1) and (2), Parliament may by law empower any other court to exercise within the local limits of its jurisdiction all or any of the powers exercisable by

> the Supreme Court under Clause (2)(4). The right guaranteed by this Article shall not be suspended except as otherwise provided for by this Constitution.

Similar laws will be available in all countries and Constitutions which guarantee fundamental rights to their citizens. In countries where Protection of Human Rights Act has been enacted, certainly, there will be provisions for effective remedy in case the human rights are violated. These rights may be seen as fundamental rights too in certain Constitutions. For example, in the Protection of Human Rights Act, 1993 (10 of 1994) enacted in India, section 2(d) lays down–

"Human Rights" means the right relating to life, liberty, equality and dignity of the individual guaranteed by the Constitution or embodied in the International Covenants and enforceable by courts in India. The very purpose of the Act has been spelt out as :

"An Act to provide for the Constitution of a National Human Rights Commission, State Human Rights Commission in States and Human Rights Courts for better protection of human rights and for matters connected therewith or incidental thereto." What is meant by "better" protection is not clear. It must have been "full" or "total" protection of human rights.

The Article 8, UDHR-1948 becomes unnecessary and irrelevant in a Declaration on Human Rights. For, it does not speak anything about the human rights and their violations. It speaks about the fundamental rights guaranteed by the Constitution and effective remedy *via* national tribunals for such violations. It may be remembered that all constitutional rights are not human rights and all human rights need not necessarily be the fundamental rights guaranteed by various Constitutions of the world. The UDHR–1948 ought to speak only about the human rights and not about the fundamental rights guaranteed by the Constitutions of the world. Various countries do have different types of Governments. Democratic countries are of different nature. There are kingdoms, theocratic countries, military rulers and so on. Accordingly, their Constitutions and fundamental rights differ. At the same time their human rights remain the same. They are universal. I, therefore, recommend to delete the entire Article 8 from the proposed new UDHR. Accordingly, the new Article may be :

> "Everyone has the right to all effective remedies by the competent national tribunals for acts or/ and omissions violating the human rights declared to be so by this Declaration and the laws applicable to the country to which he belongs."

What is meant by effective remedy? The expression is vague and as such must be clearly spelt out or specified. Is it victimological compensation/restitution? Is it awarding of punishment to the violators of human rights? Is it both? Making the Article clearer and more specific, we may write–

> "Everyone has the right for victimological compensation/ restitution through a competent tribunal for acts and omissions violating the human rights declared to be so by this Declaration or by other laws applicable to the country to which he belongs.
>
> "Further, everyone has a right to set the law into motion for the punishment of the violators of human rights by a competent human rights court."

Why do we change the fundamental rights to human rights? The reason is that the fundamental rights granted by the Constitutions in various countries need not necessarily be universal whereas the human rights are. There are theocratic countries, democracies, kingdoms, etc., and the fundamental rights in those different jurisdictions, as said above, need not necessarily be the same whereas the human rights are. They are the inalienable rights of people wherever they are. Human Rights are, therefore, to be brought into the Article 8 after deleting the expressions "fundamental rights and Constitution".

Article 8 and Criminal Justice

Every human rights violation is a criminal act and the punishment will be imprisonment, fine, etc. On the other hand, the violations of the fundamental rights in the Constitution need not necessarily be a human rights violation. Precisely therefore, the remedy may be, as said under Article 32 of the Constitution of India, anything from a writ of *habeas corpus* to *certiorari*. This is not victimological compensation/restitution. In human rights violations, there will be/should be the victim justice as well as criminal justice administered. Then only it becomes a total justice—holistic justice administration.

17

Arrest and Detention

> "No one shall be subjected to arbitrary arrest, detention or exile."
>
> (*Article 9, UDHR-1948*)

'Arbitrary' is an expression ununderstandable to many. It means: "subject to individual will or judgement without restriction; contingent solely upon one's discretion". It may also mean "decided by a judge or arbiter rather than by law or statute; using or abusing unlimited power; uncontrolled or unrestricted by law; despotic; capricious; unreasonable" etc. If this is what 'Arbitrary' means, arrest in common parlance as well as in dictionary means "to seize a person by legal authority or warrant". In law too it means the act of taking a person into legal custody, as by officers of law. Sometimes, it means an act of taking a person into custody by force. This legal power can be misused or abused. Hence, the correct approach is and should be :

> "No arrest shall be made, but upon probable cause supported by evidence."

Any arrest—arbitrary or otherwise, will have subjective contents, i.e., individual will or judgement. Whether or not the individual will or judgement has been executed with or without restriction is a matter of dispute. In arresting or not arresting a person, one's discretion plays an important role. Whether or not the discretion used is right or wrong is again a matter of dispute. Again, whether or not the arrest is made using or abusing unlimited power is a matter of dispute. In order to avoid all these confusions and disputes, the Article 9 may use the expression "probable cause supported by evidence". The reasonable men must be able to make the usual inference upon arrest that the arrest is justified under law and supported by evidence. Reasonable men may mean those who are neutral and detached people. A law enforcement officer who is engaged in the often competitive enterprise of ferreting out crime will interpret any arrest made by him fully justified whereas a neutral and detached individual will not. Probable means: "likely to occur or prove true; supported generally but not conclusively by the evidence; affording ground for belief; capable of standing a test". This is what is required in human rights laws too and that is the reason behind the proposed change in the Article 9 of UDHR–1948.

My experience and research findings give me ample proof to show that the police resort to *informal* arrests. *'Informal'* is the expression they use and it means in law nothing but *abduction* by the police officials. They make an unrealistic, imaginary and pleasing to them strategy only to show a distinction between *formal* and *informal* arrests and in effect both are one and the same, i.e., arrest. Arbitrary arrest is not in police dictionary, instead they have *informal* arrest, which is nothing but a violation of the human rights. *Informal arrest* for the police is nothing but taking a person into custody and detaining him (wrongful confinement in legal terminology) until at last he is arrested formally or released without making any record of the fact of having taken him in custody. Therefore, in order to put everything rightly and correct that aspect, I propose the amendment further in the way shown below, i.e., **"No arrest/taking in custody shall be made except upon probable cause supported by evidence."** For, I have seen police officials taking the erroneous view "take informally into custody, collect evidence and then arrest" instead of "collect evidence, have a probable cause and then arrest." This approach can be fully eliminated if the proposed amendment is made in Article 9 of UDHR–1948.

'Detention' may be of many kinds—namely, detention in (1) police custody or (2) judicial custody. Detention in police custody may be (1) in police custodial facility (popularly called in India police lock-ups) authorised by the administration or (2) in an unknown place in a clandestine way. According to law, the police can detain a person for 24 hours excluding the time required for the journey. Instances are plenty to show that the police detain people beyond the statutorily permitted 24 hours illegally or in an unauthorised manner. *Informal* arrest facilitates this sort of unauthorised practices. If the detention is for 24 hours, then, it may be for (1) 24 hours until he is produced before the court or (2) for a period less than 24 hours until the police release him from their custody. In many cases, transparency is lacking, secrecy is maintained and clandestine nature is unauthorisedly permitted and practiced. Hence, I suggest a change in the Article 9 of UDHR–1948 in the following manner, i.e.,

> "No one shall be detained in a non-transparent, secret or clandestine way. The detainee has the right to be released in all bailable offences without causing undue delay.
> No one shall be detained in custody without trial for a longer period than the period of imprisonment prescribed under law for the offence/s alleged to have been committed."

'*Exile*' means "(1) prolonged separation from one's country or home, as by force of circumstances; (2) anyone separated from country or home; (3) expulsion from one's native land by authoritative decree". I think that there has come into being a situation that the said '*expression*' in the Article 9 of the UDHR–1948 is no more required. Such arbitrary exiles are practically non-existent today so much so that it can be deleted.

Article 9 and Criminal Justice

Arrest and detention–they are found to be abused and the authority doing so is misused or abused to the maximum by vested interests. In India, the National Police Commission (1977-81) found that 60 per cent of the arrests were either unnecessary or unjustified under law. The situation may not be different in other countries too. There are laws, court rulings, instructions and standing orders to stop the abuse/misuse of the authority and they are found to be of no much conspicuous utility or value even today. The most important reason for the abuse/misuse of the authority is seen to be the absence of the expression "probable cause supported by evidence" before the arrest and an effective or meaningful scrutiny by the higher ups/media to evaluate whether or not the provision is meticulously followed.

'Detention' in its various forms and descriptions is not visibly seen because of its clandestine nature, lack of transparency and maintenance of secrecy. It can range from the momentary detention of a pedestrian to the arrest of a person (legally, illegally, formally, informally, etc.) who is suspected to have committed an offence or has been charged with the commission of an offence or incarcerated as a convicted offender. While each detention, no matter how brief or long, should be subjected to the human rights law particularly at a time deaths in custody, custodial rapes, inhuman, cruel and degrading treatments in custody, etc., are reported in plenty. The lawfulness of detention itself becomes a matter of importance and anguish today. It may determine the civil, possibly even criminal and certainly of human rights liability of the officer responible for the same. As such, the importance of my proposed changes in Article 9 of UDHR–1948 cannot be ignored or neglected. It is of importance not only in itself, but also because a decision to detain a person in an inconspicuous way, in a non-transparent manner, etc., is a decision not to show respect to the human rights of the people under custody or detention. The legitimacy and propriety of the exercise of the power to detain a person are matters of serious concern for human rights activists.

18

Trial in Fairness, Equity and Good Conscience

> "Everyone is entitled in full equality to a fair and public hearing by an independent and impartial tribunal, in the determination of his rights and obligations and of any criminal charge against him."
>
> [*Article 10 of UDHR 1948*]

I do not know why the words "entitled" "in full equality", etc., were introduced into the Article 10 of the UDHR-1948. *Equality* has already been recognized earlier in the UDHR and the fundamental human rights include *the right to equality*. Why to repeat the same thing and the tautology gives an impression that it is a *charity* shown to people and not a human right.

Full equality, part equality, less equality, etc., are meaningless as *equality is equality* as far as human rights are concerned. Human rights are the birth rights, inalienable rights of people and without which man cannot live and survive in dignity. As a physically handicapped man (one eyed man, deaf, dumb, and so on) is doubtlessly a physically handicapped man (he may not be handicapped in many other areas or may be differently abled), any person who does not have human rights is a handicapped one in every sense. Any person who is denied to have his human rights enjoyed is really a handicapped man. Enjoyment of human rights is his birth-right and, therefore, "entitlement" to human rights is unwarranted. Hence, there is no question of an "entitlement" (i.e., giving a title, right or claim to something) arising here. I propose that the entire expression—i.e., *entitled in full equality*—should be deleted from the Article 10 of UDHR–1948 to read:

> "Everyone has a right to....".

What is meant by FAIR AND PUBLIC HEARING? *Fair* means "(i) free from bias, dishonesty, or injustice; (2) legitimately sought, pursued, done, given, etc., (3) proper under the rules". As far as human rights are concerned, I, for one, think firmly that the concepts of EQUITY and GOOD CONSCIENCE too should be introduced. For, EQUITY means "(1) the quality of being fair or impartial; fairness, impartiality, (2) something that is fair and just, (3) [and in law, it means] the application of the dictates of conscience or the principles of natural justice to the settlement of controversies, (4) [and in jurisprudence, it means] a system of jurisprudence serving to supplement and remedy the limitations and inflexibility of the common law, (5) an equitable right or claim etc. These concepts are superb and precisely, therefore, I propose the following changes in the Article 10 of the UDHR 1948, as :

> **"Everyone has a right for a public trial in fairness, equity and good conscience".**

What is meant by "good conscience?" It is, as explained elsewhere, the (good) sense of what is right or wrong in one's conduct or motives, impelling one toward right action'; the ethical and moral principles that control or inhibit the actions or thoughts of an individual." While 'fairness, equity and good conscience' are introduced into Article 10 of the UDHR 1948, I am not inclined to accept a "Public" trial in all cases of human rights violations. Human rights justice consists of victim justice, gender justice, justice to terrorists/ insurgents etc. and, therefore, situations may arise owing to obvious reasons that a public trial cannot be conducted in sex related offences or in terrorist/ insurgency activities. There, it becomes necessary and inevitable to accept in-camera trials to protect the dignity of the victim of sex offences and to safeguard the interest of the country in terrorists/ insurgency activities. Therefore, I suggest a further amendment as :

> "Everyone has a right for a public trial in fairness, equity

> and good conscience, provided that in a trial for any offences against the womanhood or in cases related to terrorist/insurgency activities it may be done in-camera". In-camera means "privately".

The *hearing*–whether public or in-camera–should be by an independent and impartial tribunal. My researches in justice administration indicate that the independent and impartial tribunals are not constituted necessarily by qualified personnel to decide on human rights issues. Instances are not rare that tribunals which are under-qualified, unqualified or less qualified in human rights jurisprudence award judgements in some cases. The competency and suitability of the tribunals are of paramount importance in human rights cases. Eligibility to become the tribunal is different from the suitability and competency of the tribunal. Therefore, the proposed amendment is :

> "...... Provided further that the trial shall be conducted by an independent, impartial and competent tribunal."

It may be remembered that the competency of the tribunal along with impartiality and independence alone will decide the "quality" of the judgement. The merit of a verdict is decided by the quality of the judgements.

In Article 10 of the UDHR-1948, what is specially noticed is the introduction of "OBLIGATIONS" along with the RIGHTS. Fine, the obligations are to be read with duties as any rights without duties are meaningless. Determination of any criminal charges against one necessitates a thorough knowledge in criminal justice as well, i.e., in addition to human rights justice, victim justice, juvenile justice, social justice, equal justice, holistic justice, etc. Tribunals dealing with taxation, excise, civil, disciplinary, services cases are not competent enough to sit on judgements in human rights issues. Hence, the Article 10 of the UDHR-1948 is finally to be written as :

> "Everyone has a right for a public trial in fairness, equity and good conscience, provided that (1) in a trial of any offence against the womanhood or in cases related to terrorist/insurgency activities, it may be done in-camera;

(2) the trial shall be conducted by an independent, impartial and competent tribunal;
In determination of his rights and obligations and of criminal charges against him."

Article 10 and Criminal Justice

There are many problems for the enforcement of Article 10 in many countries. They are :

1. There exist only limited number of tribunals in many countries to decide on human rights cases and to decide on the criminal charges levelled against an individual. There are states and countries where no tribunals have been established.
2. If at all human rights tribunals are instituted, the personnel appointed are not qualitatively competent to determine the cases. They need special recruitment, training and acquisition of expertise.
3. The decisions of the tribunals are challenged in appeals and in some instances, the appeal courts set aside the decisions of the trial courts. This affects the public trust adversely on the merit, quality and competence of the tribunals administering justice and their judgements.

19

"Either–Or" Rights during a Trial

> "Everyone charged with a penal offences has the right to be presumed innocent until proved guilty according to law in a public trial at which he has had all the guarantees necessary for his defence."
>
> (*Article 11.1 of the UDHR-1948*)

The Article is framed on the basis of the accusatorial system of criminal justice. Here, the presumption of innocence is in favour of the accused when he/ she is charged with a penal offence. The issues are :

1. Before the charging of the penal offence, what is his status? In other words, what about the presumption of innocence?, i.e., either in favour of him or against him?
2. If the presumption of innocence is in favour of him, what justification is there for his arrest, remand and other pre-trial proceedings? Evidently, an innocent man should not be arrested and put to suffer the ordeals connected with the investigation of crime and subsequent pre-trial proceedings. Logically, it follows that he is presumed "guilty" during the investigation and subsequent pre-trial proceedings as well.
3. If one is presumed *guilty* during investigation and subsequent pre-trial proceedings, can he be given the status of "not guilty" immediately one day, too soon when the trial begins? The court too is aware of the ordeals connected with the investigation of crime in which

interrogation of the suspect forms a part. Allegations are plenty that the investigating officers employ questionable methods during arrest, detention, interrogation, etc. What justification is there for the ordeals and miseries to which he is subjected if he is not guilty?

4. Can the human psyche switch over from guilty to innocence so suddenly and without any reason or with a reason which tends to take a presumption in a different way. "To presume" means "to take for granted, assume or suppose" and in law, it means "to assume as true in the absence of proof to the contrary." How can the law assume something as true merely because there is the absence of proof to the contrary?" How cannot the law assume something as false in the absence of proof to the contrary? In the case of a criminal trial, there will not be absence of proof to the contrary, rather there will be the presence of proof to show that the charged is guilty and not innocent. Hence, the presumption in favour of the charged with a penal offence is of a questionable nature.
5. Why cannot the law take a realistic approach?, i.e., the one charged with a penal offence may be *guilty* or *innocent* until proved otherwise. I am not in favour of the inquisitorial system of criminal justice in which the person charged with a penal offence is presumed to be innocent. The presumption is against one who is charged with a penal offence. In my book on *Equal Justice,* I have proposed a new system of justice and I call it to be the 'Noquisitorial System". The system is realistic in the sense that the system considers the one charged with an offence to be "MAY BE INNOCENT OR GUILTY" as the case is. This "EITHER-OR" approach (i.e., Either Guilty or Innocent) gives equal opportunities for both prosecution and the accused to prove their version. The court is dispassionate and does not take sides as in the case of accusatorial and inquisitorial systems of justice. I have seen in my research studies that the accusatorial system and/or an unrealistic presumption of innocence in favour of the accused have been responsible for massive rate of acquittals. The system in my view has been instrumental for administering less justice, wounded justice, injustice and causing miscarriage

> of justice more than administering fair and just justice under an equal justice philosophy.

An act or omission is said to be an offence if and only if it violates the criminal law. There will be a punishment for every offence and, therefore, the word "PENAL" prefixed to "OFFENCE" in the Article is unnecessary and tautological: For, PENAL means "of pertaining to, or involving legal punishment; prescribing punishment; used in or for punishment, subject to or incurring punishment. Of course, one may take note of the fact that there is the expression "PENAL OFFENCE" in English language. But, I, for one, suggest that the word "PENAL" may be deleted from the Article to read as under :

> "Everyone charged with an offence has the right to be considered and treated as a person in an 'EITHER-OR status, until proved innocent or guilty as the case is...".

'EITHER-OR' there means either INNOCENT or GUILTY. In other words, either GUILTY OR INNOCENT under a NOQUISITORIAL system of justice administration. The word PENAL prefixed to offence is deleted. The Article 11.1 of UDHR–1948 reads further :

> "... according to law in a public trial ..." Here, I may add "... according to law and procedure established by law..." The 'PROCEDURE' I speak of will answer the test of reasonableness in order to be in conformity with the principles of human rights contained in the Universal Declaration of Human Rights by the United Nations. The procedure must be "right, just and fair"–must satisfy "equity and good conscience" and not "arbitrary, fanciful or oppressive".

As I pointed out in the previous chapter, I do not favour public trial in all cases because of the reasons given in the earlier chapter. Hence, I propose :

"... according to law and procedure established by law in a public trial in all cases except in those which are exempted from public trial for in-camera trial ..." The Article 11.1 of UDHR-1948 lays down further that :

". . . at which he has all the guarantees necessary for his defence." Here, I propose "rights" instead of "guarantees". Why? Rights are enforceable by courts of law whereas the guarantees need not necessarily be. The full text of the proposed Article will be :

> "Everyone charged with an offence has the right to be considered and treated as a person in an "Either-or" status until proved innocent or guilty, as the case may be, according to the law and procedure established by laws in a public trial in all cases except in those which are exempted from such trial for in-camera at which he has all the rights necessary for his defence".

Article 11.1 and Criminal Justice

Presumption of innocence in favour of the accused has been a perpetual cause for acquittals of large number of criminal cases. My researches show that it is easier to acquit an accused than to convict him. By virtue of the presumption of innocence and the doctrine of "benefit of doubt" to the accused which follows from the above presumption make the judges to acquit people as they wish. Normally no one questions the acquittal verdicts. The accused is happy and the prosecution goes after fresh cases more than making appeals and appeals against the acquitted ones. Unless gross injustice has been done or irresistible pressures from other quarters is sensed, the prosecution is inclined more to sleep on the disposed criminal cases than appealing against. Criminologists subscribe to the view that miscarriage of justice (wounded justice, less justice, etc.) comes into being as a result.

Trial in public-otherwise called public trial-ensures transparency. This really affects adversely very much in the trial of sex offences. The lawyers make use of the weakness of the victims of sex-attacks and the trial is converted into an opportunity to humiliate, victimise, harass and verbally slap the victims. This is of bad taste and everybody including the judge tolerates the ordeal. In order to ensure full justice by/*via* of human rights justice administration, one needs a lot of change in attitude, approach, laws, court practices, crafts and Evidence Acts in many countries.

20

Presumption of Innocence and Nature of Penalties

> "No one shall be guilty of any penal offence on account of any act or omission which did not constitute a penal offence, under national or international law, at the time when it was committed. Nor shall a heavier penalty be imposed than the one that was applicable at the time the penal offence was committed."
>
> (*Article 11.2 of the UDHR-1948*)

For reasons stated in the previous chapter, the word "Penal" prefixed to offence is unnecessary, meaningless and tautological. Hence, I propose to delete the same from the new Article. Good that the term "omission" is brought along with "commission" (of an act) in the above Article 11.2 of UDHR–1948. For, omissions are as important as commissions when offence is defined or described. Nevertheless, it seems to me that the expression "omission" has been forgotten when the full text was written. What is the meaning of *heavier* penalty? Penalty cannot be heavy or light in ordinary parlance and understanding. It may be severe or more severe. "Severe" means 'harsh'. In order to make the Article clearer and better, I propose an alteration in the structure as shown below :

> "No person shall be guilty of any offence for violation of the law—national or international—in force at the time of commission or omission of the act charged as an offence, nor be subjected to a penalty more severe than that which

> has been inflicted under law in force at the time of the commission/ omission of the act."

While no further amendment is suggested in the above Article, I think that the Article failed to take note of a serious omission on double jeopardy, i.e. :

> "No person shall be prosecuted and punished for the same offence more than once."

I do insist this provision too, because there are instances in which one and the same persons have been prosecuted more than once for the same offence. Although the above provision cannot be applied, there are people who face different kinds of ordeals in cases of human rights violations. For example, a police officer who violates human rights laws faces a departmental inquiry which may culminate even in the dismissal of the officer, a criminal charge before the Human Rights Courts which may culminate in punishment from imposition of fine to death penalty, a compensation case before the Human Rights Commission, etc. They—all of them—will not come under the purview of double jeopardy. Still they suffer a lot from a victimological angle. The violator of human rights here becomes an offender as well as a victim particularly when there exists no indemnity insurance schemes for police personnel who is always vulnerable to accusations—real or created. While protecting the Human Rights is a declared objective of UDHR, the fact cannot be denied that the protection against double jeopardy too must be a declared human rights. Double jeopardy must be evaluated and appreciated not only from the angle of criminal proceedings but also from the civil and victimological angles.

Further, it is very essential to give protection against incriminatory evidence. I, therefore, propose to add the following to the Article above.

> "No person charged with an offence shall be compelled to be a witness against himself."

This should be a protection against compulsion "to be a witness against oneself". If this protection is not ensured, there is every chance for the misuse or abuse of power and authority.

Why do I insist protection from (1) double jeopardy? And (2) incriminatory evidence in the UDHR ? The fundamental nature of the guarantee against double jeopardy can be traced to Greek and Roman times. It became established in the common law of England long before the UDHR was drafted and accepted by the United Nations (in 1948). Many countries in the world have incorporated this protection against double jeopardy in their Constitutions. It being the case, I am surprised to note the failure of the UDHR-1948 to have such a provision. The underlying idea here is that the state with all its might, manpower and resources should not make repeated attempts to put a person alleged to have committed a human right violation or crime to suffer embarrassment, expenditure, mental agony and many kinds of ordeal and thus force an individual to live in perpetually continuing state of anxiety and insecurity, as well as enhancing the possibility or chance that even if an individual is found to be innocent under one count, he may be found guilty on another count. It is nothing but "unfairness" to the accused. Fairness, justness, equity and good conscience demand the state to limit itself to one and only one effort to establish one's guilt. The prohibition is a protection against double punishment. The prohibition also implements the accused's interest in nullification, i.e., the nullification should have a conclusive effect.

Testimony given under a freewill is always welcome. Any compulsion to give self-incriminating testimony should be made violative of the human rights. The law must afford protection against being "forced to give testimony leading to the infliction of penalties stipulated to the criminal act committed. Immunity from the use of compelled testimony and evidence derived directly or indirectly therefrom gives protection to people.

When one reads the Articles 11.1 and 11.2, he sees the wordings that the one charged with an offence should be ensured of all the guarantees necessary for his defence. This way of loosely telling one's right is not enough although the "guarantees necessary for his defence" mean protection against double jeopardy and self-incrimination. I want to make Article specific about those guarantees which, according to me, are nothing but human rights.

Article 1.2 Criminal Justice

Many Constitutions in the world have made this a fundamental right. Nevertheless, in practical administration of criminal justice, one sees the applicability of this both in the attitude and approach of the officials towards the crime-doers and it is more so when the case is investigated by employing undesirable methods and strategies. It may be remembered that an offence today might not be an offence yesterday and likewise may not be an offence tomorrow. There is no retrospective effect for any criminal laws and if retrospective effect is given to the enforcement of criminal laws, there will be limitless prosecutions. It, itself, will be a human rights violation.

Every offence has a punishment prescribed and it is within a range, i.e., for a term which may extend to a fixed period of imprisonment or for an amount which may be a maximum fixed by law. This is decided by the punishing authority taking into account many aspects including the gravity of the offence, circumstances necessitated to the commission of the offence, victimological considerations, etc. "The punishment should be proportionate to the gravity and nature of the offence"–is a principle in jurisprudence and the discretion of the judge to decide the quantum of punishment is restricted by that principle in jurisprudence. The judge is not allowed to go beyond the quantum of punishment prescribed by the legislature and if one goes beyond the boundary so fixed by law, he violates the Human Rights law.

21

Interference to Privacy and Attacks on Honour

> "No one shall be subjected to arbitrary interference with his privacy, family, home or correspondence nor to unlawful attacks upon his honour and reputation. Everyone has the right to the protection of law against such interference or attacks."
>
> (*Article 12 of UDHR-1948*)

Problems connected with the use of the expression "arbitrary" have been discussed earlier when "arbitrary arrest" was dealt with. Again, one sees the same usage in Article 12 of UDHR-1948. It has been brought out there that the use of "probable cause supported by evidence" would be better than the use of "arbitrary" in the Article. Here too, I propose the same thing. Why? The quantum of information which constitutes probable cause-evidence which will warrant a person of "reasonable caution in the belief"—that an interference to one's privacy, family, home, etc., necessary should be there in every case. The misuse or abuse of the power to interfere in one's privacy, family, home, etc. has caused a lot of problems for people, i.e., even law abiding citizens will have to live at the mercy of the officers' whim and caprice. They enter the homes of the people at any time during night hours and sometimes repeatedly disturbing the privacy of all the members of the family. Researches show that this strategy is adopted not with the strength of any probable cause supported by evidence, but owing to the whim and caprice of the officers conducting investigation or searches. They may argue that the entire exercise has been done "not arbitrarily" and at the same time, they will not have any probable cause supported by evidence. The evidence collected by the officers or which is at their hand should be sufficient enough for arriving at an independent judgement that probable cause exists to interfere in the privacy of others. Sometimes, officers interfere in the privacy of others thinking or imagining that the people or materials which they need may be available in one's home, residence, family, etc. This type of interference affects adversely the dignity of the people who are subjected to. Therefore, I suggest a positive approach and recommend to make changes in the wordings of the Article 12 of the UDHR-1948 as :

> "No interference without probable cause supported by evidence to the privacy, family, home or correspondence will be allowed."

"Interfere" means, *inter alia,* "to take part in the affairs of others" and it can be done openly or secretly. "Private" means, among other meanings, (1) belonging to some particular person or persons; (2) concerning or restricted to only one person or specific persons; (3) not intended to be made publicly known; (4) most personal, etc. *Family* in simple words is "parents and their children dwelling together or not." It may be a nuclear family or joint family. Home means "a dwelling place in which one's domestic affections are centred". It will have sharing of live feelings, emotions, concern, care and what not for the harmony, oneness and happy living. *Correspondence,* here means communication by exchange of letters or otherwise. Privacy is a secret for anyone and everybody has great interest to keep his privacy as private and most personal. In psychology, it has been observed that there exists a special and specific area or layer in every human psyche which is known to himself and to no one else. This is essential for healthy psychological living. Forget about such unseen areas. For, a psychoanalyst or a psychiatrist may be able to look into such inconspicuous layers of human mind. A human rights activist or an advocate of human rights should not be bothered about it. At the same time, the human right laws must be concerned with the privacy of others. Even a prostitute or a sex-worker has her modesty and privacy. The home of a hardened criminal has its privacy and sanctity. The parents living in one's home should have their privacy and home for everyone is a 'sweet home'. Any sort of interference in the privacy of an individual is inherently "wrong" and should simply not be misused by Government agencies. Nevertheless, if there exists probable cause supported by evidence, there is justification to interfere in the privacy of others. Even in doing so, care must be taken not to violate the human rights of the people by intruding into their private life, private communications or by inhibiting their free association with others and expression of ideas. Whenever interference to the privacy of an individual is warranted, it must be ensured that the information thus collected is not available through other sources or by more direct means.

Interference in the privacies may be done through individuals and electronic devices. Surveillance conducted through electronic gadgets or searches conducted in person–all of them must come under the article which protects human rights. Hence, the proposed change is :

"No interference by any methods–electronic or otherwise–without probable cause . . ." Today, video cameras, mobile telephones, wireless communication devices, etc., are used or misused for interfering into the privacies of individuals. Tapping of telephone conversation, surveillance by many electronic means and methods are employed. Allegations are heard about the misuse of authority/abuse of power violating the human rights of people.

The second part of the Article 12 of UDHR-1948 is about ". . . nor to unlawful attacks upon his honour and reputation." "Honour" here means "high public esteem; fame; glory; high respects, as for worth, merit, or rank; honesty or integrity in one's belief and actions" etc. "Attack" means, among other meanings, "(1) to blame or abuse violently or bitterly; (2) to direct unfavourable criticisms against, etc." In my view, such attacks are dangerous and should not be allowed. The Article should cover areas beyond "honour and reputation". Reputation means "the estimation in which a person or thing is generally held", i.e., the good name one has. In other words, it is a favourable and publicly recognised name or standing. "Reputation" is what other people tell about a man and it is different from "character" which one has in himself or possesses by himself. Character is the "combination of moral and other traits which make one the kind of person he actually is (as contrasted with what others think of him)"–says the Random House. According to me, the areas to be covered by the Article should, in addition to honour and reputation have character, esteem, status, personality, individuality and good name, etc. Hence, the Article may be redrafted as :

"...nor to attacks upon his honour, reputation, character, status, esteem, individuality, good name and personality" ... Each one means different things and an attack on any one of them is an attack on his human rights.

The third right conferred by Article 12 of UDHR-1948 is that "everyone has the right to the protection of the law against such interference and attacks." This portion, in my view, is unnecessary as it goes without saying that everyone has the right to the protection of the law against such interference and attacks. Therefore, the final draft of the Article–12 may be :

> "No interference by any methods–electronic or otherwise without probable cause supported by evidence to the privacy, family, home or correspondence nor to attacks upon one's honour, reputation, character, esteem, status, personality, individuality and good name will be allowed."

Article 12 and Criminal Justice

In spite of court rulings and departmental orders, some overenthusiastic investigators of crime interfere with the privacy of people—allegations are thus heard. Some do so for collection of even political intelligence. Some employ cultivated sources to do so on their behalf while some others do it by themselves. Interference in correspondence is another allegation. While the investigating officers have some protected privileges to collect information and to keep to themselves the sources of information it may be remembered that their power and authority to do so are not a licence to interfere in others' privacy, home, family or correspondence without any control and restrictions. If they do so without probable cause supported by evidence, it is at their risk and peril. The UDHR is very specific about such unnecessary/ unjustified interferences. It is nothing but misuse of authority and/ or abuse of power. One's home, his family, automobile, lodge or wherever he wants to have privacy to live as per law, there he should be protected by the unwarranted governmental intrusion. As far as one's correspondence is concerned, when one puts something in his filing cabinet, in his desk drawer, or in his pocket, etc., he should have the right to have protection from unwanted intrusion of the Government. He must feel security and safety. The same is applicable to his telephone conversation, internet transactions, voice-chats, etc. Any type of surreptitious electronic surveillance or purloining of one's private papers is not acceptable. Yet the mighty Government officials do it. Surreptitious eavesdroppers are there and their acts are, doubtlessly, human rights violations. There were instances in which the right of the accused and their counsels to prepare for trial without intrusion upon their confidential relationships by agents of the police/ prosecution were reported and necessarily such intrusions are human rights violations. The policemen, at times, are posted as undercover agents. (I had such a bitter experience in my professional career too for many days.) They too may post more agents like babysitters, domestic servants, neighbours, maids, repairmen, small shop-owners and the like to have a secret watch over the people. They enter into one's privacies by ruse rather than by force. All these are of bad taste during criminal justice administration.

22

Freedom of Movement and Residence

> "Everyone has the right to freedom of movement and residence within the borders of each State."
>
> (*Article 13.1 of UDHR-1948*)

> "All who can walk are equally entitled to the use of paths and roads".
>
> (*Rig Veda, 2, 13, 2*)

This is not a human rights law, but a revealed truth in Indian mysticism. It means that it has been honoured and respected from time antiquity. Men and animals have legs to walk, birds have wings to fly, fishes have to swim and the purpose is, among other things, to acquire food for livelihood. Man has more purposes than what animals, birds and fishes have by their movement. Many Constitutions have recognised this as a fundamental freedom. In my view, there is no need to prefix *freedom* to movement. It is more than enough to say that "Man has the right to movement". I may qualify further the movement thus, i.e. :

"Man has the right to movement–vertical as well as horizontal . . ." The human rights should not be restricted only to horizontal or vertical physical movement. Vertical movement means upward movement–socially, educationally, financially, status-wise, etc. "Move" means "to pass from one place or position to another, (2) to go from one place of residence to another." I think that the framers of the UDHR-1948 had only the above simple meaning of "movement" when they drafted the Declaration. Today, physical movement from one place to another (by migration) is seen everywhere. While the human rights law allows it, one sees that the mobility may be for a social/economic/ educational, etc., cause to the upward direction. The upward mobility is not allowed or appreciated as some administrations and people become parochial in their attitude, mind-set and activities. Resultingly, they make conditions to make the upward mobility very difficult, if not impossible. If the concept of upward or vertical mobility is recognised in the Human Rights Declaration, certainly it will help a lot to enjoy the right to dignity and other rights. Vertical mobility is a *sine qua non* for social progress, happiness and harmony. Besides the vertical mobility, different from the physical mobility, there is the lateral mobility (some call it horizontal mobility) which means "of or pertaining to the side; situated at, proceeding from, or directed to a side. "There exist a lot of differences among people and such differences may be in the area of religion, caste, sub-caste, race, colour, sex, status or anything of like nature. India is a country where one could see "untouchability" among people and amidst people belonging to the same group/subgroup. In Indian Constitution, under Article 17, it is enacted: "Untouchability is abolished and its practice in any form is forbidden. The enforcement of any disability arising out of 'untouchability' shall be an offence punishable in accordance with law." Accordingly, India passed the Scheduled Castes and Scheduled Tribes (Prevention of Atrocities) Act, 1989 and Protection of Civil Rights Act, 1955. This is in addition to the Protection of Human Rights Act, 1993. If Human Rights declare that lateral or horizontal mobility is a recognised human right, then that will be good for the further development of human rights. Hence, I suggest the amendment in Article 13.1 of UDHR-1948 as :

> "Everyone has the right to movement and mobility–physical, vertical and lateral..."

Physical movement and mobility alone will not ensure equality, dignity, etc., unless the people are given vertical and horizontal movement/mobility.

The second part in the above Article (Article 13.1 of UDHR-1948) speaks about the residence within the borders of each State. "Residence" here means "(1) the place, especially, the house, in which a person lives or resides; (2) dwelling place; (3) staying in a specified place while performing official duties", etc. I think that it is necessary to specify the nature of residence–i.e., owned, rented, leased out, mortgaged, etc. Why do I think so? There are states which do not allow the migrants from other states to own a residence. Is it not a violation of human rights?–to live in dignity? Why not a migrant be treated equal before the law? Hence, my suggestion is to alter the Article to read :

> ". . . and residence owned, possessed, rented, mortgaged or leased out–within the borders of each State."

Article 13.1 and Criminal Justice

The freedom of movement or the right to movement (physical) is often denied to people owing to *hartals, bandhs*, etc., organised by vested interests, pressure forces or power centres. Resultingly, people cannot move freely and the ruling governments, it is alleged, take an indifferent and sometimes encouraging attitude to such human rights violations. The terrorists, insurgents, naxalites and so on cause anxiety to people who want to move. The bomb blasts, terrorist-attacks, shootings etc. in trains, buses, public ways, railway stations/cabins, etc., make movement very difficult causing fear and anxiety. What does the criminal law do there?–or what can it do? Policemen are attacked, injured and killed; the innocent are caught and butchered; women and children are murdered in bomb blasts and other kinds of attacks. Human rights and enjoyment of human rights become illusions, perhaps, in some practical situations. There are human rights laws, but are seldom enforced with vigour, earnestness and sincerity. Criminal justice system becomes sterile or shows a frozen attitude.

Do the people enjoy human rights as far as their residence is concerned. The attacks and manslaughters in selected areas in cities/towns become a concern for the human rights activists and judges administering human rights justice. Even police headquarters, police stations, individual police, prosecuting and adjudicating officials are attacked at their residences and in such a deplorable state of affairs, what can or what do the criminal justice, human rights justice, victim justice systems do? The Declaration is fine in theory and the problem is in the practical field. And the criminal justice system is concerned about them !

23

Nationality and Citizenship

"Everyone has the right to a nationality."
(*Article 15.1 of UDHR-1948*)

"No one shall be arbitrarily deprived of his nationality nor denied the right to change his nationality."
(*Article 15.2 of UDHR-1948*)

"Everyone has the right to leave any country including his own and return to his country."
(*Article 13.2 of UDHR-1948*)

'Nationality' simply means membership in a particular nation or country. Is 'nationality' different from "citizenship"? A citizen means a native or naturalised member of a state or nation who owes allegiance to its government and is entitled to its protection (distinguished from alien): 'Citizenship' means "the state of being vested with the rights, privileges and duties of a citizen". The Universal Declaration of Human Rights–1948 speaks only about nationality and nothing about his/her citizenship. Why? In Constitutions of many countries, there will be Articles on citizenship and not about 'nationality'. I, for one, suggest that the Article 15.1 of UDHR–1948 must be amended to include *citizenship* too along with *nationality* as under :

"Everyone has the right to a nationality and citizenship." Why do I suggest so? Citizenship has many rights, privileges and duties attached to it and it is the birth right of everyone to have such rights in order to enjoy his/her nationality and citizenship.

Moreover, the right to acquire the citizenship of another state should also be a human right. Hence, the Article should be further amended by adding :

> "Everyone has the right to voluntarily acquire the citizenship and nationality of another country, if he/she so desires and as per the law established."

'Arbitrarily' used in the Article 15.2 of UDHR-1948 is not couched in clarity. Hence, I suggest the following change :

> "No person shall be either deprived of his nationality and/or citizenship or denied the right to acquire the same of another country except according to procedure established by law and on legal grounds supported by evidence."

'Legal grounds supported by evidence' means that a person who enjoys the rights of nationality and citizenship may be denied of his rights to acquire the nationality and citizenship of another country only under the laws that are made by the legislature/ parliament of the country to which the rights to change the nationality and citizenship are sought.

Article 13.2 of UDHR-1948 relates to one's right to leave any country including his own and return to his country. Here, I suggested to add "lawfully" after 'any country'. Why do I suggest so? Instances are plenty to show people leaving one's country illegally. Illegal migration is a problem and precisely, therefore, they are not entitled to claim any of the rights which those who lawfully enjoy the nationality and/or citizenship may claim. Hence, the suggested amendment is :

> "Everyone has right to leave any country lawfully including his own and lawfully return to his country."

Articles 15.1, 15.2, 13.2 and Criminal Justice

No one is born in vacuum. Everyone has parents-known or unknown to the child born. It simply follows, therefore, that everyone has a right to the nationality of the country where he/

she is born. Once the nationality is fixed, he may be entitled to have the citizenship. This is the reason why many Constitutions in the world categorically say–

"Every person who is born in the territory" of a particular country has a right to citizenship. Therefore, no person is born as an orphan or as a destitute. There are countries which use the expression "destitute children, orphan children" etc. in their Children Acts. Of course, the Children Acts are intended for the welfare of children, but to call a child-citizen of a country to be an 'orphan or destitute' is, to my view, a violation of human rights, i.e., right to dignity. In laws dealing with delinquency and delinquent children, the expression "orphanhood" is defined. The expression "destitute" is seen. This is of bad taste. There are "orphanages" established by NGOs aided by the Government. There are Government run orphanages too. The citizens of a country should not be humiliated to this extent or should not be treated in a degrading manner. Hence, the expression "orphanages" should be avoided. Likewise, there are houses for the destitutes established by the NGOs aided by the governments or run by the Government. The nationals who are the citizens in a country should not be put down by calling them destitutes living in houses for the destitutes. It affects the human dignity. Every child is the child of the nation and, therefore, in criminal justice administration, he/she has a right to be treated with dignity as the most wanted child. Everyone, the old and the infirm, should be treated with dignity as no one is a destitute. It is necessary to make the attitude of calling someone "destitute" or "orphan" because of his/her economic or other conditions ought to be made punishable under law. Every citizen has a right to be treated with dignity.

In criminal justice administration, problems come when foreign nationals infiltrating into other countries to commit crimes (including terrorist activities). There are countries to which criminals escape after the commission of crimes and live there happily as such countries do not have extradition treaties signed with the country of the criminal who has escaped. While human rights laws recognise and respect the nationality and citizenship of the people, why are some countries reluctant to enter into extradition treaties? In criminal justice administration, countries which respect human rights should come forward to enter into extradition treaties with other countries which respect and honour human rights as declared by the UDHR-1948.

Illegal migrants are there everywhere and some of them remain so for many years. I am aware of such migrants who have been staying in a country for several decades and some of them are above 70 or 80 years of age. They live with their children, kith and kin and one day, too soon, they are asked to go back to their country of nationality. Some political leaders come forward to support them and plead for humanitarian treatment to such old, infirm and God-forsaken people. Of course, such people have a valid ground for getting the right for nationality and citizenship on humanitarian grounds. If the authorities deny their right to change their nationality or to acquire citizenship, will it not be a violation of the human rights declared by the UDHR-1948 ?

There are national laws for the acquisition of citizenship, change of nationality, leaving one's country and returning to his country, etc. In the light of what has been discussed above, is it not necessary to think about enacting new laws and amending the existing laws to go in tune with the Universal Declaration of Human Rights–1948 relating to nationality/citizenship. For example, if a personnel of another nationality, living in a different country for 10 or more years, will he not have the right to change his nationality on the grounds of his long stay in a different country? Can we treat the denial of his right to change the nationality on that lone ground to be a human right violation ?

24

Right to Marry and Found a Family

> "Men and women of full age, without any limitation due to race, nationality or religion, have the right to marry and to found a family. They are entitled to equal rights as to marriage, during marriage and at its dissolution."
>
> (*Article 16.1, UDHR-1948*)

What is meant by full age? It may mean age of being a *major* as per law. Why not the same be written as "Men and women who are not a *minor* under law . . . ?". The expression "Full age" is vague and not couched in clarity. Is it the chronological age?—psychological age?—emotional age? Nothing is clear here. To be due to "is the phrase and the usage of "due to" is not correct. Therefore, I suggest that the phrase may be substituted by "owing to", "thanks to" or "because of". Why should there be that clause "without any limitation due to race, nationality or religion . . . "? The entire matter should be deleted to read :

"Men and women who are not minor as per law have the right . . ." Again, the usage "men and women" though correct is unnecessary. As in other articles, it may be better to say "Everyone" and thus may be rewritten as :

"Everyone who is not a minor as per law . . ."

The Article 16.1 of UDHR-1948 gives to people the right to marry. Like the right "to marry", the people should have a *right not to marry as well*. Therefore, it may be further written as :

> "Everyone who is not a minor as per law has the right to marry and found a family just like everyone has the right not to marry and found a family."

If "full age" does not mean "not a minor", but the age fixed by a state to be the "full age of marriage", there is no harm in writing the Article thus. Since in many countries, the age of consent is fixed at the age when a person gets the status of "not a minor under law", I prefer to write "not a minor under law". This is a time of 'Uni-sex' marriages(?) and there is a view that "uni-sex" marriages(?) should be legalised. It is a matter of dispute whether or not one can call a uni-sex marriage to be a "marriage" at all ! Marriage in simple terms means "the social institution under which *a man and a woman* establish their decision to live as husband and wife by legal commitments, religious ceremonies, etc. Some religions consider marriage to be sacramental and *up to death*. The law may treat it as *contractual* which may be terminated at any time. Whatever that be, the marriage is and should be between *a man and a woman*, i.e., between two sexes of complementary nature. As some countries have legally recognised uni-sex "marriages"(?) it is necessary to make the marriage between "man and woman" to be the birth right of people. Accordingly, the Article may be spelt out as :

> "Everyone who is not a minor as per law has the right to marry a person of complementary sex and found a family . . ."

Polygamy, polyandry, etc., are still in vogue in various forms. Hence, the question is: "Is the human right to marry limited to marrying only one person of the complementary sex (or is it a human right to have recourse to monogamy only) or is it a human right to have recourse to polygamy or polyandry as the case may be. In my view, monogamy only is the birth right and, therefore, the Article should specify the fact that the birth right to marry a person of complementary sex is limited to only monogamy and not polygamy or polyandry. Hence :

"Everyone who is not a minor as per law has the right for a monogamous marriage with a person of complementary sex . . ." Remember that male sex and female sex are complementary to each other and not opposite to each other although some writers use "opposite sex" when they think about male and female sexes. In my view, they are complementary and, therefore, the usage 'complementary" in the Article.

"Family" has many meanings such as :

1. Parents and their children, whether dwelling together or not;
2. the children of one person or one couple collectively;
3. the spouse and children of one person;
4. any group of persons closely related by blood, as parents, children, uncles, aunts and cousins;
5. all those persons considered as descendants of a common progenitor;
6. Chiefly British Approved lineage especially noble, titled, famous, or wealthy ancestry; and
7. a group of persons who form a household under one head, including parents, children, servants, etc. The litany is very long depending upon the culture, custom, etc., prevailing in various countries.

In all those meanings given above, one may see parents, children, spouse, descendants, household, etc., and it is in these senses the word "family" is used when "human rights" are taken into account? The family, in my view, is and should be a basic unit of the society comprising of man and woman with enduring sex relations and upbringing of the children (if there are) born in that wedlock. Of course, there can be nuclear families or joint families. There can be families with or without children. There can be families formed on the basis of polygamy or polyandry. Let the sociologists deliberate on those points and issues. As far as human rights are concerned, the founding of family means and includes "enduring sex relations" and in such a noble concept (as the basic unit of the society), unisex marriages(?) have no meaning. There may be "unwed" mothers who live with their children or people keeping their concubines and living together with or without children. There may be a paramour, i.e., an illicit lover, especially of a married woman–from whom children are born and they live together or people who have adulterous relations and living together with their children. The family as contemplated by the concept of human rights means and includes only those understood in the traditional way and as explained above in the traditional sense.

The use of "They are entitled" may be deleted and substituted by "the husband and wife." The marriage must be legal and parties to the marriage must enjoy the rights of "husband and wife". Instances have come to my notice of people living together under a misconception that they are married legally. The "stamp paper" marriages in India are examples in point. People go to a Marriage Registrar's Office and register a document written in a stamp paper stating that they are married and they live together henceforth as husband and wife. Certainly, they do not have the legal status of a "husband and wife" as per law and that is the precise reason why I suggest the amendment "The husband and wife", instead of "They" in the newly proposed Article. I do not like to say "entitled" as they do have the Rights. The proposed Article will be–

> "Everyone who is not a minor as per law has the right for a monogamous marriage with a person of complementary sex and found a family just like everyone has the right not to marry and found a family. The husband and wife have equal rights as to marriage, during marriage and at its dissolution."

Presently, the wife of dissolution is entitled to get maintenance from her earlier husband. If husband and wife have equal rights at the dissolution of marriage, problems may arise. Therefore, my considered view is to delete the words "and its dissolution" from the Article to read :

> ". . . as to marriage and during marriage".

Article 16.1 and Criminal Justice

Marriage, family, family life, etc., are sacred concepts. It is found by me from my studies that 70 per cent—a little less or a little more—of crimes (traditional) take place in or around the family/ family life in India. Suicides within the family, attempt to commit suicide, family-suicide, family murder-suicide, domestic violence of various types, dowry harassment, dowry deaths, hootch production, consumption of alcohol, child rapes, incestuous sex-relations, sadistic sexuality, pervert sex relations, neglect of children, etc., are just a few among very many crimes connected directly or indirectly with one's family life. Though the criminal justice system takes note of this fact, many a time, a number of crimes which takes place in the four walls of the family or in its victimity may not come to the attention of the subsystems including the police and court. Family courts are established everywhere in many countries. Nevertheless, one doubts very much whether or not they function in the way they should be. Are the judges in the family courts suitably qualified and professionally competent to sit on the seat of the tribunal to pronounce judgements in family courts?- may be a question of dispute–no, most of them are not. Therefore, it is necessary to frame specific laws prescribing the eligibility, suitability and competence of the judicial functionaries to administer human rights justice to family-cases. Likewise, are the police officials investigating family cases suitably qualified and trained? Do they investigate family cases with proper attitude and professionalism in work? One may listen to many women, women's organisations and women's commissions (i.e., statutory body established for the welfare of the women) demanding specially qualified women police officials to investigate family cases involving harassment to women, dowry deaths, forced abortions, child rapes, etc. It is time now to think aloud to allow the women's demand to ensure the protection of human rights to women. What about the prosecutors? Should there be women prosecutors to prosecute family cases in which the women are the victims/the accused?

Should the criminal justice system think of enacting more and more laws to ensure human rights and their protection within the married life, domestic atmosphere and families? If needed, they must be thought of and enacted. The family offences are many and will include disorderly conduct, menacing reckless endangerment, harassment, assaults, attempted assaults (between spouses, between parents and children, between members of the same family or household), wife-beating, torture by wife/husband on the spouse/parents/children (some parents, either individually or on mutual agreement between the father and mother poison their children, throw them to water, kill them by electric shocks, etc.) and the United Nations which declare human rights to people to marry and found a family ought to think about perfecting the criminal justice system to protect the human rights thus stated in UDHR-1948. Just by simply stating that they have the equal rights as to marriage, during marriage and its dissolution may not be enough. The United Nations may specify in clear terms about the rights the couples have, the children have or their parents have, etc., in family life. What about their rights as to marriage, during marriage or at its dissolution? For example, the women get maintenance allowance at the dissolution of the marriage when men who deserve such a maintenance from their wives (who have good income) are not entitled to. Why to have such a discrimination? Again, what about the custody of children when divorce/separation is granted? Usually, the mothers get the custody until the child becomes a major. Is it necessary to have such a strict law which is discriminatory? Why cannot the father be entrusted with the care and custody of children in deserving cases? It has been noticed that the children who are entrusted with the mothers at the time of dissolution, sometimes, suffer from neglect and abuse. They, purposefully or otherwise (includes financial difficulties) fail/refuse to look after the basic needs of the children so entrusted. Sometimes, the children living under the care and protection of their (divorced/separated) mothers are found to exhibit incorrigible, ungovernable, habitually disobedient behaviour beyond the control of their mothers. What to do then? Though the UDHR–1948 declare the right to marry and found a family to be the human rights of everybody, it seems to me that the Declaration is silent about many of the problems which follow the enjoyment of such rights by everyone. Hence, there is the immediate need to bring out special international law to ensure domestic rights at marriage, during marriage or at its dissolution.

25

Marriage, Consent and Will

> "Marriage shall be entered into only with the free and full consent of the intending spouses."
>
> (*Article 16.1, UDHR-1948*)

"Freedom" has two special areas and they are "Will and Consent". "Will" means :

(1) the faculty of conscious and particularly of deliberate action; the power of controlling the mind has over its own action; *the freedom of will.*
(2) The power of choosing one's own actions; *to have a strong will.*
(3) The act or process of using or asserting one's choice; volition.
(4) The wish or desire; *to submit against one's will.*
(5) Purpose or determination, often hearty or stubborn determination; wilfulness: to have the will to succeed.
(6) The wish or purpose as carried out; or to be carried out: *to work one's will.*
(7) Disposition, whether good or ill, toward another.
(8) And "at will" means "at one's discretion or pleasure; as one desires . . ."

The Article 15.2 of UDHR-1948 does not say anything about the "will" of the parties to a marriage. It speaks only about the "consent" which is certainly different from the "will". The word or concept "will" contains "voluntary" which means "done, made, brought about, undertaken, etc., of one's own accord or by free choice." There is an exercise of one's free choice there. In law, *voluntary* means "acting or done without compulsion or obligation; unconstrained by interference"; done by intention, and not by accident.

"Consent" means :

(1) To permit, approve or agree.

(2) Comply or yield. A consent may be given without the "Will". External forces may work in consent and there may not be any elements contained in the concept "voluntary" when consent by force is given. St. Thomas Aquinas (1225?-74), an Italian scholastic philosopher spoke about "Will" and "Consent" as the faculty or function respectively of human mind. Therefore, one's "will" as well as "consent" to marriage would surely be ascertained or ought to be ascertained before his/her marriage. In Catholic church, this is done during the betrothal ceremony and again before the solemnization of marriage. As the *consent* does not necessarily contain the will (i.e., the voluntary-free-choice), both are to be included in the Article on human rights.

"Free Will" and "Free Consent" are not one and the same. There exists the "Freedom of Will" and there is nothing called the "Freedom of Consent". "Will" is a *Faculty* of the human mind whereas the "Consent" is a function of the human mind.

What is the meaning of "Free and Full Consent"? There is nothing called the *free consent* and *free consent* does not mean that the consent is free from all road-blocks. The road-blocks can be physical, psychological, social, financial, professional, occupational, communal, religious, educational, cultural and what not? Instead of "free consent", if "free will" is used, it means the power of choosing one's own action, i.e., freedom of will. Often, in law, the usage is "Against One's Will" and "With or Without One's Consent".

"Full" means–(1) filled, (2) containing all that can be held, (3) complete, entire, maximum, etc. How can a Consent be filled?– or can contain all that can be held? Or can be complete? The expression "full consent" means "complete, entire, etc., and therefore, my suggestion is to put "Will" and "Consent in the Article to read:

> "Marriage shall be with the free will and full consent of the aspiring parties."

Why do I delete the expression "spouses" from the Article? Spouse means "either member of a married pair in relation to the other; one's husband or wife." When the plain meaning of the word "spouse" in dictionary is what is given above, there is no meaning in the expression "intending spouses". When an idea can be expressed in a better and more understandable way, why to go for ambiguous or confusing terms and expressions?

"Intending spouses" needs explanation. "Intend" means "to have in mind as something to be done or brought about." Since the Article begins with the word "marriage", it is better to use the expression "parties" to a marriage than "spouses" to a marriage. Of course, "intending spouses" conveys some idea, nevertheless, "aspiring parties" in my considered view gives a better and a more meaningful idea. "Aspire" means "to be eagerly desirous, especially of something great or of high value." This is a time one sees divorces, judicial separations and desertions are on an abnormal increase and one of the reasons for the high rate of divorces/desertions is the decline in the values connected with marriage and marital life. Think about unisex marriages and the ridiculous way they are accepted by some. Marriage is something *great and of high value* and in order to create these sublime and lofty ideas in people, I purposefully suggest "aspiring" instead of "intending" in the proposed Article.

What is this "entering into marriage" . . . of intending spouses? "Enter into" means "to begin participation in; engage in". No. I do not want any such "beginning participation in" marriage. Though I do not want to make any comments about the sacramentality, perpetuity, or the contractual nature of marriage, I am to say that the expression "entering into marriage" is disregarding and violative of human dignity. One marries another and he/she does not enter into a marriage (as stated above 'to begin participation in'). Human rights to the aspiring parties to a marriage mean that they have the birth right to marry and, therefore, the suggestion to amend the Article in the way stated above in the newly proposed Article by me.

Article 16.2 and Criminal Justice

Instances are plenty to show that girls of marriageable age–less or more–are kidnapped, abducted or forced to marry some people whom they do not want to marry. Girls are cheated, coerced, pressured or threatened to marry some people whom they do not want to marry. Sometimes, boys too are subjected to such cheatings, coercions, pressures and threatenings. In all such instances, the marriages are not with the free will and full consent of the aspiring parties. Once the marriage has taken place, consummation of marriage follows. The parties to the marriage thus become psychologically upset and the only way out is to go for divorce. The human right to marriage is only with the free will and full consent of the aspiring parties and if marriages take place against the above stated declaration contained in the UDHR-1948, then the question is: "Are the victim of such a marriage entitled to get victimological compensation?" If not, necessary provisions of law should be enacted. What about the criminal law? The criminal law in some countries may make such acts punishable under law. If not, necessary provisions under the criminal law must be enacted to make the act penal. The abettors, supporters, instigators and those who aid the solemnization of marriage and the guilty party to the marriage deserve to be punished under law. Marriages can be registered under the Special Marriage Act. The provisions in the Act are very clear. But, there are instances of people ignorant of the provisions of the said Act get the marriages registered in a stamp paper in the registration offices and not before the marriage officer of the registration department. These kinds of stamp paper marriages are not legal marriages. As such, the *so-called* couples do not get any right for inheritance, succession, etc., if one of the parties die prematurely. Therefore, the criminal justice system may take note of this malady and make laws to punish everybody aiding the parties to the marriage to register a legally unacceptable marriage. What is seen today is that the "so-called couples" get themselves separated by means of desertion. In other words, one of the parties after a few days/months/years of cohabitation/sexual life leave the other party. Resultingly, the deserted may not get any maintenance allowance. If children are born in such illegal "marriages", they are called "illegitimate"–a term degrading the dignity. The "woman" does not have any inheritance right. She becomes "forsaken" and will be looked down upon by others. Everything happened under a misconception or misunderstanding that a really legal marriage has taken place by registering a document in the registration office. The document writers, officials in the registration department, witnesses to such illegal marriages and all who aid the registration need to be punished for the crime they jointly commit. The Government is responsible for the illegality committed and the subsequent miseries caused.

The free will and full consent stated in the Article may be given by the aspiring parties under utter ignorance about the provision of law. The will and consent given in such situations are not free or full at all. How can the will and consent given under deception or misunderstanding be considered as free? Instances have been reported that the aspiring parties to a marriage go to a temple and put garlands and *kumkums* (in India) in the presence of *pujarees* and they think that it is a valid marriage under Hindu Marriage Act in India. The *pujarees* know that such marriages are not legal. The people who aid or perform such invalid marriages too must be brought under the operation of the penal laws with punishment. There may be invalid marriages similarly performed in other countries too. Since the Article in the UDHR-contemplates only valid marriages, naturally the performance of marriage in the illegal way is a human rights violation. If the aspiring parties are ignorant of the national laws about legal and valid marriages, then they must be entitled to get victimological compensation. If an invalid marriage has been performed under misconception, misunderstanding, pressure, ignorance, coercion, cheating, etc., then the parties to such marriage must be entitled to get protection when the marriage has been dissolved or one of the parties has deserted. The criminal courts, victim compensation tribunals, family courts must be empowered to order support to the other by the deserting party, issue orders fixing the custody of children, of visitation and protection by the deserting parent. The amount, conditions and duration of payments for support must be specified. Orders of visitation must set times and conditions for visits with children.

When divorces are granted the court issue orders of protection and maintenance. In some cases, the orders are violated. In such instances, penalties for the violation of orders must be prescribed in the penal law itself. The same provision should be made applicable in cases of desertion (i.e., the poor man's divorce) in valid as well as invalid *'marriages'*. There is a view that the courts should have the power to issue an order of sequestration of the property of the one ordered to extend the monetary support and the income therefrom may be used for defaulted support payments.

26

Family and Protection by Society

> "The family is the natural and fundamental group unit of society and is entitled to protection by society and the state."
>
> (*Article 16.3 of UDHR-1948*)

Is family a natural group unit of society? "Natural" means: (1) of or pertaining to nature; (2) existing in or formed by nature; (3) in accordance with the principles of nature, (4) as formed by nature without human intervention; (5) in accordance with human nature, (6) in accordance with the nature of things, (7) inborn, etc. Whatever may be the meaning one may find out in a dictionary for "natural", it goes without saying that the "FAMILY" is a man-made or created social institution and precisely, therefore, it is not/cannot be a *natural* group unit of society. A *family* is created in different ways by different societies in different parts of the world in different times. As FAMILY is created by man (society), one may delete the wrong expression in the Article 16.3 of U.D.H.R.–1948. The next question is: "Is family the fundamental group unit of society? "(1) Fundamental means serving as, or being an essential part of, a foundation or basis; basic; (2) of pertaining to or affecting the foundation or basis; (3) essential part, etc. Alright. As the family is the basic group unit of any society, the expression "fundamental" is fine.

Instead of "natural", I suggest "inevitable and necessary". Why? Inevitable means: (1) Unable to be avoided, evaded, or escaped; (2) certain, necessary. According to me, a society without "families" cannot exist and survive. A society without the "man created institution like family" will be no *society* at all. It will be like the life of animals. Family is *necessary*. 'Necessary' means, again 'essential', 'indispensable', existing by necessity', etc. I may argue for the inclusion of *necessary* too in addition to 'inevitable' in the Article to read :

> "The family is the inevitable, necessary and fundamental group unit of society..."

Thus, the expression NATURAL in the original Article (16.3 of UDHR-1948) is deleted and substituted by INEVITABLE, NECESSARY there.

What is the meaning of "Protection by society?" *Society* is a faceless mass and as such, it is like the word "PUBLIC" which means nothing in this context. There will be many sub-societies in a given society and that is the precise reason why the very definition of *society*, given by sociologists, contains such concepts. The meanings given in a dictionary may be :

1. An organised group of persons associated together for religious, benevolent, cultural, scientific, political, patriotic, or other purposes.
2. A body of individuals living as members of a community.
3. Human beings collectively associated, or viewed as members of a community.
4. A highly structured system of human organisation for large-scale living that normally furnishes protection, continuity, security and a national identity, etc.

As far as the human rights are concerned, no society, whatever may be its organisation and structure cannot be/should not be expected to offer full *protection* just like the State. If the society gives full protection, it is fine. At the same time, it is the obligation of the state to do so. Hence, in my view, the *society* has no obligation to offer full protection to the FAMILY whereas the state has. The state has its infrastructure, manpower, legal authority, resources, fund and no society enjoys such powers and authority which the *state* has. Therefore, the Article 16.3 of UDHR-1948 may be rewritten as :

> "The family is the inevitable, necessary and fundamental group unit of society and it has the right to be protected by the State."

I delete the expression: "is entitled to" from the original Article owing to the reasons explained in other chapters for the deletion of "entitled" from other Articles too. "Right to Life" is a declared human right and the same right is extended to the FAMILY when it is taken as a fundamental, necessary and inevitable group unit of a society. The society can or must cooperate with the *State* for the protection of the human rights of "Families" in a given society. Society here means the individuals constituting the sub-groups or sub-societies in a given society. In spite of the society or irrespective of the social responsibility/ obligation to offer protection to families, the State has the prime responsibility to do so.

Article 131 and Criminal Justice

There are different types of disorganised families about which the criminal justice system ought to take note of. Researches show that poverty in families, unemployment, overcrowding etc., have been causally connected as factors responsible for the commission of delinquencies by children. Moreover, disorderly conduct, harassment, menacing, reckless endangerment, assaults, consumption of alcohol, loose character of parents, strict mothers, conflicts between spouses or between parent and child or between members of the same family or household, neglect of children, abusing or victimising of children, etc., have some direct or indirect impact on the causation of delinquency. If family is to be respected and honoured as a family, it should have a responsible parenthood and harmonious atmosphere of a home for the children to develop their personality in the most desirable way with an upright conscience. Since the protection of family by the society and State is considered as a human right by the United Nations, it goes without saying that any negligence or refusal to provide protection on the part of the society and state will be a human right violation.

How to protect the family by society and state? There are very many ways and methods to do so. I used to think that a fight against poverty, unemployment, underemployment, etc. is a method of offering protection to family life. Any development in industry, agriculture, education, science and technology, transport and communication is a method of protecting the family. Any positive investment for the welfare of the society is a positive investment for the protection of the family. For example, the problem of unemployment can be eradicated by creation of employment in any form or description. The problem of poverty can be eradicated by means and methods calculated to raise the per capita income of individuals and families. The state will have to encourage investors and entrepreneurs to cooperate with the developmental activities of the state. No, a state cannot itself offer protection to every family by providing jobs and employment to all living within the territory of the country. Individuals and institutions should come forward. If the state is not offering full support to such activities by individuals and institutions, it will be treated as a human right violation.

This is a time family suicides, family murder-suicides, run-away children from home, truant children, disruption in family life, neglect of the old and the infirm, euthanasia, abortions and assisted suicides, dowry harassment and deaths, persecuting the helpless and the defenceless in the family set-up, calculated murders and simulated suicides at homes, etc., are found to be on the increase. Protection of family by society and state means protection of the family from all these crimes and ailments. What does state do to protect the families from all these problems? The state may establish homes to accommodate children, women, the old and the infirm if they need state care and protection. The state can encourage, support and aid NGOs to work for family welfare, conduct marital therapy sessions, family group therapy sessions, alcoholism or drug treatment programmes or anything of similar nature for the protection of families. The health of the family, education of children, medical treatment to the needy and the poor, etc., are important and many of such things can be arranged at government levels. What about the leisure time activities and entertainment? The government can censor the visual media from showing programmes which may promote anti-family life values, violence, eroticism, perverse sexuality, unethical transactions, etc., or put reasonable restrictions on the visual media. The government and society can make use of the print and cultural media to promote values which will be developing family ties with the members living under the same roof. The criminal justice system can help a lot to develop positive attitude to family life. Everything that may disturb the family life in the negative way can be made penal. The prisons and correctional services can initiate many strategies to keep the prisoners' family relations warm. Visits to family and retaining the conjugal relations of the prisoner undisturbed may be steps initiated to protect the family. Parole system and ticket to leave the prison system may be encouraged. Probation may be considered as an alternative for imprisonment. For, it is found that the probation in deserving cases is always better than confinement in prisons for the protection of family. As such, there is a view that the probation should be granted in maximum number of cases, if it is possible.

Society and the state have many responsibilities to protect the family. I am to say that when family life is challenged by conditions of hardship, maladjustment, sickness or rejection, the society and the state must come forward with constructive programmes to assist the families. The society and the state are called to serve the people and the common good. The state can initiate many legislative measures to protect family life. To quote from Evangelium vitae of Pope John Paul II: "Any government which refused to recognise human rights or acted in violation of them would not only fail in its duty; it decrees would be wholly lacking in binding force." Here, it is the responsibility of the government to protect the family. If the government fails or refuses to do so, it will be a calamity indeed.

27

Property of All Kinds and Descriptions

> "Everyone has the right to own property alone as well as in association with others."
>
> (*Article 17.1, UDHR-1948*)

"Ownership" is "(i) the state or fact of being an owner; (2) legal right of possession; proprietorship". "Owner" means "a person who owns; proprietor" and "own", accordingly means, "of, pertaining to, or belonging to oneself or itself (usually used after a possessive to emphasise the idea of ownership, interest, or relation conveyed by the possessive). According to the meanings seen in the dictionary, an owner can be the proprietor. A proprietor means "a person who has the exclusive right or title to something (i.e., an owner). *Owning* a property is different from *possession* of a property. In the case of possession, one gets only the *possession rights* and not the *ownership rights*. There may be a situation in which one and the same person may enjoy the rights of ownership as well as possession. There may be situation of one becoming a mortgagor and the other becoming a mortgagee. A mortgagor is not an owner of the property. As mortgage in law means only "a conveyance of property to a creditor as security", every mortgage confers some rights for the mortgagee to enjoy. Likewise, there may be the leaser and the leasee. A lease is a contract or instrument conveying property to another for a specified period or for a period determinable at the will of either leasor or leasee in consideration of rent or other compensation. The leasee has certain rights over the property and he can enjoy them.

I do not understand why the Article 17.1 of the UDHR-1948 has restricted the birth rights of people only to their ownership, i.e., only to own property. Why cannot the birth rights be extended to the enjoyment of property as owner, mortgagee, lessee, possessor, licensee, invitee, etc.? Or, are they not the birth rights of the people? Only one's ownership is his birth right? I propose, therefore, to make the following changes in the existing Article 17.1 of the UDHR–1948 as :

> "Everyone has the right to lawfully enjoy property as owner, mortgagee, leasee, possessor and licensee".

Why do I say lawfully? The purpose is that one has a birth right to enjoy property only in a manner allowed or permitted by law; not contrary to law, i.e., legally or recognised by law; sanctioned by law, legitimate or enjoying according to the law. "Enjoy" here means to "have the benefit of"—nothing more or nothing less. *Enjoyment* in law means the *exercise of a right*—nothing more or nothing less. Enjoyment of property is in many ways and all of them are one's inherent rights.

"Property" needs not necessarily be the movable or immovable property alone. It can be intellectual as well. Today, there exists intellectual property and precisely, therefore, it is necessary to use "enjoy" in front of property. It will cover the intellectual property rights and many other rights which are different from mere property rights. Therefore, the amended Article may be like :

> "Everyone has the right to lawfully enjoy property of all kinds and descriptions . . ."

Patent rights, copyrights, electronic rights, translation rights, or any such rights will come under "property of all kinds or descriptions." Perhaps, when the United Nations prepared the UDHR-1948, these rights were not well recognised as they are today.

While there is nothing wrong in using "in association with" in the Article, I, for one, may prefer to put "*along with*" instead of "in association with". Along with means "in company or in agreement" and is often used when one speaks about the *enjoyment of rights*. It is sweeter to hear *alone and along with* than *alone and in association* with. Accordingly, the Article may read:

> "Everyone has the right to lawfully enjoy property of all kinds and descriptions as owner, mortgagee, leasee, possessor and licensee, either alone/or along with others."
>
> "As well as" means "and", I may like to put 'or' instead of "as well as" to make the idea clearer and more specific. The idea must be "either or" and not "as well as". It will then mean "either alone or along with others."

Article 17.1 and Criminal Justice

The Penal Code in any country will have provisions making thefts, misappropriation of property, extortion, dacoity, forgery etc., offences. Even in the Code of Hamurabi and Moses' *Ten Commandments*, the provisions to own property alone or in association with others is seen. This is a human right recognised and respected from time antiquity. The entire criminal justice system protects or attempts to protect this right of the people. Dispossession of another's property, no doubt, is a violation of human right. While accepting the above fact by the criminal laws of any country, the truth remains that the antique penal laws do not take into account the modern and current methods and nefarious ways some unscrupulous people amass wealth or dispossess others of their property. Today, one may see Nexus Crimes in which the leaders (political, labour, administrative, religious, etc.) establish unholy linkage with the bureaucrats and with the aid and support of go-betweens and bandits, unprincipled men, *dadas and goondas* amass a lot of wealth in an unbelievably huge manner. The financial loss to the society cannot be easily calculated. It may be said in a special way that these nexus partners do not dispossess any particular person of his property, rather, they do dispossess all from owning their property. Presently, the nexus crimes are not treated as crimes under the penal laws in many countries. While the law admits criminal conspiracy as a crime, it, however, does not make nexus crimes (The nexus partners are the leaders–bureaucrats–businessmen–go betweens and *dadas*) crimes even today. What about the *consensus crimes* in which many people join together after making a consensus to commit crimes and thereby to amass wealth or dispossess others from owning the property. Corruption in Government service is a consensus crimes in that sense. In corruption, the consensus partners make money by adopting a give and take approach. For example, in enforcement crimes, the enforcement crime partners dispossess the government—i.e., the general public—of its property. What is due to the government is not given in full. The enforcement crime partners pocket them and become richer and richer in life. In criminology or better in the Economics of Crimes–one's undue wealth is another man's loss in money. In enforcement crimes, the loser is always the general public. What about the white collar crimes? They also pickpocket others and challenge their right to own the property. Nevertheless, the criminal justice system does not treat nexus crimes, consensus crimes with financial motives, enforcement crimes and corruption in government services, white collar crimes, etc., as human rights violations. The Penal Codes in many countries are dealing only with property offences which are of a traditional nature. Even organised crimes, Mafia, Costra Nostra, etc., are not capturing the attention of the human rights laws and criminal justice system.

The criminal justice system in any country, normally, may be expensive. To get justice from the system is really expensive. It is observed that many who approach the system to get justice or many who are dealt with by the system to administer justice become paupers in life. In a way, the system itself dispossess the people of their property. Today, political parties, labour unions, (government) sponsored trade unions, students' unions, religious group (supported sometimes by the ruling political parties) conduct demonstrations and damage public and private property to find victory for them. They damage the private vehicles, shops and establishments, public transport vehicles, etc., and their activities are nothing but violating the human rights of the people to own property. The organised strength and the muscle powers of the political parties (sometimes of the ruling government in a democracy) organise *hartals, bandhs*, etc., to express their protests and to exhibit the organised defiance to authority. The entire transport system is paralysed and the shops/establishments are closed so much so that the loss caused to the people and the public exchequer will be several hundreds or thousands of rupees (pounds, dollars). According to the organisers of the *bandhs, hartals,* etc., such dispossession of property, damage to property or questioning the very ownership of people on their property are not human rights violations, rather are inevitable, desirable, necessary and highly recommendable strategies in a democracy to express their protests and to exhibit their organised defiance to authority. Whatever that be, the criminal justice system takes a lenient and tolerant attitude to such human rights violations in which the very right of the individuals and the general public to own property either by oneself or in association with others is questioned. This is of bad taste and, therefore, must be remedied or rectified.

28

Acquisition of Property and Authority of Law

"No one shall be arbitrarily deprived of his property."

(*Article 17.2, UDHR-1948*)

Again, 'Arbitrarily' comes in the Article 17.2 of UDHR-1948. As repeatedly stated by me earlier, the concept is not couched in clarity. What is the exact meaning of the word "Arbitrarily deprived of" one's property? When the Constitution of India was amended, it was clearly stated that :

> "No person shall be deprived of his property save by authority of law."

Again it was specified–

> "No property shall be compulsorily acquired or requisitioned save for a public purpose and save by authority of a law which provides for acquisition or requisitioning of the property for an amount which may be fixed by such law or which may be determined in accordance with principles and given in such manner as may be specified in such law."

I think that an Article similar to the amendment effected in the Constitution of India is necessary to make matters clearer and more specific. Accordingly, I propose :

> "No one shall be deprived of his property of all kinds and descriptions save by authority of law."
>
> No property shall be compulsorily acquired or requisitioned save for a public purpose and save by authority of a law which provides for acquisition or requisitioning of the property for an amount or compensations which may be fixed by such law or which may be determined in accordance with principles and given in such manner as may be specified in such law."

Along with "an amount", it is necessary, sometimes, to fix compensation in the form of "other land, job, etc." This too must be specified in the amended Article. The rights in relation to the enjoyment of property will include any rights vesting in an owner, possessor, proprietor and sub- or under-proprietor, tenure holder, mortgagee, leasee or other intermediary and so on. The rights of the owner, possessor, mortgagee, leasee, tenant, etc., are real rights and instances are there that the might and muscle power are used to deny their rights. This is of bad taste.

Article 17.2 and Criminal Justice

Some people collect together under some political leadership and with their muscle power take possession of land to make roads– this is seen in many parts of the world. The administration including the police keep a distance from the disturbed spot and keep their eyes close to what is happening in and around the area. This sort of an indifferent or silently promoting attitude by the administration and subsystems in criminal justice administration, is, indeed, a sort of incitement and encouragement to involve in *arbitrarily* depriving of one's property. If *arbitrarily* depriving of one's property is a human right violation (in UDHR-1948), then this sort of evil activities are violations, however, noble may be the objectives/purposes behind such activities. What is happening in the educational sector? The educational authorities with the knowledge and connivance of the political administration, pressure the people to pay through their nose under some heading or another. This is nothing but a sort of dacoity committed to arbitrarily deprive people of their property under the colour of providing education or under the cover of doing a noble thing. If depriving of property arbitrarily is a human right violation, certainly this comes under such violations. But the criminal justice system seems to take a tolerant or indifferent attitude to such violations. The courts of law now impose some restrictions on the acceptance of capitation fees for admissions to educational institutions and the governments make rules prescribing the fee-structure, etc., they are seen more only on papers and not in practical reality. Arbitrarily depriving the property is visibly seen everywhere in the educational field–so visible that even the children of the political leaders, police functionaries, prosecutors, judges and prison authorities are willingly becoming victims of such human rights violations.

It seems to me that the Article 17.2 of UDHR-1948 is very narrow and sees the arbitrarily depriving of property only in the limited sense, i.e., of the immovable property only. This is not correct. The arbitrarily depriving of property can be in different ways and should be taken in a wider perspective. For example, what happens in hospitals? They extort money from the people under various headings. The tests, scans, hospitalisation, etc., may not be necessary in some cases. Nevertheless, some hospitals do them to make money. They amass wealth by arbitrarily depriving people of their property and the criminal justice system seems to take a light attitude to such nefarious activities. How to bring all these human rights violations under the penal laws of the country? For example, the Blade Companies (i.e., extracting exorbitant interest for the loans by loan sharks), false investment schemes (i.e., accepting investments by giving promises to pay unbelievably high interest rate and incentives), N.O.C./ Visa rackets, etc., are just a few among very many methods of arbitrarily depriving others' property. When I say that "no one shall be deprived of his property of all kinds and descriptions save by authority of law.", I mean that the criminal justice system must come forward to control the loan sharks, false investment scheme and so on from committing frauds on people. Instances are reported that people who are made victims of such arbitrarily depriving of their property committing suicides in large numbers. Sometimes, human rights activists come to the scene to save such unfortunate people in life. The political leadership too may come forward. But, the criminal justice system seems to show an attitude of reluctance to interfere in such situations. There are commercial and cooperative banks which charge 36 per cent interest for the credit card holders and there are moneylenders who charge 300 or 400 per cent of interest for the loans they advance. They do so right under the nose of the legislature, police, courts and jails. They extort their interests by the help of *goondas* or *dadas* and the criminal justice system, though is aware of such deprivings of people's money/property, keep a blind eye to such throat cuttings (meter-interest is the expression used by the common man). Meter-interest means that the interest goes up like an electronic meter installed to measure the electricity. It runs like a high speed motor vehicle even when a mobile phone is charged or not in use. If it is a human right violation, it should be made penal.

Again public interest should not be a vested interest. Instances have been reported that certain *personalities* in the ruling governments may very much desire to deprive certain people of their property. They may bring "public interest" to satisfy their "vested interests". Such rulers in government may have not only the muscle power but also the system power which is called the organisational strength. Making use of or misusing the organisational strength to deprive the property of individuals who are helpless and defenceless are really infamies and violation of human rights. Many a time, these rulers enjoy immunity from legal proceedings against them. They are 'public men' and the whole criminal liability, if any, will be fixed on the Government servants who are forced to dance according to their tunes. Whatever that be, the criminal justice system ought to be concerned about all these facts when it executes the human rights laws.

29

Religion and Freedom

> "Everyone has the right to freedom of thought, conscience and religion; this right includes freedom to change his religion or belief and freedom, either alone or in community with others and in public or private to manifest his religion or belief in teaching, practice, worship and observance."
>
> (*Article 18, UDHR-1948*)

"Freedom of thought"–and one can think in the way he wants. There is no control over the thoughts one has. I used to tell my students: "We eat the same food; live under the same roof; talk the same language; but what a variety of thoughts we have !" No one can say that one must think in this way or that way. Thinking is an internal happening and no one can know with certainty what others think about. The thoughts can be normal, abnormal, desirable, undesirable, realistic, unrealistic, human rights friendly or human rights unfriendly, etc., and so long as they remain in the human mind, there is no harm. There is no need to declare that the right to freedom of thought is a human right. Everyone has that capacity and human right. Hence, no one can exert the least pressure on a person compelling him to think in a particular way when he wants to think in a different way. It being the fact and reality, I propose to delete the entire expression "right to freedom of thought". The expression has no meaning in human life.

What about the "freedom of conscience"? I can understand to some extent what is meant by the expression "Freedom of Will" but I am quite incapable of understanding what is meant by "freedom of conscience." *Conscience* is a concept and is comprised of the superego norms or the do's and don'ts. Of course, this concept used by the philosophers, theologians, psychologists, psychoanalysts, criminologists and so on may be helpful to explain why human beings behave in a particular way. Their explanations may be challenged and may be issues of disputes. Forget about it. Except in the Universal Declaration of Human Rights by the United Nations, I have not come across the usage called "Freedom of Conscience" and that too as a right. I think that those who coined the expression "Freedom of Conscience" and those who accepted the same in the UDHR-1948 needed more information about the very concept of Conscience. They might not have the information that the conscience is formed in an upright way in the right direction by several agencies who are called "conscience formators". The 'formation of conscience' is a widely discussed topic by the theologians, psychiatrists, moralists, philosophers, jurists and so on. In such a state of affairs, there is no meaning in the very expression "Freedom of Conscience" and it is meaningless to declare that as a right or a human right. I propose that the entire expression must be deleted from the UDHR that is to be enacted now. It may be more appropriate to say that everyone has the freedom to act as he thinks and enjoy or suffer the consequence.

Yes, Freedom of Religion is a right to be recognised. I, therefore, propose–to accept, profess, practise and propagate religion."

> "Everyone has the right to freedom to or not to accept, profess, practise and in a lawful way propagate his religion."

The right to freedom "not to" means that one has the freedom to be a rationalist, atheist, deist, theist or agnostic, etc. The right to freedom is just like one's right to freedom for not accepting or professing a particular religion.

Article 18 of UDHR-1948 speaks about changing one's "religion or belief". Though "*belief*" means a 'religious tenet or tenets (e.g., the usage *Christian tenet*), it is, more often than not, a word used to mean 'an opinion, doctrine, dogma, etc., held as true. I prefer to use "Faith" instead of "Belief" in the amended Article. Faith means "belief in God or in the doctrines or teachings of a religion." It also means "a system of religious belief". Hence, the amended Article can be :

> "..., this right includes freedom to change from one religion or faith to another as well as to remain irreligious or non-religious."

"To change religion or belief" means to me that the Article in the UDHR-1948 presumes that everyone has a religion. No. There are people, as said above, who are irreligious, agnostic, non-religious, rationalistic, or atheistic, etc. They too must have human rights. As such it is found necessary to put as well as to remain "irreligious or non-religious" too in the Article.

"Teaching, worshipping, observing", etc., seen in the Article may be incorporated in the Article as follows :

> "Everyone has the right to freedom to or not to accept, profess, teach, practise, promote 1, worship and in a lawful way to propagate his religion or faith in, and to manifest his religion or faith in worship and observance either alone or in community with others in public or private or both taking due care and caution to maintain religious tolerance and harmony."

Article 18 and Criminal Justice

Criminal justice system cannot and will not punish a person for exercising his freedom of thought. 'I can think the way I want; but I cannot express or exhibit my thoughts in the way I want; If I express my thoughts, be prepared to enjoy or suffer the consequences–either positive or negative.

Again, the criminal justice system has nothing much to do with the freedom of conscience. As I said earlier, in my view there is nothing called freedom of conscience. There is the conscience in man, but "freedom of conscience" is something ununderstandable to me and, therefore, I do not want to have any discussion on the freedom of conscience and criminal justice.

Yes, the criminal justice system has something–many things– to do with the freedom of religion, especially at a time, when there are Government sponsored and promoted communal riots and atrocities committed in the name of god/s and religion. The allegation often raised may be that there is secularism only in the Constitution and lips of the religious leaders/adherents to a particular religion. There is communalism, fanaticism and fundamentalism in many parts of the world. The criminal justice system treats the atrocities committed in the name of a religion just like it deals with any crime of traditional nature. If the freedom of religion is a human right, then the atrocities committed in the name of religion or communalism are violations of human rights. There are countries in the world and they compensate the victims of communal riots and religious bigotry. I have made extensive studies on communal riots that took place in the State of Kerala (India) from 1956 and I have noticed that many a time, wild fire comes from the sparks. In other words, very insignificant issues that may be normally ignored by an ordinary man of prudence get ignited and spread like wild fire when religion comes to play its role in a diabolic manner. Making a mountain from a mole-hill may be the strategy employed by the religious fanatics and fundamentalists. What does the criminal justice system do here? When communal is prefixed to a riot, murder, arson, etc., the act itself becomes holy and not criminal. The personnel employed in the criminal justice system may not be totally free from their communal outlooks and religious affiliations. Therefore a treatment by calling a spade a spade in matters relating to religions is difficult, if not impossible. Whatever that be, the criminal justice system, it seems to me, is not very much concerned or enthusiastically earnest in ensuring the freedom of religion and thus protecting the human rights.

'Freedom to change one's religion' again is a matter about which the criminal law is very much concerned. Every religion, it seems, makes its own efforts to discourage their members to change their religion to another and at the same time makes attempts to attract people professing a different religion. They have reason for the same. If their attempts do not involve commission of any crime as per law, the criminal justice system shows no special interests. Let everyone in any religion do anything to effect changes in other to accept another religion–this is the attitude of the criminal justice system. If the attempts cause any law and order problems or commission of crimes as defined in the penal codes, the attitude is that the criminal justice administration has nothing much to do there.

The Article 18 of the UDHR-1948 allows anyone to manifest his religion or belief in teaching, practice, worship and observance.

The criminal laws insist that the manifestation of one's religious faith or worship should not cause any crimes or law and order problems. Nevertheless, the history shows and proves that the manifestation of one's religious faith or belief in public has been a cause of irritation for some professing other religious faiths or beliefs. It has resulted in communal riots and religious intolerance. Some people become emotional to the extent of becoming irrational in some cases. Massive destruction of property, arson, assault, manslaughter may be the consequence. Cases may be registered and investigated.

If freedom of religion is a human right, then the freedom of not being religious is also a human right. The criminal justice system is, thus, bound to protect the freedom of the rationalists, atheists, empiricists, deists, agnostics, and so on to live in their philosophy, to change it, to manifest it, to teach and promote it, etc., in a lawful way. The tribals may have their gods and their special rituals or practices. They have a right to protect them as those who do not belong to the tribal community protect their interests. However, the criminal justice system will not favour any observances/practices which cause damages to people's human right to life, equality, freedom and dignity. For example, untouchability in any form based on religious beliefs will not be tolerated. In the Indian Constitution, it is given as a fundamental rights, i.e., "untouchability is abolished and its practice in any form is forbidden. The enforcement of any disability arising out of 'untouchability' shall be an offence punishable in accordance with law". Likewise, the practice of Sati in India is forbidden. The criminal justice system also takes note of sacrificing human beings for pleasing the deities or gods. Thus, the freedom of religion does not mean that anything can be done under that banner. Criminal justice system accepts communal harmony and religious tolerance as the highest values to be followed.

30

Freedom of Opinion and Expression

> "Everyone has the right to freedom of opinion and expression; this right includes freedom to hold opinion without interference and to seek, receive and impart information and ideas through any media and regardless of frontiers."
>
> (*Article 19 of UDHR-1948*)

Freedom of opinion and expression is a human right. But it should not be an unrestricted freedom. There can be reasonable restrictions put on the freedom. Therefore, I suggest the following amendment to the existing Article :

> "Everyone has the right to freedom of opinion and expression subject to the condition that the said freedom should not be exercised in violation of any reasonable restrictions imposed by national and international laws on the exercise of right conferred by this Article in the interest of the sovereignty and integrity of a nation, the security of the state, friendly relations with foreign states, public order, decency, morality, public interest or in relation to contempt of court, defamation or incitement to an offence or in contravention of the principles of human rights of the people."

This is a time of terrorism and insurgency. There are individuals and organisations promoting and propagating terrorism. One sees the state sponsored or activated terrorist activities and all of them justify their views, opinions and activities. The freedom of opinion and expression is not for terrorist/ insurgent activities. Instances have been reported that the state sponsors and promotes communalism, religious fundamentalism, political vandalism and racial or ethnic bigotry. They express their views and opinions against those who voice against their stubborn and complete intolerance to any creed, belief or opinion that differs from theirs, etc., and all such activities cannot be brought under this Article.

The Article 19 of UDHR–1948 tells about "the freedom to hold opinion without interference." What does the expression "without interference" mean?–interference from whom?–interference for what? Nothing is clear and, therefore, I suggest deletion of the said portion from the Article. The next part of the Article may contain the expression "to hold opinion" and can be rewritten as follows:

> "This freedom includes the right to hold opinion and to seek, receive, enrich and impart information and ideas through any media or otherwise and regardless of frontiers of any kind"

I have put 'enrich' and otherwise in the amended Article. Receiving an information/idea does not really mean "enriching". That is the reason why it is included–Media–electronic, print, cultural, etc., are effective means for imparting information/ideas. But, *whispering campaigns* during elections, religious conventions, etc., assume a lot of importance in these days. As such, it is very necessary to put "otherwise" in the new Article. Frontiers may be geographical. It may be cultural, socio-cultural, legal, ethical, ecological, etc., and, therefore, it is better to express it in the following ways, i.e., frontiers of any kind.

Article 19 and Criminal Justice

Criminal justice system accepts one's right to freedom of opinion and expression. What does an opinion mean? In dictionary, it means (1) a belief or judgement that rests on grounds insufficient to produce certainty; (2) the expression of a personal attitude or judgement; (3) a judgement or estimate of a person or thing with respect to character, merit, etc. There may be other meanings as well. The criminal law accepts the fact that one has the right to freedom of opinion and expression, but should not be a libel or slander. Libel in law means 'a defamation by written or printed words, pictures, or in any form other than by spoken words or gestures'. It is a crime to publish a libel. For, it is defamatory or maliciously or damagingly misrepresents facts. A slander is again a defamation, calumny, i.e., a malicious, false statement or report. In law, a slander means "defamation by an oral utterance rather than by writing, pictures, etc."... In libel or slander, one misuses his freedom of opinion or abuses his freedom of expression. Whatever that be, both are violations of human rights.

Opinion has no frontiers. "My opinion is my opinion and nobody can or may claim the credit for the same"–but once my opinion is out or expressed, then it goes or travels beyond any geographical boundaries, cultural frontiers or time-limitations. Opinions expressed millennium back still rule the world and an opinion may change the entire world and vision of the people. Criminal justice system does not have any difficulty to accept the view that everyone has the freedom to hold an opinion without interference. Nevertheless, if the opinion is against the interest of the sovereignty and integrity of a nation, or inciting communal riots or religious bigotry, security of the state or friendly relations with foreign states, public order, decency, morality, public interest etc., then the criminal justice system will or will have to interfere. The issue here is: "Is the criminal justice system powerful enough to interfere with vigour in such situations?" The penal laws and the criminal justice system came into existence in some countries during the nineteenth century or earlier or during the early period of the twentieth century. In such a situation, is the outlived system capable of interfering effectively with people's freedom of opinion now? If they are weak or powerless then they must be made stronger. Newer legislations may be required.

No doubt, the people have the freedom to seek, receive and impart information as stated in the Article 19 of UDHR-1948. What to seek? Where to seek? What to receive and what not to receive? How to receive? What to impart and how to impart information? If the seeking, receiving or imparting information is in a human rights unfriendly way, necessarily the criminal justice system will or will have to interfere. Today, terrorists are at work and when I turn back to 12th July, 2006, I remember to have heard the T.V. news telecast that more than 169 people were killed in a bomb blasts in Mumbai, organised allegedly by some terrorist groups. Afterwards, the same thing is repeated over and over again. The criminal justice system will have to interfere with seeking, receiving and imparting information among the terrorists, insurgents or enemies of the state/nation. If necessary, new legislations will have to be enacted.

Media have all the rights which an individual has and I do not think that the media enjoy more or special rights which individuals do not have in any country. The criminal justice system may interfere with the freedom of any media if the contents are not acceptable for the larger interest of the country and people. Criminal action should be initiated against the media, if that is needed. Allegations are plenty to show that the media violate the human rights of people. The media which have commercial interests may publicise any news with views which are human rights unfriendly. The views may be their opinions, but the opinions may be defamatory in character. The affected victims whom such media caricature rush to criminal and civil courts with suits. The media action may be punished and the courts award compensation to the affected parties. Of course, the procedure is expensive and time consuming so much so that the poor and economically weak people may suffer the sufferings. There is a view that the violations of human rights by misusing/ abusing the media power/freedom of opinion should be dealt with severely. The affected victims of such misuse/abuse must be permitted to approach the courts with less expenditure and the disposal of the case must be speedier than what happens today in many countries. People misuse the internet media and recently a court in India punished the culprits for misusing/abusing their freedom to express their opinion in a defamatory manner *via* internet. The cultural media too violate human rights by expressing the views in a defamatory manner. Some politicians in India raised their protest against the mimicry artists to misuse/abuse the cultural media for damaging the name of some political leaders. Human rights activists too subscribed to the politicians' views. Yes, the right to the freedom of opinion and expression becomes a topic of vital importance for the criminal justice system now and years to come.

31

Peaceful Assembly and Association

> "Everyone has the right to freedom of peaceful assembly and association".
>
> [*Article 20.1 of UDHR-1948*]

"The right to freedom of peaceful assembly" is, no doubt, a human right. The assembly may be peaceful and without arms, but the objective may be objectionable. Therefore, the Article needs amendment in the following way :

> "Everyone has the right to freedom of peaceful assembly for any objective which is not against the sovereignty and integrity of the state or which may affect adversely the public order or morality".

Why do I say so? Instances are reported and people assemble apparently in a peaceful way in the pretext of praying together or to celebrate a festival, etc., and the purpose may be to disturb public peace at the same or at a subsequent time. Communalism and religious bigotry may be strengthened by such so-called peaceful assembly in the beginning. Those who have vested interests or interest in the vote-bank exploit the communal feelings and some governments most unfortunately are blamed or found to silently promote them. Some Constitutions in the world, though allow the right to assemble peaceably and without arms as fundamental rights, put severe and reasonable restrictions on the exercise of that right. In the international level too, similar restrictions must be imposed on people who want to assemble peacefully.

"Freedom to form associations and unions" may be a fundamental right in many Constitutions of the world. This freedom may be with some restrictions. What type of restrictions? The restrictions must be reasonable which signify that the limitations imposed on a person should not be without probable cause supported by evidence. The interest of the sovereignty and integrity of the country, public order, morality, etc., are grounds on which reasonable restrictions on the exercise of the right to freedom of association are imposed in some Constitutions. Therefore, I may propose that the same restrictions should be imposed on people when they want to enjoy the freedom for association. The amended Article may be :

> "Everyone has the right to freedom of peaceful assembly and association for any objective which is not against the sovereignty and integrity of the State or which may affect adversely the public order or morality".

Whatever is made applicable to the "Assembly and Association" ought to be applied to unions which may be a trade union, an organization of workers or a labour union. The students' unions too come under this category. Their unions are not simply an association of people. They have special and specific purposes. Instances are there that their union strength is misused/abused even for disturbing public peace, morality and integrity/ sovereignty of the state. They too must come under the purview of the Article to read :

> "Everyone has the right to freedom of peaceful assembly, association and union for any objective which is not against the sovereignty and integrity of the state or which may affect adversely or are likely to affect adversely maintenance of public order or morality".

Further I propose to annex the following clause to the above Article, i.e.,

> "Public order shall be presumed to have been affected adversely or shall be deemed likely to be affected adversely, *inter alia*, if any of the activities of any assembly, association

> or union directly or indirectly, is causing or calculated to cause any harm, danger, alarm, a feeling of insecurity, unsettling of human mind or anxiety among the general public or any section thereof or a grave or widespread danger to life, property, freedom, liberty or public health".

I insist this clause to be added to the existing Article as I find that the power of the "Assembly, Association and Union" is widely misused/abused by vested interests. A situation has now emerged that any injustice done under the strength and support of an organized union, association or assembly is always justified whatever may be the justness or morality. This is of bad taste.

Article 20.1 and Criminal Justice

The human rights to the freedom of assembly create a lot of headache for the law enforcement officials, to the court and prison authorities. The freedom of assembly is misused/abused to an extent of causing injury to policemen on duty. It is statistically seen that nearly 600 police personnel are injured seriously or otherwise during an year in Kerala State having a little more than 50,000 police officials. Attacking the policemen on duty cannot be treated as the exercise of the human right to assembly. Criminal justice system finds to handle such violent and human rights unfriendly gathering of people. The so-named assembly in temples, mosques and churches become violent assembly and any serious action may adversely affect the communal harmony or cause communal riots. In my career, I have noticed many people making false claims about the peacefulness of their assembly and accusing the police and other organs of the criminal justice system responsible for causing atrocities on them. The media too may support their false claims as they have more of commercial/ business interests than human rights interests. When the people and the media express hostility and dissatisfaction, the criminal justice system feels that they are at their wit's end–what to do and how to go about? Many so-named *peaceful* assemblies are not really peaceful! Peaceful in name and violent in strategy and action ! What is peace is not known to them! What is violent in the eye of the criminal justice system may be peaceful to those who form the assembly. They justify all their actions as necessary, moral, human rights friendly and fair. It is observed that riots by the so-called peaceful assemblies in the State of Kerala were going up in an alarmingly incredible way causing serious law and order problems for the police and the courts. Similar situations are seen in other parts of the world too.

Right to the freedom of association is a declared human right in UDHR-1948. The associations can be with various vicious or destructive objectives including to involve in the human rights violations and for the commission of crimes. There are associations for *goondas, mafia criminals, nexus criminals, enforcement crime-doers,* and so on. The criminal justice system cannot tolerate such associations and it will have to fight with such gangs, crime-syndicates and organized criminals.

An association is an organized strength and depending upon the objectives and leadership, it may turn out to be a law and order problem. An association is a Constitutionally permitted group, but every association has a potential to create law and order problems. There are associations with enviable objectives, but are in reality very dangerous organizations. They have hidden agenda and they involve secretly in activities which are harmful to the integrity of the nation or are promoting fundamentalism or are interested in terrorism and insurgency. Hence, the governments put them in the black list. They need to be closely watched and continuous surveillance may be required. Hence, while the right to form peaceful assembly and association is a declared human right, it goes without saying that some unscrupulous people misuse/abuse their freedom. The criminal justice system ought to have to keep a watchful eye on their activities including crimes. If Naxalites form an association, then they need to be carefully watched as they involve in murdering people. Fundamentalists have associations, but fundamentalism is an evil in society. If criminal laws are to be enacted to check and control the activities of certain dangerous associations, they should be done. After committing atrocities and cruelties on innocent people, some of these terrorists/fundamentalists seem to claim the credit for such inhuman acts. I do not call them 'associations' although some form associations to involve themselves in destructive acts and activities. They take law in their hands and involve, instigate, abet, encourage and prompt cruelties on mankind. The criminal justice system should be active and must be activated to meet the situations.

32

Associations and Unions

> "No one may be compelled to belong to an association."
> (*Article 20.2 of UDHR-1948*)

"Belong to" means "to be a member, adherent, inhabitant, etc." and in that sense, no one may be compelled to belong to an association. Instances are plenty to show that people who do not belong to a particular *association* are compelled to support, offer help, contribute, patronize, aid, etc., and the victims of such compulsions enjoy no option but to suffer or yield. Instances have been reported that those who resist to patronise, support, aid, etc., are shuffled, attacked, injured or killed as the case may be. In some instances, damage is caused to their property, dependents, reputation and dignity.

"Compel" means "(1) to force or drive, especially to a course of action, (2) to secure or to bring about by force, (3) to force to submit, (4) unite by force, (5) to have a powerful and irresistible effect, influence, etc." It means that there is no harm in inciting, persuading, exhorting, etc., people "to belong to an association". Where does "the inciting, persuading, exhorting", etc., stop and compelling begins is a matter of dispute. It being so, one needs to clarify the "compelling" or to qualify the "compelling" to make matters clearer. Hence, I propose

> "No one shall be compelled by inciting, persuading, provoking, exhorting or forcing to belong to an association. No person who is not a member of such an association is necessitated to support, offer help, contribute, patronise

> or aid, etc., of the said association and its activities without his free will and full consent."

"Association" means "an organisation of people with a common purpose; friendship, companionship." O.K. Any association will be different from a Union which may be specially, *inter alia,* defined as "an organisation of workers; a labour union; a trade union", etc. Therefore, it may be better to add union too along with association to read :

> "No one shall be compelled by inciting, persuading, provoking, exhorting or forcing to belong to an association, assembly or union.
> No person who is not a willing member of such an association, assembly or union shall be necessitated to support, offer help, contribute, patronize or aid, etc., of the said association, assembly or union and their activities without his free will and consent."

Article 20.2 and Criminal Justice

I understand that more than the physical force, psychological forces are used to compel people to become members of some association. For example, a person may be harassed, troubled in many ways, isolated from others, threatened, degraded till he becomes a member in some associations. Many people, I am told, join some service associations (unions) just to get support from others who work with them. Do they join with their free will and full consent? They may not. Yet, so long as there exists no complaint about compelling, the criminal laws do not have any application. There are many associations formed on the basis of religion, art, culture, locality, religion, residence, castes, sub-castes, etc., and usually one does not visibly see any compelling forces making a person to become a member in the said associations. However, there may be persuasion, inciting, exhorting, etc., repeatedly making people to think about joining the association. Such incitings, persuasions, exhortings cannot be treated as compelling forces until and unless there arise some complaints against the people doing so. Until some complaint is received the criminal law cannot be set into motion. Compelling a person to become a member of an association by inciting, persuasion, exhorting, etc., can be made penal, if necessary. This may make the criminal justice system to activate itself against such evils, if they exist. The problem arises with some terrorists' associations. It is reported that the terrorists forcefully abduct or kidnap people and forcefully make them to become members in the terrorists' group. I do not call such groups to be "associations" in the conventional sense of the word. Yet, in some sense they are associations. How? The terrorists register associations with very noble objectives (apparently) and they enlist people to be the members of such associations. Gradually, they brainwash them with their philosophy, outlook and mind-set and thus their method is intellectual infiltration. Can we call such brainwashing or intellectual infiltration to be a sort of "compelling to be a member of an association?" If brainwashing/intellectual infiltration is for terrorist activities/insurgency or similar acts against the security of the State or against the safety of the people, then certainly the criminal justice system ought to react. Such kinds of brain washings/ infiltrations are to be taken as offences or compelling forces to become members in such activities of terrorists/ insurgents. Of course, many terrorists organisations/ associations are blacklisted and banned. Still, they operate in some form or another in many parts of the world. Many associations, unions, assemblies, etc., are not engaged in terrorist or insurgent activities. At the same time, allegations are plenty to show that they cause terror in people. Hence, criminologists rightly call them to be institutions responsible for promoting terror causing 'isms' in society. *Attimary* (i.e., extorting money by labour union members for doing nothing. This is seen more in Kerala State than in other States). *Nokkucooli* (This too is compelling people to pay exorbitantly to labour union members for doing nothing, seen in Kerala), donation fixing, donation splitting, etc., by many associations/unions, etc., are examples in point. They must be made punishable under law.

33

Participation in Government

> "Everyone has the right to take part in the government of his country directly or through freely chosen representatives."
>
> (*Article 21.1 of UDHR-1948*)

The "Everyone" used in the Article above means *anyone* regardless of his/her age. All democratic countries have put the lowest age limit to vote. This is necessary for the free exercise of one's freedom. There are countries which do not allow the convicted in the prison to vote. Why? At the same time, those who are convicted, but not incarcerated to a correctional institution, do vote. This is discrimination and not justifiable under law/morality. There was a time some countries allowed only those who were above some economic status to vote. It was like a sort of double treatment to citizens who had the right to equality and dignity. If the suspected, the arrested, the detained, the convicted (but released) and so on have the right to take part in the government of their country, directly or through freely elected representatives then that right should not be denied to the citizens who are suffering punishment (in the present terminology, who are being corrected) in prisons. What is the rationale for such a denial of this sacred right to those imprisoned? Hence, the Article must be clearly spelt out as :

> "Everyone including those in an institution of personality development of the state, has the right to vote and take part in the government of his country, directly or through freely chosen representative."

Instead of "chosen", I prefer to call "elected" as the word "elected" is used in democratic countries and certain other jurisdictions ruled by kings, queens or princes. "Chosen" means "selected from a number; preferred". People's Representatives Acts available in many countries in one form or another use the word "*elected*" instead of the word "*chosen*". "Elected" means selected by vote, as for an office is concerned. It is in this sense, the word "chosen" is put in the Article. Removing it, the amended Article will read :

> "Everyone including those in an institution of personality development of a state has the right to vote and take part in the Government of his country, directly or indirectly, through freely elected representatives."

Article 21.1 and Justice

Are the people able to take part in the government of his country directly? The obvious answer is 'no'. Why? The candidates to an election are not decided by the people. The top level political leadership makes decisions about the candidature of the people. There is allegation that the candidates are nominated without people's participation. Resultingly, a candidate unknown to the constituency is sometimes nominated to contest in the election and the people have no option but either to vote or not to vote for him in some countries. "Don't argue, vote or don't vote"–is the attitude of the political leadership. In one instance, the father, son and daughter were nominated and many people complained that it was an injustice done to the voters in the constituency. They said that it is a violation of the human right and the voice of the people was not listened to or attended to. In order to protect the human rights of people, many suggested to introduce pre-election voting of aspiring candidates by the common voters. The aspiring candidates who want to contest in an election must be chosen by the common voters. Otherwise, justice cannot be ensured and the very purpose of the Universal Declaration will be defeated.

Are the people able to exercise their voting power freely? The voters are purchased and many are given liquor, edibles and gifts to cast their votes in favour of a candidate/against a candidate. There are laws to ensure free elections, but the laws are not strictly enforced. Huge amount of money is pumped into and once an Election Commissioner in one of the large democracies in the world commented that the corruption among the political leadership has its roots in the corruption during elections. The businessmen, companies, the affluent, the social higher ups, the religious leaders, vested interests spend lavishly any amount of money to manipulate the voters and to make advantages for them. Will these strategies ensure free elections? Will the voters be able to elect their representatives? Naturally, the present system of elections in some countries violates the human rights of people. There are election offences defined in the laws, but how much of the law is enforced?

The political parties announce an election manifesto with a lot of promises which cannot be materialised. Once the government is formed, the ruling political party may conveniently forget the election manifesto and the voters cease to have any say in what they do even though they have elected their representatives to the legislature. The empty words and hollow utterances remain to be so. The elected representatives and the ruling government have accountability for what they promised. This is, doubtlessly, a violation of the human rights. They rule the people with strategies which are secret or clandestine. There is no transparency in actions and the voters helplessly suffer them. This is injustice, but nothing can be done either to get victimological compensation or to call their representatives back. The elected representatives may behave like *kings and* above grammar, but the voters have no option but to submissively tolerate them.

Allegations are plenty to show that some of the representatives amass wealth through nefarious activities and the voters who send them to the legislature become unwelcomed spectators for the entire show. The voters are ignored and vested interests rule the people ! Victimisation results; yet nothing can be done.

Administration through people's participation has become a cliché and what is seen today is that their elected representatives establish unholy nexus with bureaucrats, businessmen, *goondas* and so on to amass wealth and to involve in nexus crimes, organised criminality, crime syndicates, etc. People who vote for them become an unwanted lot and the human rights of people, it seems, are found to have been written on waters. When I see how the elected representatives and the ruling political party act after the *so-named* free election, I remember what Pope John Paul II has said in his Encyclical "Evangelium Vitae"–On the one hand, the various declarations of human rights and the many initiatives inspired by these declarations show that at the global level there is a growing moral sensitivity more alert to acknowledging the value and dignity of every individual . . . . On the other hand, these noble proclamations are unfortunately contradicted by a tragic repudiation of them in practice." This is what is seen in the political arena. There is a total denial of the people's rights by their representatives and it occurs in many democratic countries which loudly proclaim human rights as sacred and inalienable. There is an attack on the voters' rights to the extent of jeopardizing the very meaning of democratic existence. Most unfortunately the "freely" elected representatives of the people question the very power of the voters and thus the general public are subjected to the will of the stronger. Again, to quote Pope John Paul II, "In this way democracy, contradicting its own principles, effectively moves towards a form of totalitarianism. The State is no longer the *common home* where all can live together on the basis of principles of fundamental equality, but is transformed into a tyrant state, which arrogates to itself the right to . . . ignoring the human rights of the electorates to vote and freely choose their representatives".

34

Equality of Opportunity for Government Jobs

> "Everyone has the right of equal access to public service in his country".
>
> [*Article 21.2 of UDHR-1948*]

This Article is about the equality of opportunity in matters of public appointments or employment. The expression "access" means the ability or permission to approach, enter, speak with, or use." In my view, simply an "access to public service is not enough. Hence my proposal is to redraft the above Article to make matters clearer and more specific as :

> "There shall be the right to equality of opportunity for all in matters relating to employment or appointment to any office under their country."

This is not enough. Why? The expressions "Equal Access" or "Equality of Opportunity" may not convey the idea fully. Hence, I propose a clause as under :

> "No one shall, only on grounds of race, colour, sex, language, caste, political or other opinion, social or ethnic origin, property, birth, residence, decent or any of them be ineligible for or discriminated against in respect of any employment or office under the state."

Nevertheless, in many countries one notices backward classes of people who are not adequately represented in the services of the state. For them and their upliftment, some reservations of appointments or posts may become essential or necessary. Therefore, a clause to that effect must be put under the Article as :

> "People belonging to the backward classes of citizens and who are not adequately represented in the services under the state have a right to reservation of appointments or posts in favour of them."

Who belong to the 'backward classes'? This should be decided objectively and realistically in every country. For, those who are in the backward classes in one country need not necessarily be so in another country. There should be special and specific criteria for deciding the backwardness of people in every country.

These people who are handicapped religion-wise, caste-wise, economically, socially, racially, physically etc. cannot come up in education and life unless they get special reservations. It is not a leniency shown to them, rather is their right to get such reservations. They do not want any charity or sympathy. What they want is the recognition of their human rights.

Moreover, there may be religious or denominational institutions and the incumbent of an office in connection with the affairs of any such religious or denominational institution ought to be people professing that particular religion, faith or belonging to that particular denomination. There is no meaning in a rationalist, atheist or a person professing another religion, faith or belonging to another denomination to occupy such posts or claiming appointments under the state. Therefore, I propose another clause to the above Article as :

> "No one other than a person professing a particular religion, faith or belonging to a particular denomination, has any right to claim appointments or posts in connection with the affairs of any religious or denominational institution or to become a member of the governing body thereof."

Putting all together, the amended Article will be :

"There shall be the right to equality of opportunity for all in matters relating to employment or appointment to any office under their country.
No one shall, only on grounds of race, sex, language, caste, political or other opinion, social or ethnic origin, property, birth, residence, decent, or any of them be ineligible for or discriminated against in respect of any employment or office under the state.
People belonging to the backward classes of citizens and who are not adequately represented in the services under the state have a right to reservation of appointments or posts in favour of them.
No one other than a person professing a particular religion, faith or belonging to a particular denomination has any right to claim appointments or posts in connection with the affairs of any religious or denominational institution or to become a member of the governing body thereof."

Article 21.2 and Justice

Public commissions are appointed by the countries. More often than not, the appointment is based on political considerations. Allegations are heard that some members of the Public Commission purchase their positions with ulterior motives. What is more? In such deplorable situations, if the allegations are not false, the appointments of the members of Public Service Commission will be on the basis of political considerations or on the strength of the money power or other influences. The human right of equal opportunity to public services is thus defeated and the declaration is seen more on paper rather than in reality and practice. Merit of the candidates to public office becomes a wishful thinking and nothing more when the members of the Public Commissions are 'personalities' of suspicious integrity. The Public Service Commissions and the Procedure of Recruitment—they work in a system and as such is a means and not an end—, the means to the selection of the right candidates possessing quality and merit become suspicious and questionable. Instances are plenty to show litigations before the courts of law after the selection of candidates to some posts every now and then. But the value of recruitment to public service stands or falls with the values which it embodies and promotes. Of course, values such as the dignity of every aspiring candidate, respect for his inviolable and inalienable human right of equal access to public service and the acceptance of the best suitable and most competent person as the end of the selection, etc., are doubtlessly fundamental for good and efficient civil service. If and when the members of the selection board are people with no respect for human rights, then the selection procedure and the system themselves will be shaken in their foundation and will be reduced into a mere mechanism for selecting candidates who are not worthy, but are submissively obedient to the political whims or are aggressively susceptible to corruption and corrupt practice. This indeed is a violation of human rights and injustice shown to the deserving candidates to public offices. If the recruitment and its procedure are not built upon the values of equal access to public service, then the entire system proves to be illusory. If the system is defective, then the candidates selected will also be defective in many situations. They may be the candidates most capable of manoeuvring not only the members of the selection board that is supposed to work for the betterment of civil service. In such situations, the expressions "human right of equal access to public service" become simply empty words to be laughed at. It is an illusion to think that one can build a good civil service just by making a declaration meaning nothing much in practice.

Once the house of the Chairman of a State Public Service Commission was raided by the police, they could unearth money worth Rs. 40 crore of Indian rupees. He made income abnormally disproportionate to his known sources of normal or legitimate income. How? It is through continuous violation of the human rights ensured in the UDHR.

This is a time people in many parts of the world make demands for the appointment of "Sons of the Soil" for public offices. Many governments and public undertakings yield to such demands, whether desirable or not. Countries where unemployment is a serious problem, the survival of the fittest works. The survival is decided not always by the quality of candidates, but by the money powers/other influences. I will be able to cite any number of such cases in which the candidates to public offices have contaminated the entire atmosphere with corruption and corrupt practices.

All said and done, persons with upright character, values, personality traits show extreme respect and honour to human rights and select the best candidates who are qualitatively meritorious. Introductions and recommendations do not work with them. Vested interests and undesirable political pressures do not come to them. Money and material benefits do not influence them. Such people will be–and they alone will be–able to administer human rights justice to the just recruitment of the best candidate to public offices.

35

Will of the People and their Right to Suffrage

> "The will of the people shall be the basis of the authority of government; this will shall be expressed in periodic and genuine elections which shall be by universal and equal suffrage and shall be held by secret vote or by equivalent free voting procedures".
>
> [*Article 21.3 of UDHR-1948*]

The "WILL" of people is not only the basis of the authority but also the *source of power* for the exercise of that authority to the government. A *will* without the *power* cannot exercise an authority. Therefore, I propose the following change :

"The will of the people shall be the basis and source of power for the authority of government..." Source of power means the *energy* and without the energy, no government can exercise its authority. It is always said: "the merit of the exercise by a government is the quality of the exercise of the authority vested on it by the people. The quality of the exercise of the authority is decided by the people of the country." Since the authority is vested on the government by the people, the people alone can provide the energy to exercise the authority. That is the reason why the "source of power" is added to the "basis" in the Article above. Basis here means the foundation, the bottom or base of anything; anything on which something is based; fundamental. A base alone will not be enough.

"... this will shall be expressed ..."—that is what follows next. Somehow or other, I do not like the word "expressed" there. Why? "Express" means "9(1) to put (thought) into words; (2) to show, manifest, or reveal, (3) to set forth the opinions, feelings, etc., of (oneself), (4) to represent by a symbol or formula, etc." Instead of "expressed", I prefer to use the word "exercised". "To exercise" means "to put (faculties, rights, etc.) into action, practice, or use." In this sense, one may say "to exercise the freedom of speech". Again, to *exercise* means "to make use of (one's privileges, powers, etc.)" and one may say "to exercise one's constitutional rights." To *exercise* again means "to discharge (a function) and one may say "to exercise the duties of one's office". Taking into account the various meanings given for "to express" and "to exercise", I, for one, am inclined to use the word "exercise" instead of 'express" as the former contains freedom (of speech), Constitutional rights, duties of one's office, etc. while the latter does not have all such concepts, meanings and inner meanings. Showing, manifesting, revealing, putting thoughts into words, etc., given as the meanings of "express" do not comprehend many concepts which are seen in the word "exercise". Hence, I propose-

"... this will shall be exercised..."

"In periodic and genuine elections which shall be by universal and equal suffrage and shall be held by secret vote or by equivalent free voting procedure." "Secret vote" does not necessarily mean "secret vote by a ballot". Ballot means "the method of secret voting by means of printed or written ballots or by means of voting machines. "Voting by ballot" is to be used instead of just saying secret vote. Secret vote can be done by S.M.S. (mobile phones), internet or even by telephone calls or by telegraphic messages. In order to avoid all such confusions, it may be written as :

> "... held by secret vote by ballot or by equivalent free voting procedure." Perhaps, equivalent free voting procedure may include internet, S.M.S., telegraphic messages, etc., provided they are done freely and secretly without revealing one's identity.
>
> "The right to vote by free ballot means that one has a right to vote for a particular candidate, if he so decides. Instances are there that some people want to vote for "no one". He may very much like to express his freedom showing that

> he does not want to vote for anyone in the list. That too is a right. Hence, it is necessary to confer such a right. "Everyone has the right of freedom to vote for none in the ballot paper." This right is otherwise called, the right of "not voting to anyone".

Earlier, it was brought out that the will of the people is the basis and source of power for the authority of a government. The people who have the will to elect their representatives ought to have a right to recall them if they fail or refuse to fulfil the aspirations of the people. The *right to recall* their representatives is a human right. Hence,

> "This will shall be exercised by expressing their right to call back their representative elected by a free election."

Putting everything together, the amended Article will be :

> "The will of the people shall be the basis and source of power for the authority of government. This will shall be exercised in periodic and genuine elections which shall be by universal and equal suffrage and shall be held by secret vote by ballot or equivalent free voting procedure. This will shall be exercised by expressing the right to call back the representative held by secret vote by ballot or equivalent free voting procedure; this will shall also be exercised by casting one's vote to none in the ballot sheet or calling back the representative already elected".

Article 21.3 and Justice

People are the Government and the Government are the people. This is a nice idea and an enviable concept. Today, in many countries one may see political parties coming into power and ruling the nation. As a result, we can see the will of the political parties and not the people and not that of the people becoming the basis of the authority of government during the period the said political party is in power. In certain constituencies, sometimes, the total percentage of the voting population may be less than 50 percentage and a representative is elected. One cannot, then, say that he represents the people—not even the majority of the people. Whatever that be, once a political party comes into power, the government thus formed will rule the people in accordance to the policies and programmes of the political party it may represent. The political party in opposition may raise their protests by organising anti-government processions, conducting *dharnas, hartals, bandhs,* etc., and they do so for getting political mileage for them. Majority of the people—both in the ruling political party or in the opposition—are silent spectators of what is going on. The neutral people may be disinterested in government authority. Hence, the declaration that the will of the people shall be the basis of the authority of the government is questioned by some human rights activists. If it is the human right declared, then the authority exercised by the political parties of the ruling government for satisfying the vested interests of the politicians will be violations of human rights. It is seen that some political parties are richer than the ruling government. The government may be financially weak whereas the political parties may be financially sound. What is done by one government (of a particular political party/ies) will be undone by another government (of another political party/ies). If that cannot be done, then an attitude of indifference, causing delay, neglect, etc., may be shown. The Human Rights Declaration says that the will of the people will be expressed in periodical and genuine elections which shall be by universal and equal suffrage. Is this true? In a way, the people are condemned to vote for this candidate or that candidate fixed by the political party leadership on considerations which may be different from or other than the will of the people. A lot of people may not vote at all. There was a time in India when people who were land owners only could vote. Today, owing to democracy and human rights consciousness, anyone, except the convicted inmate staying in an institution of personality development, who is 18 years of age or above can vote. The question here is: "Are the elections genuine?" The Election Commission may like them to be conducted in a fair, free and genuine way, but the political parties and their religiously ardent workers may not honour the Election Commission's earnestness. They may do many things to win the election and they will make the elections far away from being genuine. Booth capturing, personation, corruption and corrupt practices, malpractices, etc., may be incredibly in vogue and a number of election petitions may be filed before the courts of law after every election. What is more? Injustice and human rights violations do take place during the election and the ruling governments are accused of for involving in undesirable practices during the elections. "All is well that ends well"–this may be the attitude of political parties, ruling governments, opposition, vested interests and all those who are interested and involved in elections. They are not, it seems to me, concerned with the human rights justice during elections. Win the elections by any means seems to be the often resorted strategy!

36

Social Security and Personality Development

> "Everyone, as a member of society, has the right to social security and is entitled to realisation, through national effort and international co-operation and in accordance with the organisation and resources of each state, of the economic, social and cultural rights indispensable for his dignity and the free development of his personality."
>
> [*Article 22 of UDHR-1948*]

"Free development of his personality" is a fine concept, nevertheless, this right must be "in the right direction and with an upright conscience with acceptable values and morality." Free development of one's personality needs not necessarily be with desirable personality traits or characteristics. What is meant by the expression 'Free Development'? Development of Personality is understandable, but free-development is something ununderstandable to me. There are agencies and socialization agents who devote a lot of time and energy for the proper development of human personality. Proper development is different from free development of human personality. Proper development means the development in the right direction with an upright conscience.

"... as a member of the society" means "as a responsible member of the society." Everybody is a member of the society, but one needs not necessarily be a responsible member. A responsible member means a person who enjoys his status performing fully his role as a responsible member of the society, i.e., a responsible member in letter and spirit, in meaning and in content, etc. A responsible member can claim his rights along with his duties which he must perform for the welfare, human coexistence and individual happiness. Hence, the said Article should be amended to :

> "Everyone, as a responsible member of the society has a right to social security..."

The right to be enjoyed by him will have meaning only if he performs his duties. Duties and responsibilities are on the other side of his rights. Hence, the Article may be further elaborated to–

"... along with his obligations and duties for claiming social security..." One has a right to claim social security only if and if only he fulfils his obligations and takes up the duties in the way he must. For example, a terrorist, an insurgent, a traitor, an unpatriotic fellow and so on cannot and should not make any claims for social security. The social security claims ought to be genuine and the genuineness is decided by the sincerity in performing one's duties and obligations. The Amended Article will be-

> "Everyone, as a responsible member of the society has a right to social security along with his sincerity to fulfil his obligations and duties for claiming the social security. He is entitled to realisation through national effort and international cooperation and in accordance with the organisation and resources of each state, of the economic, social and cultural rights indispensable for his dignity and the free development of his personality in the right direction and with an upright conscience with acceptable values and morality."

Article 22 and Criminal Justice

What is social security? In India, many farmers committed suicide because of heavy social and economic insecurity. They had bank loans which they could not repay. A government in a South Indian State sanctioned some amount of money to the dependents of those who committed suicide. It was an incentive for some farmers who told the media that they would commit suicide for obtaining the fund from the government. This sort of social and economic insecurity can be seen in many parts of the world. Richer and very powerful nations attack other countries and destroy the social security feelings of the general public. I have heard the head of an affluent and highly developed country making a telecast that his army action in a particular country was intended for better living and social security. I have witnessed the bombings and seen women, children, the aged and so to say all being killed in military operations along with destruction of their culture, civilisation, buildings, and so to stay everything. Countries which speak in loud voice with a wide mouth committed atrocities and human rights violations which only human imagination could conceive of. It was indeed cruel injustice.

What about the terrorists and insurgents? They may make social security impossible. When I listen to a T.V. news telecast and I hear the Mumbai bomb-blasts in the railway stations killing more than 200 innocent, helpless and defenceless civilians whose bodies are shattered. Whether or not it is cross border terrorism from the neighbouring country, it is no doubt a cruel atrocity on people and an unpardonable act of diabolism. What kind of social security may be given to people if the governments in power promote terrorism?

There are terrorists and insurgents (not sponsored by the governments in power) who make human life miserable and anxiety-causing. People are afraid to go to markets, to travel in omnibuses and trains, to walk on roads, to live peacefully at home. Why? *Bandhs and hartals*, political party sponsored agitations and aggressions, threats by the criminals, dacoits, naxalites, chain snatchers, kidnappers and so on—uncertainty caused by the lethargy and inaction by police—all these and many more factors in society make the social security indeed very difficult. Some governments may offer some financial help to the unemployed, to the underemployed, to the financially handicapped, to the aged, to the infirm and sick, to the victims of natural calamity, etc. While accepting them as social security measures, one will have to accept the fact in fairness that social security and safety of human life are threatened by many destructive forces committed to destroy the people. While the Universal Declaration makes social security a human right, many governments, political parties, vested interests, criminals, law enforcement officials, terrorists, insurgents, and so on 'simply ignore it, nay, destroy it'.

Adulteration of food, pollution of environment, air and water, contamination of diseases including AIDS, etc., make social security a wishful thinking. Some governments watch these in a helpless way while other governments make small investments to ensure social security from adulteration, pollution and contamination of diseases. Some governments make their revenue from the income received from the sale of liquors to people and thus allowing slow killing of the entire population. The hootch is readily available. Sex tourism is practised in some parts of the world. Starvation is seen. The national wealth is plundered by vested interests by corruption, corrupt practices and other nefarious activities. Guerrilla warfare may be encouraged making the people anxious about their next-minute existence. Amidst all these insecurities, what is the meaning of talking more about the social security. To talk about social security and its realisation through national effort and international cooperation, etc., becomes a *tamasha* and not a human right for many—becomes an injustice instead of human rights justice for them.

37

Right to Work and Protection against Unemployment

> "Everyone has the right to work, to free choice of employment, to just and favourable conditions of work and to protection against unemployment".
>
> [*Article 23.1 of UDHR-1948*]

Everyone has the right to work and also he has an equal right 'not to work'. Why do I say so? In many strikes, *hartals* and *bandhs* organised by political parties, it may be virtually impossible for many willing to work employees to go for work. If they go for any work, it is likely that they are physically manhandled or psychologically attacked by the mad adherents of political parties. Likewise, trade unions/labour unions declare strikes and organised defiance to authority by many means and methods. They do not allow the willing to work employees to work on those striking days. Even public undertakings and government owned corporations go for strikes and total stoppage of work. Most unfortunately and desperately enough there are government sponsored strikes, *bandhs* and *hartals*. There are political parties of all magnitudes, communal and fundamentalist organisations, students, businessmen, traders, regional power points and pressure centres, etc., declare *bandhs* and *hartals*. The right to work is questioned by those who claim that they have a right 'not to work'. Sometimes, the governments in power accept their right 'not to work' and accordingly, do nothing to protect the rights of the people willing to work. Recently, a court of law convicted a few people who attacked those who came to work on a *bandh* day. On conviction, the government in power dismissed them from service. After six months, another government came in power and all the dismissed employees were taken back as if they were not dismissed. Hence, I propose that the Article must be rewritten as– "Everyone has a right to work and 'not to work'. . ."

". . . to free choice of employment, to just and favourable conditions of work . . ." In some countries, choice of employment is an impossibility. It is so because "the beggars cannot be choosers." Free choice of unemployment comes only when the employments are plenty. What is happening in many developing or even in developed countries? There exists dearth of employment opportunities, and the exercise of freedom for the choice of employment does not practically exist or is non-existent. Hence, the question of "free choice of employment" does not often arise.

"Just and favourable conditions of work" stated in the existing UDHR-1948 may be an expression that is not clearly understood. What is just for Paul may be unjust for Peter. Likewise, what is just in Padua may be unjust in Paris. Who decides or can decide whether or not the conditions of work are just and favourable? Hence, it must be made clear in the Declaration itself. I propose

"Just and favourable conditions of work decided by the national and international laws." Why do I say so? What is found to be just and favourable in one country, as said above, may be unjust and unfair or unfavourable in another country. There should be an international standard and consensus in the area.

"Protection Against Unemployment" is a human right. How to decide the *unemployment status* is really a problem and precisely, therefore, this provision is misused or abused. Countries where employments are plenty, there may not be any great difficulty to decide the unemployment status. But, countries where unemployment and under-employment are very serious problems, the question of deciding on the unemployment status does not arise. Many are unemployed and how to ensure "protection against unemployment?" What may be seen today is that the governments give "unemployment wages" to those who are *said to be* unemployed. The amount so given is often so meagre that one does not have any protection whatsoever against unemployment worth mentioning. It has become almost an impossible task to perform or to find actualisation. Still, it is a human right to be recognised and respected. I may suggest that the protection ensured against unemployment must be extended to underemployment as well, I propose :

> "Everyone has the right to work and an equal right not to work with its consequences, to free choice of employment, to just and favourable conditions of work decided by the national and international laws and to protection against unemployment and underemployment."

Article 23.1 and Criminal Justice

Organised defiance to authority is manifested in different ways and sometimes without any justification thereby violating others' right to work. Strikes, justifiable and unjustifiable–occupy the most important position. Every strike results in the loss of many crores of rupees/dollars not only to the employers but also to the general public. Stay-in-strikes, hunger-strikes, token strikes, quickie, lightening strikes, regulation, work to rule, pen-down strikes, tool-down strikes, go slow, picketing, boycotts *hartals, bandhs,* political strikes, sympathetic strikes, stay-in-strikes and thus a long litany of strikes affect directly or indirectly others' right to work. The strikes are organised by an effective and powerful minority whose vested interest may prohibit others to exercise their option to work. This is injustice and I have seen many unwilling workers crying over their fate to objectionably participate in strikes which they really do not want. The employers may declare lockouts or even close the company for good so much so that the strikers–willing or unwilling–lose their jobs. Some of them have committed suicide as a result. No doubt, it is injustice done to them, their family and to humanity at large.

The workers want just and favourable conditions of work. The Government has to maintain law and order during the strikes. But, sometimes, the governments will not be prepared to offer protection because the strikes are organised by the political leaders (They are trade union leaders as well) who support the political party in the ruling government. Instances are plenty to show that the 'willing to work' employees are physically attacked and psychologically harassed by the striking employees supported by the political as well as trade-union leadership. The police and the government machinery may watch the show as silent spectators or sometimes as active promoters. Where is the human rights to work declared by the United Nations if this is what happens at the ground level?

Not all strikes result in violence, but many of them may manifest a potential for it. Violence erupts when (1) bitterness exists between the *willing to work* employees and the striking employees if the former exhibit their preparedness to work; (2) violence is deliberately employed–encouraged–to deter the willing to work employees, (3) an incident or misunderstanding which momentarily influences the striking employees to attack the willing to work employees or those who already work. The striking employees may establish pickets and they may violently protest the entry of willing to work employees. They may *gherao* the employees who come to work or are working. Instances have been reported that the willing to work employees have been beaten up, seriously injured, etc., by those who *gherao* them or by their *goondas* when they get out from the striking spots. It is illegal to do so and is a violent violations of the human rights perpetuating injustice. During the demonstrations/processions, the striking employees may resort to verbal abuse of the willing to work employees in the form of obscene remarks, taunts, ridicule, etc. Placards, posters, printed materials and cartoons ridiculing the fellow workers (who work), leaflets and handbill may be lavishly employed without maintaining any dignity or decorum. They outrage the very respectability of other employees. Flags or posters may be mounted on wooden or metal sticks. Some unruly strikers may even spit on the fellow employees who work. Instances are reported that the employees who strike burn the property/houses of the working employees.

Right to work is as sacred as the right to *not to work*. The employers resort to many tactics to deter, coerce and compel the employees who do not want to work. The hired *goondas* of the employers may even murder the labour leaders who lead the striking employees. They may employ any unethical and atrocious strategies to deter the employees who strike and paralyse the factory. The union leaders are beaten up and sometimes, the management enters into secret or sweet-heart agreements with the union leaders to defeat the employees. Literally, the management purchases them and so to say, there are many underhand dealings and unethical strategies employed by the management, employees and the employees who oppose the trade union activities, employees who protest the management, employees who sympathise with those who strike, etc. In other words, the area of employment and the work are contaminated with injustice and human rights violations of many types and all descriptions.

Right to work is a human right. In some places, the organised union workers do not allow the new comers to work in the job they do. This is seen in many areas. For example, the head-load workers in an Indian railway station do not allow a new worker. If one of the head-load workers wants to leave the job or wants to retire from his work he sells his right to work to a new comer who spends money to purchase the right. The same work culture is seen amidst organised auto-ricksaw drivers, *attimary* labourers, way-side sellers and so on. Governments too impose restriction on the basis of residence to potential employees.

Right to free choice of employment is another declared human right. As stated elsewhere, 'Beggars cannot be choosers' and in a country of unemployment or in a state of underemployment, what is the *foolish* meaning of the expression "Right to choose employment". Exercise of this right is virtually not possible and practically not feasible. People out of despair accept some or any job and in utter despair work in their job and in such a deplorable state of affairs, the Article seems to have no impact or effect in many undeveloped, underdeveloped or even in developing countries. It is a *nice to hear* Article and a curse to willing to work population.

Protection against unemployment ! What type of protection? Highly qualified people are unemployed and they cannot work with pleasure and willingly like labourers and coolies. They have a dignity and their dignity must be protected. What type of protection is given to employees who do not work? Substitute for an employment is another employment. There is no substitute for unemployment. Presently, some governments give a nominal amount as unemployment wages. It is not a protection, but a charity to the unemployed.

Employees in countries where unemployment is an acute problem may accept jobs desperately under conditions they cannot work with pleasure and safety. Even children are employed in hazardous conditions and dangerous environments. They have no choice of employment and the human rights to the choice of employment becomes a practical impossibility. Though workmen's compensation laws are available in some countries, they are observed more in violations and not in observing the provisions of the law. Policemen are attacked and are seriously injured while they are on duty. There are countries where there exists no provision of law to compensate the losses to them while they are on duty. While the law is seriously concerned with the compensation to be paid to the victims of human rights violations by policemen, the allegation often heard is that the law is not concerned with the compensation to the loss or injuries sustained by policemen while they are protecting the human rights of the people entrusted to them.

"Hire and Fire" policy is accepted by many managements and they extract work from their employees under conditions of anxiety about the continuance of job. The employees are terminated from service by giving a short notice of termination or by offering a nominal amount in lieu of the notice to be issued. As soon as they are dismissed or their service is terminated under a Hire and Fire Policy, they are not offered any protection against unemployment. In jails where the incarcerated work, there exists no question of any "choice of employment". The incarcerated are to do any job they are given. There was a time, the incarcerated were pressured to do some hazardous job without any remuneration (wages) and without any purpose. Drawing water from a deep well in big buckets and pouring it back to the well was a type of work given to them. Again, digging pits from morning and filling the pits by mud in the evening was another work given to the incarcerated. The question of working, not working, changing the work, etc., does not arise in prisons. The caged prisoners are to work as slaves under conditions which violate the human rights declared by the United Nations. The pictures shown on the T.V. screens about the works done by the prisoners of war and by the incarcerated human beings show how violently are the Articles in the Universal Declaration of Human Rights violated. If they are not injustices, then what are they?

38

Equal Pay for Equal Work

"Everyone without any discrimination, has the right to equal pay for equal work."

[*Article 23.2 of UDHR-1948*]

"Equal pay for equal work." No doubt, it is a human right; but how to decide the equality of work"? It may be virtually very difficult, if not impossible. In prisons, what is the pay? It was almost like extracting free labour from the confined convicts. Until recently, in India, the prisoners who were employed did not get any wages worth mentioning. Likewise, the prisoners were working under controlled conditions like slaves in many countries. Some human rights activists approached the courts to get decent wages for their work, but in vain.

There exists no criterion to decide the equality of work. One may look at the nature of the work and in certain places, the equality of work is decided by the nature of work. The remuneration is fixed sometimes on the basis of the sex of the worker rather than on the nature or type of work. For example, the helpers to construction work. The men get a higher pay than women and if the construction work is done by the convicts [There are states where the prisoners are employed by the Public Works Department, (PWD)]. In prisons, they are paid little or no wages. Children are employed by many in places including hotels, cottage industries, small scale industries, workshops, etc., and they do very hard labour for which they are given only food and accommodation. When the turnout is taken, they produce enviable output, but no wages. Here, the age of the employee becomes a criterion to decide the wages. Employees in the urban area are paid higher wages than what is given to the employees in rural areas for doing the same work. Here, more than the nature of work, the geographical nature of the place of work is taken into account. As a result, there is migration to cities from villages causing serious social problems. My view is that there is no meaning in making a sweeping declaration like the one given in the UDHR-1948. My proposal is :

> "Everyone, without any discrimination, has the right to minimum wages for a work. The minimum wages will be fixed by the national laws and standards made from time to time.
>
> Everyone, without any discrimination, has the right to equal pay for equal work throughout the territory of a State.
>
> The convicted in an institution for personality development have a right to get a pay equal to what is given for the same or similar work outside the institution".

Article 23.2 and Criminal Justice

Everyone has, without any discrimination, the right to equal pay for equal work is a human right. Nevertheless, what happens in the area of child labour? (Child labour is prohibited in some countries) The children who are employed are not paid anything at all except food by some employers. Some children are asked to work long hours and are paid very meagre wages. Their poverty is exploited. Forget about the wages and think about their working conditions. Deplorable indeed! Even the adults are not given decent wages. Women are harassed and sexually exploited. The inmates in prisons are pressured to work and they are paid only nominal wages. If at all they are given equal pay for equal work, the pay thus paid is far away from being reasonable. The question of paying equal wages comes into being only if they are paid at all! The problem here is that they are under-paid or not paid at all. Food for work may be a government sponsored programme and there too, the question of paying equal wages for equal work, without any discrimination, does not arise. Human rights are violently violated in such situations and the human rights justice is grossly denied. Governments are aware about such malpractices and miscarriage of justice. Nothing is done to remedy the situation; rather is allowed to continue. Bonded labour is still in existence in some form or another. The employer gives a loan and the loanee or a dependent of the loanee is treated as a bonded or caged labourer until the loaned amount is paid back. More often than not, the labourer cannot pay back the interest on the loan, forget about the principal amount. In some instances the labourer is auctioned to another employer under whom the loanee is expected to work. There are temple servants. The girls are entrusted to the temple as a religious practice. They work there without accepting any wages and many a time becoming victims of religious prostitution.

Women are discriminated against men. They do the same job, but they are paid less than men. Why? No justification to discriminate on the basis of sex. There are government jobs, jobs in public undertakings and quasi-government institutions, private sector, etc., and there the women are discriminated. The disparity between the employees in private and public sectors may be incredible. For example, an engineer working in the software area is paid exorbitantly by private companies, the same job done by an engineer in government service is paid less. Likewise, employees in government service get a lot of benefits privileges, but are denied to the employees working in some private enterprises. In countries where unemployment and underemployment are problems, there will not be equal pay for equal work. People having the same qualifications and merits get different wages. The perks and privileges may be different in public and private enterprises. What is worse is the difference in the wages/ pay between the employees doing the same job in different States in one and the same country. There exist differences in the wage structure, perks, privileges between the employees working in the Central Government and State Governments in the Federal system of government. Although the Universal Declaration of human rights makes equal pay for equal work a human right of the people, it seems that such a declaration is nothing but empty words. Countries which are the signatories of the Declaration do not care much or anything about their commitment to the United Nations' principles. Resultingly, gross injustice is perpetuated when the United Nations watch the drama helplessly.

39

Just and Favourable Remuneration

> "Everyone who works has the right to just and favourable remuneration ensuring for himself and his family an existence worthy of human dignity and supplemented, if necessary, by other means of social protection".
>
> [*Article 23.3 of UDHR-1948*]

"Ensuring for himself and his family an existence worthy of human dignity"–this is something which cannot be guaranteed. A family means a lot and it can be a large family or a small family. It can be a nuclear family or a joint family. How to ensure an existence worthy of human dignity to himself and his family? I propose that the entire portion may be deleted from the Article to read :

> "Everyone who works has the right to just and favourable remuneration fixed by the national laws respecting international standards. The remuneration so fixed for the work will be considered sufficient to ensure for himself and his family an existence worthy of human dignity."

How "to supplement, if necessary, by other means of social protection"? What are the "other means of social protection?" When one gets just and favourable remuneration fixed by the national laws and respecting international guidelines, the question of supplementing other means of social protection does not arise.

This provision should be made applicable to those who work in the prisons during their period of incarceration. Work in the prisons is for their correction, reformation, rehabilitation, resocialisation and reintegration. Just and favourable remuneration will certainly enhance the possibility of correction and rehabilitation in the desired direction in a speedier way. Presently, it seems, there exists no national or international law worth mentioning fixing the just and favourable remuneration for the inmates in prisons.

Article 23.3 and Criminal Justice

What is the just and favourable remuneration? The difference between the lowest employee in a department and the highest employee in the same department in government services is found to be unbelievably huge in some countries. The government may feel that the difference is insignificant when the reality is quite frustrating indeed! The lower levels of employees may have a larger family with many dependents while the higher levels may have smaller families having fewer members with little or no liabilities. I have noticed that more employees at the lower strata in government services committing suicides, family suicides, family-murder suicides owing to their financial problems and liabilities than those employed at the higher levels. The meagre pay given for a hand to mouth existence in countries having unemployment is a severe problem which cannot be treated as just and favourable remuneration ensuring for himself and his family an existence worthy of human dignity. The governments in such countries may be financially weak so much so that the declaration making the remuneration just and favourable for oneself remains to be an unachievable wish or task for them.

In some countries the governments have fixed just and favourable remuneration "ensuring for himself and his family an existence worthy of human dignity". But, what is seen there may be that they make the remuneration just and more favourable to the employers than to the employees. The employers insist and get a receipt for *just and favourable* remuneration, but they give only meagre remuneration just necessary for their hand to mouth existence. Helplessly and silently, they receive the remuneration cheating them as well as the United Nations and speak about the remuneration with the tongue of a human rights activists. What is found to be *just and favourable* remuneration by the government becomes unjust and unfavourable in the prisons. It may be reiterated that the government policy is deplorably frustrating and painful as far as the just and favourable remuneration is concerned. There is unpardonable exploitation of free labour and injustice done to the helpless in the prisons.

Human dignity is relative—that is what many employees say. What is this human dignity? It is the most nebulous term which can never be clearly understood. What is the human dignity of Peter will be different from the human dignity of Paul although both perform the same job, live together in the same culture and work environment. "A cobbler needs not look above the shoes" is the attitude of the employers to human dignity. The employees should not compare their dignity with the same of the management. A comparison will frustrate them. As far as there exist no objectivity or objective scales in deciding human dignity of the employees and the same of the employers, they argue that the expression "worthy of human dignity" is meaningless. These interpretations and thoughts make them to violate the human rights law in the way they want and thereby to commit injustice. What is meant by "supplemented, if necessary, by other means of social protection"? There may be the insurance coverage, medical reimbursement, welfare contribution, contributory provident fund, etc., for employees working in factories, firms, companies, government, public undertakings, etc. What is going on in the case of seasonal employees, labourers, coolies, farmers and so on? They do not have any social security schemes in many countries although they pay taxes to government. Recently, some governments have started some welfare measures for some of them. But that is not enough. This is an area where injustice is perpetuated.

40

Trade Unions and their Activities

> "Everyone has the right to form and to join trade unions for protection of his interests".
>
> [*Article 23.4 of UDHR-1948*]

"For the protection of his interest"–this is a dangerous declaration. The protection of the employees' interests may be important. But it must not be harmful or detrimental to the interests of the employers. What is seen today? Trade unions, with political support, put unrealistic demands and with their muscle power make attempts to see that their demands are approved by the management. If not, they declare strikes, damage property and cause many problems and instances are plenty that the managements cannot but wind up their industries. Trade union leaders become helpless in such situations and some of the trade union leaders are looked down upon by the employees as they are found to be people of suspicious integrity and earnestness. The trade unions are good for collective bargaining and the objectives of trade unions are not destruction, but construction. Nevertheless, some unscrupulous trade union activists encash on the weakness of the management as well as of the employees. Hence, the Article needs amendment.

> "Everyone has the right to form and to join trade unions for the protection of his interest and for the promotion of harmony between himself and the management."

The right shall be exercised for the mutual benefits of the employers and employees and for the development of the nation as a whole in an atmosphere ensuring co-operation and unity of purpose for betterment.

Trade unions are very powerful. The employees are as important as the employers in nation-building. But, unfortunately, they organise *hartals, dharnas, bandhs,* destruction of property, etc. Some of their strikes were declared to be illegal. Whatever that be, the Article should have a clause stating that the right of an individual in forming or becoming a member in the trade union should not be misused or abused for the purpose of serving self-interests. Hence, the Article should have a clause :

> "The right to form and to join trade unions for the protection of one's interest shall be subject to reasonable restrictions imposed by law and shall not be against public interest and nation's development."

Article 23.4 and Criminal Justice

The expression "protection of his interest" creates a lot of problem and becomes a cause for injustice. After all, the employers and the employees are complementary to each other. What I observe is that some of the employers have money power and some of the trade unions of the employees have muscle power supported by the politicians with vested interests. They fight each other causing damages and financial loss to the employers and government. In some instances, the employers wind up their business and the employees go to the streets and wander around jobless. The trade union leaders are unable to open the factories closed and in one instance, near to my home town, I found the unemployed "employees" of a company committing suicide, family suicide and family murder-suicides and it happened owing to an excessive trade unionism for the sale 'interest of the employees' in the factory.

The human rights to trade unionism, if not properly understood, will cause great calamity. Public undertakings and government owned business institutions have perished owing to too much of trade union activities detrimental to the mutual benefits of the employer and employees. The police, prosecutors and so on consider labour cases as insignificant. Labour unions/ trade unions with a tunnel vision and only parochial interests have became instrumental to the total destruction of some employers' dreams and finance. Human rights and the rights to have human rights should not be misused or abused to cause injustice by misuse of authority or by abuse of power.

Excessive trade union activities are not enjoyment of human rights, but are destroyers of human happiness and social welfare. The investors and employers will be hesitant to come to a field where there is excessive trade unionism. Many political leaders who have come to power in the ruling governments have been instrumental to make the trade unions to commit atrocities on the employers/ their property, to create disputes, strikes, organised defiance to authority and thus they become trade union leaders. If the investors do not come forward to invest money, it will affect adversely the industrialisation. I have witnessed such a sad state of affairs because of excessive trade unionism by vested interests. It is an injustice done to human society and young generations to see that the investors are expelled by misinformed trade union activists about their role in the establishment of human rights and their enjoyment. The number of criminal cases registered against trade union leaders and trade union activists are many. At the end when the dispute is settled, the trade unions misuse their organisational strength to pressure the governments to withdraw the cases registered against them. Political parties, supported by trade unions, having their eyes on vote banks see to it that all cases are withdrawn and thus they enjoy a sort of immunity from the liability in criminal cases registered against them. The damages caused by them to private property, to public property and to the property of the employers may be unimaginably huge and finally an agreement is reached that the sufferer (i.e., the employer, the government, etc.) will suffer the losses caused by the trade unions and the employees. Thus, they get immunity from paying compensation to the damages or losses caused by them. Thus, they get double immunity in trade union activities. The winners in most of the situations will be the trade unions. I do not know whether or not the enjoyment of human rights declared by the United Nations in the above Article contemplates the double immunity, i.e., immunity from criminal liability and immunity from paying compensation to the damages/losses caused by them–enjoyed by the trade unions in addition to the enjoyment of human rights by them. In any case, in my view, it is nothing but injustice caused by trade unions, vested interests and politicians.

41

Leisure and Working Hours

> "Everyone has the right to rest and leisure, including reasonable limitation of working hours and periodic holidays with pay."
>
> [Article 24 of UDHR-1948]

"Eight hours to work, eight hours to sleep and eight hours to other activities including rest and leisure'—this is an accepted principle in many cultures and societies. If someone works more than 8 hours, then he is eligible to get overtime pay or allowances. In Indian police, one sees 24 hours of work and it creates discomfort and murmur among the policemen in countries where such a law is in force. There are employees who enjoy more holidays than the days they work. There are employees who do not work at all during their working hours, but enjoy rest and leisure. There are employers who work in target oriented jobs and they cannot take rest and enjoy leisure until their target is reached. There are employees who cannot leave the work in between and, therefore, the human rights declared by the above Article needs amendment as under.

> "Everyone has the right to rest and leisure for 8 hours a day and this right shall be exercised depending upon the nature of the work and subject to reasonable restrictions. Everyone who works beyond 8 hours has a right to get overtime pay or allowances."

Article 24 and Criminal Justice

Employers are not very happy to give leisure for their employees, because, they consider time and work as money and business for them. They do business and profit is their motive. Though 8 hours' work is generally accepted, many a private employer wants to see that their employees work more. This is resisted by the employees and their trade unions. Nevertheless, 'Hire and Fire' policy is adopted by many private employers so much so that there is an excessive content of uncertainty in many jobs. A study conducted by me amidst the employees in software field, I understand that the employees are under severe stress and work tensions and they are working in a target-oriented work culture. Rest or no rest, leisure or no leisure, they want the target to be finished within a time-frame. This is seen more in Asian countries than in America and Europe. In police department in India, the law is that the police personnel are on duty for 24 hours a day. Though they are entitled to get weekly off, more often than not, they are denied of such "offs" on the ground of real, simulated or non-existing emergencies. In some firms, companies or factories, one may not find any facility for enjoying leisure time. In many government departments, rest and leisure may not be officially given; but the government employees enjoy them in many ways. They may not do the work or if at all they do the work, they do it leisurely at their will and pleasure. Many of them do not have any accountability to anyone or if at all the supervising officials insist for accountability, they are helpless to enforce their decisions. The government servants' unions and associations, backed by political parties in power or opposition, are so powerful that the supervising personnel are *de facto* restrained from exercising their power or enforcing their decisions. This may be due to the existence of a defective work culture in government services. The subculture of work seen in the government services permits the employees to procrastinate their duties and work causing unpardonable delay in services. Some people say that the government employees procrastinate until the opportunity is lost. They do so, sometimes, to make an income through corruption and corrupt practices. What to do? It may be a curse and the general public are condemned to suffer the procrastination, delay and injustice. In the technical sense, they are not at rest or are not enjoying leisure, but in reality they are at rest and they enjoy a lot of leisure. The Article in the Universal Declaration of Human Right might not have thought about such types of inertia, inaction, no work, procrastination, undue delay, unauthorised absence, French leaves, absentism, irresponsibility, unaccountability, excessive abuse of unionism, etc., when it declared the right to rest and leisure as a human right. Injustice comes when the employees are irresponsibly conscious about their rights and not all concerned with their duties and obligations.

Right to rest and leisure is denied to many labourers who work under risk-masters. Instances are plenty to show that the poor and the ignorant people are pressured to work from 6 O'clock in the morning till 9 O'clock in the night without rest and leisure. The coolies and daily wage labourers under the contractors in many parts of the world are forced to work without rest, leisure and proper wages. The same is applicable in the case of children and women. Their work is exploited by the powerful and the affluent or even by politicians. There was news in the media in the recent past that a Minister in the ruling Government in India paid very little wages to his labourers who worked in his farm. When the journalists asked the Minister about the injustice done (in paying nominal wages and in not allowing them to enjoy leisure) to the labourers who were to work as slaves to the political leader (He has *goondas* and muscle power), he leisurely and with pleasure said: "Who told you that I paid only nominal wages? I did give them a cup of black coffee at 11 O'clock everyday." Fine ! The labourers secretly complained that the black coffee was without sugar. What an injustice ! The Minister who was expected to protect human rights was violating the right to rest and leisure under the colour of his political position and under the cover of his muscle power.

Countries where poverty and unemployment are acute problems, slave-like labourers are available and they work under strenuous pressure without rest and leisure time, under the hot sun and in heavy rain, in utter starvation or semi-starvation. They may work under inhuman working conditions and without enjoying even creature-comforts which cows, dogs, buffaloes and other domestic animals enjoy. What about the domestic servants? They are pressured to work without rest and leisure time and in some cases subjecting themselves (if women) to sexual exploitation in various ways. Worse is the condition of women in some families. Wives—that is how they are called—who are called unpaid labourers in some countries—are to work hours together without rest and leisure time. In countries where dowry system still rules marriages, housewives are harassed in the name of dowry. In India, dowry deaths are reported. If death does not take place, there will be torture, inhuman and degrading treatment in addition to the excessive labour they are forced to do. In the name of dowry, some women are killed and the death is presented as a suicide—or better, simulated suicide. In such a work culture and domestic life, the human right to rest and leisure becomes an unattainable desire. What to do to overcome this sort of injustice?

It seems to me that the U.N. Article is concerned with the organised sector of labour than the unorganised section. A huge majority of people including children and women are working in the unorganised sector. How to implement or enforce the objective of the Article in the unorganised sector? There is exploitation and the governments are helpless to enforce the Article there. Child labour is a menace in many developing or underdeveloped countries. Women are forced to work without any sort of rest in very deplorable working conditions with inadequate pay, in unhealthy environments, without toilet facilities or drinking water, with insufficient and qualitatively inferior type of food, poor accommodation and health care. What happens in prisons? While rest and leisure may be granted to them, many prisons do not have rest places and leisure time activities. The governments do not seem to have any commitment to honour the human rights declaration. Is it not an injustice to do so with caged prisoners in the so-named institution for personality development?

The Article speaks about reasonable limitation of working hours and periodic holidays with pay. This is possible again in organised sector of labour. In one and the same country, one government may allow leave travel concessions for pleasure while another government may not offer any such facilities for the employees. There is discrimination among employees working in the same country under different governments. The same position exists even in the case of periodic holidays with pay. In some cases, the employees have many more holidays with pay than in some other cases. There exists no uniformity in such matters so much so that the human rights declaration is not properly recognised and respected. This is injustice and the employees show their displeasure and cry for justice. Their cry becomes a cry in the wilderness. In the unorganised sector, no question of enjoying holidays with pay arises. If they do not work, they do not have the pay—nothing more and nothing less. It seems that there exists no social protection given to them even when they are sick or hospitalised. With them, the Article and its enforcement is a closed chapter—written only on papers. Injustice is perpetuated and nothing is done to remedy the aching or desperate situation.

42

Standard of Living and Social Security

> "Everyone has the right to a standard of living adequate for health and well-being of himself and of his family including food, clothing, housing and medical care and necessary social services and the right to security in the event of unemployment, sickness, disability, widowhood, old age or other lack of livelihood in circumstances beyond his control."
>
> [*Article 25.1 of UDHR-1948*]

"Standard of living adequate for health and well-being of himself and family including food, clothing, housing and medical care", etc., may not be enough. I, therefore, add "protection of human rights" after health in the above Article to read "Standard of living adequate for health, *protection of human rights* and well-being of himself . . ." Why do I say so? United Nations have declared the Universal Declaration of Human Rights, but they have not declared that the right to enjoy human right is another human "Right" of the people. Many Constitutions in the world specifically put the Fundamental Rights of people in the beginning. They also put the *right* to get the fundamental rights enforced through the courts of law is another fundamental right. Like that the right to human rights ought to have been made a separate Article in the UDHR-1948. But, that was not done. At the same time, one cannot ignore it. Therefore, I put it in this Article. Why?

One's *Standard of Living* means that he lives like a "man" and not like an "*animal*" though there are "animal-men or *men-animal*" (living amidst us) as the case may be. In order to ensure the standard of living, the right to have the human rights ought to have been made another *Right* in a separate Article or in the articles already declared.

"Food, clothing, housing and medical care . . ." may not be enough. What about the "Socialisation" or one's right for socialisation? If human beings are not socialised, then they cease to become human beings or social beings. Like Kamala and Amala, 7-year old girls got from Indian forests, people will live like animals if they are not provided with opportunities for adequate/effective socialisation. Just like medical care, socialisation too is very essential for the well-being of human beings. The amended Article, therefore, will be :

". . . including food, clothing, proper socialisation, housing and medical care..." In my view, socialisation and that too "proper socialisation" is more important than food or shelter (housing) to live with dignity.

". . . Event of unemployment, sickness, disability, widowhood, old age . . ."—fine. But, some important areas overlooked may be "accident, natural calamities, attacks—military or otherwise—, abuse of power, misuse of authority . . ." Why do I say so? Accidents are so frequent in these days that motor vehicle accidents themselves kill millions of people, maim them and cause serious injuries and disabilities to people and their dependents. Accidents create a worse situation than unemployment and sickness, etc. Natural calamities cause further problems. Earthquakes, tsunami, flood, draughts, hurricanes of all descriptions may be the *Acts of God,* yet are severe problem creators. The after-effects of such natural calamities must be brought under the purview of the operations of human rights laws.

Attacks—military and otherwise—are to be viewed seriously. The communal, racial, terrorist attacks are known to all. What about the military attacks? Innocent people are killed in large numbers. Children, women, old men and so on are attacked just because they belong to a particular religion, community, race, ethnic origin, region, country, etc., and these attacks are more serious than old age or widowhood. Abuse of power and misuse of authority–both are serious problems. The ways in which the power is abused and authority is misused are many and various and all departments of the government from animal husbandry to zoo and museums involve in such abuses and misuses. Resultingly, the people suffer and their right to live with dignity is disturbed.

Putting everything together, the amended Article must be :

> "Everyone has the right to a standard of living adequate for health, protection of human rights and well-being of himself and of his family including food, clothing, proper socialisation, housing and medical care and necessary social services and the right to security in the event of unemployment, sickness, disability, widowhood, old age, accident, natural calamities, attacks—military or otherwise—, abuse of power, misuse of authority or other lack of livelihood in circumstances beyond his control."

Article 25 and Criminal Justice

There are countries where poverty is the most painful problem. People die of poverty. There is no sense or meaning in preaching a sermon before the poverty-stricken people. It is a crime and injustice done to them. Standard of living adequate for health and well-being of himself and of his family—what an exalted expression indeed ! It is an injustice to talk about eating cake when the poor man do not have anything to eat. We do see such human skeletons in the visual media and we read about them in the print media. If we tell about "standard of living adequate for health and well-being of himself and of his family", they may become violent and atrocious. They may commit manslaughter when they listen that it is their birth right (human right) to have such amenities (luxuries for them) like food, clothing, housing, medical care and necessary social services. Many exploit the resources of the country for their personal benefits and take an attitude "let a million people die of poverty, we want the whole national wealth." What do the ruling government do to eradicate poverty and what does the international community do to satisfy the basic needs and creature—comforts for them? It is easier said than done and even on the 64th year of the Universal Declaration of Human Rights-1948, the situation goes from bad to worse in some parts of the world.

Right to security in the event of unemployment, sickness, disability, widowhood, old age or other lack of livelihood in circumstances beyond his control'—this declaration has been a great *tamasha* ever since the Universal Declaration of Human Rights has come into being. What kind of security do the governments offer for their citizens? A big 'zero' in many countries ! The unemployed turn to crimes when they do not have income. Studies conducted in India and elsewhere show that many a juvenile delinquent hails from families which are financially poor or where unemployment is a severe problem. No one turns to them and some opt for committing suicides in such conditions. What kind of security do the sick receive? If they are rich enough, they are fine; otherwise they live under the mercy or charity of the people around them. The governments may establish some treatment centres/hospitals where there may not be doctors to treat, medicines to administer or facilities for laboratory tests, etc. Health area is contaminated with corruption and malpractices. The fund allotted by the governments for the treatment of the sick (poor) may be pocketed by the *nexus* criminals and many people go after quack doctors, fake physicians and frauds in medical sciences. Disability is not attended to in many parts of the world. Mental disorders are treated not by psychiatrists but by quack "doctors' who commit fraud on the mental patients. Widowhood is looked down upon and a widow becomes a liability/a bad omen for many. Remarriage for them is indeed very difficult in many cultures. They may be forced to live in prostitution and sex work for the maintenance of their family. Old age is an inevitable reality, but the old are forsaken. Highly costly old age homes may be there for the rich and the affluent. Money matters a lot. What about the poor and the needy? They die of hunger, neglect, or unconcern and become victims of total unwantedness. They are the "human waste" and are treated as garbage. They become subject matter of novels, films and T.V. serials. Is it not injustice to become cruel to these helpless and defenceless lots when the Declaration makes the high sounding principles of human rights? Some countries favour euthanasia (mercy killing) for the old and the infirm or who suffer from incurable diseases. They consider it to be a holy thing (not a sin) to be done and shockingly enough those people who advocate mercy killing are "honourable men" who promote and propagate human rights and human rights declaration. Hypocrites indeed !

43

Motherhood and Children

> "Motherhood and childhood are entitled to special care and assistance. All children whether born in or out of wedlock, shall enjoy the same social protection."
>
> [*Article 25.2 of UDHR-1948*]

Motherhood and childhood are given special attention in the UDHR-1948. Good. Nevertheless, why not the special attention be given to the womanhood itself. Women are attacked throughout the world and even little children of tender age are abused, victimised, exploited and sexually attacked. The *virginhood* itself needs special attention. Hence, I may say :

> "Womanhood, virginity and motherhood are entitled to special care, assistance and protection."

The childhood needs special care, protection and assistance particularly at a time the children are neglected, abused, victimised, exploited, etc. There are children who are destitutes or suffer orphanhood. There are children abandoned, maimed for begging, tortured, sexually exploited etc. Even parents do so ! Hence, they need special protection, care and assistance. The amended Article, therefore, will include :

> "Infancy and childhood are entitled to have special care, protection and assistance."

Like some of the children, the old are abandoned, neglected, exploited, abused and victimised. The *oldest old*, the *older old*, the *middle old*, the *old*—all of them have different, different problems affecting adversely their life to live in dignity. I propose that the Universal Declaration of Human Rights may include :

> "The old, the young old, the middle old, the older old, the oldest old and their oldness are entitled to have special care, assistance and protection depending upon the nature and age of different categories of the aged."

For, the type of care, protection and assistance needed for the *oldest old* (85 years and above) must be different from the same offered to the old (Above 60 and below 65 years of age).

One may say that there are no orphan children in any country. Every child is a child of the state and the concept of orphanhood ceases to have any meaning and relevance in these days. Likewise, there is no meaning in saying the "children born in or out of wedlock". To say so may be necessary to decide the legitimacy, inheritance of property from their parents, etc. and not for the enjoyment of human rights. Therefore, in my considered view, the wordings or expression, "All children whether born in or out of wedlock" is unnecessary, unwarranted and attaching stigma to the dignity of children. Such expressions are not needed when human rights are declared. I propose to delete the said expression in the Article 25.2 of the existing UDHR-1948 to read:

> "All children will enjoy the same care, social protection and assistance."

Article 25.2 and Justice

I see unwed mothers in society and they want to enjoy such a status. They want a motherhood without husbands or without legally wed or outside a legal marriage or better want a motherhood with their children not knowing anything about their "father". They want "Fatherless children" and theirs too is motherhood—so sacred that they too have a right to enjoy special care and assistance. According to the Universal Declaration of Human Rights, they are entitled to receive special care and assistance. Is it a human right to opt for unwed motherhood and claim special care and protection? The mothers who may enjoy human rights ought to have been concerned with the childhood of their children who need to develop their personality in the right direction under the control of both parents. Motherhood is a special status and motherhood without a known fatherhood for their children is not motherhood at all or motherhood proper.

What about the motherhood of those women who desert their husbands on no justifiable reasons at all? What about the motherhood of those women who divorce their husbands for no justifiable cause at all? It is one thing to see desertions/divorces of the kind stated above and it is quite another thing to have genuine desertions/divorces on justifiable grounds. What kind of special care and assistance should be given to the motherhood of women who do not accept the dignity of husbandhood for them and fatherhood for their children? Enjoyment of human rights should have the support of "JUSTICE" behind it.

Many children die of poverty and malnutrition. Unborn children are aborted without any prick of conscience—both inside and outside the wedlock. There is high level infantile mortality. Girl children are neglected. Through scans, sex determination is made and the female foetus is aborted. Infant girls are murdered by smothering, by poisoning, by choking, by starvation and thus the atrocities committed on children in general and girl children in particular are numerous. A girl in some culture (particularly where dowry system is in existence) is a liability and what protection do the governments provide to safeguard the life of these innocent, helpless and defenceless (born and unborn) children? There are countries where abortion is made legal and there are moralists who justify miscarriage of unborn children. Girls are discriminated in some culture and countries and they are denied of education, good and nutritious food, clothing and life comforts. They are exploited sexually and abused in other ways. What type of human rights is ensured to children when the Declaration proclaims that they have a right to have social protection?

Legitimate children are denied of special care and protection. Undeniably, the illegitimate ones are neglected and the governments/ NGOs construct special homes for their welfare. Doubtlessly, it is a nice attitude shown to children. Nevertheless, in many so-named homes, the children are treated like "illegitimate children after all; orphan children after all; destitute children after all." If the allegations are true, they are treated in a cruel, inhuman and degrading manner—even without adequate food, accommodation and clothing. They are punished in deterrent ways by inflicting corporate punishments so much so that some children run away from such so-called homes. What about the children who face problems with law? Formerly, they were called delinquent children. Though Juvenile Justice (Care and Protection of Children) Acts are enacted in some countries they remain as dormant Acts. There is no commitment, no enforcement of law, no training given to the law enforcement officials and officials of judiciary so much so that the Act becomes sterile in every sense. Child labour is in vogue, abuse of children, exploitation of children, misuse of children, denial of free education for children at least at the elementary stages, neglect of children, etc., are seen everywhere, while the administration conducts enthusiastically seminars, symposia, workshops, etc., for the betterment and upliftment of children who need special care and protection.

Injustice in all descriptions done to children is not reacted against because the children are incapable of any such reactions. This is taken as their weakness and the governments close their eyes to these hard realities. United Nations have brought out the Rights of the Child. But how many member States honour them? No doubt, it is time now to react against the callous indifference shown to the injustice to children.

44

Education and Reservation

> "Everyone has the right to education. Education shall be free, at least in the elementary and fundamental stages. Elementary education shall be compulsory, technical and professional education shall be made generally available and higher education shall be equally accessible to all on the basis of merit".
>
> [*Article 26.1 of UDHR-1948*]

"Education" is not only academic, but also social, cultural, moral, religious, etc. What I learn by reading the Article is that the education referred in the above Article is only about academic education. It is not enough. Hence, I propose the following amendment :

> "Everyone has the right to education—academic, social, cultural and moral—in formal, informal or non-formal ways. Education on human rights and their utility, applicability and relevance ought to be compulsory and the education shall be free at least in the elementary and fundamental stages."

Why do I insist that the education on human rights and their utility, applicability and relevance ought to be compulsory? I have noticed that the above topics are not presently included in the syllabus or course contents of elementary and fundamental education in some States. Resultingly, many do not know what are the human rights and what are their utility, importance, relevance, etc., even when they come for higher education. Most unfortunately I listen to highly educated police officials, journalists, medical officers, prison authorities and even lawyers and professors of law talking about human rights and their utility in different ways and certainly not in the way the United Nations have in their minds. Some confuse them to be the Constitutional Rights while others speak about them to be the Civil Rights. Of course, both can be the human rights, but human rights are universal, basic and inalienable while the Constitutional rights are only for those who come under the jurisdiction of a particular Constitution in a particular country. The civil rights too are applicable to the citizens of a country as per the law. The human rights are doubtlessly more than the Constitutional and civil rights of the people. Sadly enough, the course contents of the Teachers' Training or Teacher Education do not contain human rights so much so that many who pass out of the teacher training institutions have little or no information on human rights. Hence, the Article should have :

> "Education on human rights should be compulsory for teacher training courses—both induction and inservice—and they should be included in the course contents of teacher education programmes, training of police, prison and other law enforcement officials, degree/diploma courses of universities, secondary and higher secondary courses, law colleges and judicial academies."

'Researches' are not very much encouraged. I do not observe any researches worth mentioning being conducted in many government departments including police, prisons, education, law enforcement and judiciary. Even higher education centres and universities do not have enviable facilities to conduct researches especially in the areas of human rights. Hence, I propose–"Technical and professional education shall be made generally available. Researches should be promoted and researches on human rights shall be encouraged in government departments, universities and centres of education, training and higher learning".

The Article above speaks about 'merit', but does not say anything about what constitutes the merit. Today, the expression merit is so much confused that some governments conduct special entrance examinations to decide the merit of students intending to prosecute further studies. Some governments have other ways and methods to decide the merits of students. Many a time, they are of questionable validity and are not free from criticisms and protests. I propose an amendment to make matters clearer :

> "Higher education shall be equally accessible to all on the basis of merit decided by entrance tests or other objectively valid assessment scales."

However, there is a problem here. While accessibility to higher education is a human right to all, the fact remains that there are some people whose interest should be protected in the area of education. They may be the women, socially handicapped, economically poor or very poor, minorities, members of the suppressed and oppressed classes/communities (for example, in India they may be the members of the Scheduled Castes or Scheduled Tribes), etc. Therefore, I propose :

> "Provided that nothing stated in the above Article will prevent a member-state from making any provision for the reservation of seats in educational institutions in favour of any backward class of citizens which need special care and protection in the field of education."

The amended Article may be :

"(1) Everyone has the right to education—academic, social, cultural and moral—in formal, informal or non-formal ways. Education on human rights and their utility, applicability and relevance ought to be compulsory and the education shall be free at least in the elementary and fundamental stages.

"(2) Education on human rights should be compulsory for teacher training courses—both induction and inservice and they shall be included in the course contents of teacher education programmes, training of police, prison and other law enforcement officials, degree/diploma courses of universities, secondary and higher secondary courses, law colleges and judicial academies as well as in special training programmes organised for judicial functionaries by the other institutions and agencies.

"(3) Technical and professional education shall be generally available. Researches shall be promoted and the findings of researches shall be acted upon. Researches on human rights shall be encouraged in government departments, universities and other centres of education, training and higher learning.

"(4) Higher education shall be equally accessible to all, on the basis of merits decided by entrance tests or other objectively valid assessment scales.

"Provided that nothing stated in the above will prevent a member-state from making any provision for the reservation of seats in educational institutions in favour of any classes of citizens which need special care and protection in the field of education."

Article 26.1 and Criminal Justice

Go to an educational institution and see the atrocities committed there. If the allegation is true, many educational institutions have become violators of human rights in very many ways. Students boycott the classes, organise strikes, damage public property and property belonging to educational institutions, attack teachers and other fellow students, create an atmosphere of terror making it difficult or impossible for students to study and teachers to educate. Instances are plenty to show bombings, stabbings, assaults and attacks, arson and abuse of students' muscle power. The destructive energy is utilised to damage the education system. Everything is done in the name of betterment and in the pretext of ensuring human rights. Drugs are brought and sold. Girls of tender ages are tempted to become susceptible to pervert sex activities. Alcohol plays a role. Activities centring around goondaism may be seen. Ragging in an inhuman way and in the most atrocious manner is going on. As a result, some children become psychic wrecks in the sea of life. Even manslaughter, rapes, homosexuality, masturbation, nudity and show of naked parts, compulsory sex-shows, drug-consumption and *what not* do not take place in the name of ragging in educational institutions ! Truancy and vagrancy among children studying in primary schools are noticed. The governments, managements, teachers are aware of these evils in schools and colleges, but all of them show a sort of tolerating—sometimes frustratingly encouraging—attitude to such situations. Why do they promote and perpetuate injustice in schools and college campuses? Some go to the extent of telling that terrorism and insurgency have their roots in universities and institutions of higher learning. The student activists in terrorism/insurgency in some parts of the world cause irreparable damages to the culture and civilisation.

The governments in democratic countries are formed by political parties. The political parties of the ruling government and of the opposition sponsor the unions and associations of students and they encourage them in all types of activities which will be of political advantage to them. Hence, the political parties sponsor the aggression and atrocities in schools and colleges. Don't have the governments in power a responsibility to create an atmosphere in school and college campuses for the students to study? The governments have, but seldom do they exercise their power and authority to establish peace in schools and campuses. Why? The peace will be detrimental to the development of their political interests. All of them want to fish in troubled water.

What about the management of schools and colleges? It seems that many a management has business interests more than social commitment or real educational commitment. Education today has been commercialised and has become costly. The government owned schools and colleges do not come up to the mark or expectation of the people so much so that the private sector educational institutions mint money by their inputs which are not human rights friendly always. These unscrupulous private managements have clandestine understandings with the political parties in power or opposition and all of them together violate the human rights. Is it not injustice to do so?

What about the teachers? Some enter the service through the back doors. They have no suitability to become teachers although they may possess the needed eligibility. Allegations are plenty that there is corruption in appointment of teachers by private managements as well as by Public Service Commissions. Merit and quality are not counted in appointments. Although the allegation may not be true *in toto*, the development of such a feeling among the people is of bad taste.

What about the equal accessibility of all to educational institutions on the basis of merit? This is not possible and no government has, it seems, any determination to see to it that the human rights declared by the United Nations should be respected. The children of the politicians and bureaucrats who are qualitatively inferior or do not possess real merits get access into educational institutions in very many ways which are of questionable nature. Education being a costly affair, equal accessibility to all on the basis of merit is an impossible proposition as the rich and the affluent can have an easier accessibility than the poor and the needy. Instances are not rare that the poor and the needy committing suicides after their admissions to the professional and technical institution on the basis of their financial weakness. The banks do not come enthusiastically forward to assist the poor and the needy although the governments say "this and that" with an eye on the vote bank during the next election. Whatever lofty and sublime ideas are declared by the United Nations about education, educational institutions and accessibility to education on the basis of merit, the fact remains that there exists a lot of violations of human rights in the area and thereby justice is denied to many in all parts of the world.

45

Education, Personality and Peace

> "Education shall be directed to the full development of the human personality and to the strengthening of respect for human rights and fundamental freedoms. It shall promote understanding, tolerance and friendship among all nations, racial or religious groups and shall further the activities of United Nations for the maintenance of peace."
>
> [*Article 26.2 of UDHR-1948*]

"Full development of human personality"–the concept is vague and not couched in clarity. Full development can also be in the negative direction. There are some tribes in which the education is given for the development of criminal personality. Such tribes were, once upon a time, called *criminal tribes* in India. Whatever that be, the concept should be made proper and clearer. Hence, I suggest :

> "Education shall be directed to the full development of human personality in the right direction with an upright conscience rightly formed."

It has been brought out in the Article 26.2 of UDHR-1948 that the education should be "to the strengthening of respect for human rights and fundamental freedoms". Fundamental freedoms are included in the concept of human rights. As such, as said elsewhere, that can be deleted. I may prefer to add the following instead of that, namely, '*person in the other*'. Accordingly, it becomes :

"... respect for human rights and the *person in the other*". *Person in the other* means the *essence* in the human person. In other words, it is nothing but an *I-Thou* relations and not an *I-It* relationship.

"It shall promote understanding, tolerance and friendship ..."—excellent. Nevertheless, I may insist to establish and promote "harmonious human coexistence" which I do not find among people who understand, tolerate and maintain friendship with others. Therefore, I may amend the Article.

"... It shall *establish* and promote understanding, tolerance, harmonious human coexistence and genuine friendship among all nations, racial and religious groups ...' I find some nations promoting terrorism and attacking other nations although they show an apparent friendship, tolerance and understanding. Hence, I may add "genuine friendship" instead of friendship only.

"... shall further the activities of the United Nations for the maintenance of peace." I wish to add "vision, commitment and activities" and thus, it shows :

"... shall further the vision, commitment and activities of the United Nations for the *establishment* and maintenance of peace." Putting everything together, the Article will be :

> "Education shall be directed to the full development of human personality in the right direction with an upright conscience rightly formed and to the strengthening of respect for human rights and the person in the other. It shall establish and promote understanding, tolerance, harmonious human coexistence and genuine friendship among all nations, racial and religious groups and shall further the visions, commitment and activities of the United Nations for the establishment and maintenance of peace."

Article 26.2 and Criminal Justice

There is an allegation that Naxalism, terrorism and insurgency develop sometimes in educational institutions. True or false the statement is, the fact remains that some of Naxalites, terrorists and insurgents are really educated people with a high I.Q. They are the people who are capable to intellectually infiltrate into others their philosophy of Naxalatism, insurgency and terrorism. There are university graduates, diploma holders, postgraduates in the list of convicts incarcerated to the prisons. When the Universal Declaration of Human Rights speaks about the full development of human personality, a question arises about the direction of the development, i.e., to the negative or positive?; to the constructive or destructive? Governments, educational institutions and teachers have a responsibility to see to it that the development of the personality is in the proper direction. If not, it will be an injustice and violation of human rights. When one studies the personality development of children in schools, he may be shocked to see that they develop their personality not in the way 'Universal Declaration of Human Rights' desires them to develop. If media reports are true, the school going children develop special affinity to criminality. Some of them exhibit violence and organised defiance to authority. Some take to drugs while others go after carnal pleasures and erotic satisfaction. Some are after violating the human rights of fellow students. Mass copying during public examinations, attacking of teachers, avoiding responsibilities, wasting time, engaging in vagrancy and truancy, destroying public property, organising *dharnas, bandhs,* road-blocks and agitations of all sorts, committing suicides, involving in pervert sex-activities, drinking alcohol, enjoying pornography, obscene literature or photography especially that having little or no artistic merit, disrespecting parents and teachers, etc., are just a few among the various ways they develop their negative or undesirable personality. Universal Declaration of Human Rights says about promoting understanding, tolerance and friendship, etc. Are the governments serious about the development of proper human personality? The political parties want to politicise the students, the criminal elements want them to become members in a criminal culture, the communal forces make all attempts to convert them into communalism, the fundamentalist organisations go after young blood, the terrorists want them to be enlisted in their group and the governments and their political parties, many a time, keep away from inculcating the finer points in establishing and developing tolerance and friendship among all religious, racial and linguistic groups in the society. The impact is intolerance and lack of friendship with other fellow beings. Educational institutions are plenty, but how many of them are earnest in developing human rights friendly attitude among the students? Any investment on character building and human conscience formation is an investment for the development of human rights attitudes and activities. But, seldom do some of educational institutions care such aspects of human personality development. What is happening at the higher education levels? In countries where unemployment is a serious problem, students become aimless in life. Some students go after target fixed education so much so that they do not just care values in life. Selfishness develops and many of them live in an island isolated from human contacts and interpersonal relationship. These human islands are found to lack enviable personality traits, values and human contacts. That is not personality development. It is perversions in the development of proper personality. The injustice done to the student population now will certainly affect the higher education adversely for merely 30 or 40 years to come or more.

46

Education and Joint Right of Parents and Children

"Parents have a prior right to choose the kind of education that shall be given to their children."

[*Article 26.3 of UDHR-1948*]

Parents have a *right* and it is a *prior right*. But, the child too has a right to choose the kind of education. What is seen today is indeed very strange. The parents take a decision and choose the kind of education for their children. The education has thus become "target oriented". Children who do not have an aptitude for medicine go to medical colleges to become medical doctors. Likewise, children who have traits, aptitude and motivation to become teachers go for engineering, law, management or fashion technology. Therefore, the Article needs an amendment.

"Parents have a joint responsibility with their children towards their education and a *prior right* to choose the kind of education that shall be given to their children." This must be further qualified by—"The children have a joint responsibility with their parents towards education and together they have a right to choose the kind of education that shall be received by the children. They have the right to change the kind of education they have chosen with their parents if that is found necessary."

Article 26.3 and Criminal Justice

Children complain always that their parents fail to or refuse to recognise and respect the aptitude and interest in studies. Children who show special aptitude to language or culture are forced to study engineering and technology. Likewise, children who are interested to study commerce are compelled to study medicine. Countries where admissions to professional courses are purchased, the parents spend any amount of money to ensure a seat in colleges and the children are pulled or pushed into or dragged to undertake courses to which they have least interest, psychological disliking and repulsion. According to the parents, they want status, job potentials and income after the academic course for their children. The Universal Declaration of Human Rights says that the parents have a prior right to choose the kind of education that shall be given to their children. According to many children, the right conferred to the parents by the United Nations to choose the kind of education that shall be given to their children is of bad taste and does more damage to children than what they otherwise would have obtained. The parents who invest huge amount of money on the education of their children have expectations and they always entertain a sort of target-oriented education. The children who cannot suitably respond to the expectations of their parents or the children who get low scores/credits during the examination become frustrated in life and they, at times, commit suicide in Kerala State where suicides of students have become a social problem. The parents are not prepared to make any compromises as far as the education of their children is concerned. Some borrow money while others take bank loans. Unable to repay the loans, some of them commit suicide and a few of them opt for family suicide/family murder-suicides. What type of human rights do they enjoy? Parents who exercise their right to choose the kind of education for their children, it is found, take more troubles, than the students to make them what they want them to be. Doctors, engineers, chartered accountants, management experts, computer scientists, scientists, professors—all these are the aspirations of the parents who can afford to spend money. They are on the one side, and on the other side, there are parents who are poor and helpless. They do not exercise their option to choose the kind of education for their children. Resultingly, their children continue to be little educated. Thus, one sees two types of children in many societies. The creation of two types of citizens is an injustice and a violation of human rights—say many in society.

There are cultures and countries where the parents do not allow their children, especially the girls, to study much. They do not exercise their right to choose the education for their daughters. Their vision is: "Girls need not study much." Since the parents are given the prior right to choose the kind of education to their children, the parents may/will exercise their powers to the disadvantage of their girl-children educationally. If a parent does not want to exercise his power/refuses to exercise the power conferred on him by this Article, then his children will suffer the consequence of his decision. Therefore, there is a view that the responsibility or the right should be for both parents and children together. Or, better, it must be a joint responsibility to avoid injustice committed on children in their education.

47

Cultural Activities and Scientific Advancement

> "Everyone has the right freely to participate in the cultural life of the community to enjoy the arts and to share in scientific advancement and its benefits".
>
> [*Article 27.1 of UDHR-1948*]

Cultural life may be the life of the dominant culture to which each and every child belongs. In addition to the dominant culture, there may be sub-cultures too. Hence, the Article may be re-written :

"Everyone has the right freely to participate in the dominant as well as special cultural life of the society and community to which he belongs." Participation in the special cultural life does not mean one's taking participation in any criminal or gang activities. For, children, who participate in the cultural life of some criminal gangs become delinquents. Therefore, it is necessary to specify the type of life in the culture. Thus, the amended Article will have—

"... cultural life (which is not criminal or violative of the norms). Thus, the amended Article will read:

> "Everyone has the right freely to participate in the dominant as well as in the special cultural life (which is not criminal or violative of the norms) of the society and the community to which he belongs" and "to enjoy the arts, to enrich by its literature, to keep up the moral traditions, to follow the customs and share in scientific advancement and its benefits."

Every subculture in dominant culture will have its own literature, traditions and customs. They must be honoured and respected.

Article 27.1 and Criminal Justice

The own cultural activities of a community may be dying in many countries owing to the influence of mass media. In any country, there may be a lot of cultural activities in the form of folklore dances or other types of indigenous nature. They are called "native" cultural activities. Some have become extinct now, i.e., they have ended or died out. They have become obsolete. Some are in the process of extinction. Some governments take interest to nurse and nurture such extinctive cultural activities while some other governments ignore them. While the human rights to freely participate in the cultural life of the community is declared in the Universal Declaration of Human Rights, the fact remains that there exists no such special cultural life of the community in some countries or if at all it exists, it is in a state of extinction. The administration seems to show an attitude of indifference. Therefore, in order to do justice to the Article, the governments should invest money to promote the special cultural life of the community. The cultural life of the community becomes today articles of curiosity in exhibition stalls and university departments undertaking special researches in that specific area.

The culture in any country is tradition-bound and it accepts the non-material values. In the world of material culture, people who love and promote non-material culture are looked down upon. They are not encouraged and as such the non-material culture is overpowered by the material culture. It being the case, the right to participate in the material culture is more favoured by many than the right to participate in the non-material culture, i.e., in the cultural life of the community. It may be an injustice done to the special cultural life of the community and may not have any option other than accepting, recognising and respecting such a new culture and cultural life.

Pre-marital interactions, nursing of the aged and infirm parents, joint family system, food habits, dress and etiquette, prayer life, festivity and local festivals, respect to women, patriarchal or matriarchal system, matrilineal or patrilineal inheritance, etc., may be peculiar to a particular community. Let them enjoy all the privileges of such a system. They have a right for it. Nevertheless, the problem arises if the cultural life of a community is detrimental to the welfare of the larger society and culture. For example, the *sati* practiced in India, the untouchability perpetuated in India, the polygamy/polyandry practiced in some communities, sacrifice of animals/man to please deities, dedicating female children to please goddesses, etc., are to be prohibited by law although the Article in the Universal Declaration of Human Rights does permit the right to participate in the cultural life of the community. No. there are criminal tribes, i.e., the denotified tribes, and they had a life of crime practised and perpetuated in the cultural life of their tribes (community). The human rights declared in the Article UDHR-1948 gives a free licence to participate in a life of crime accepted and respected by the cultural life of the community. This is nothing but injustice in every letter of the word. The cultural life of the community should be moral and must be acceptable to the larger culture in the society. The sub-culture in some of the government services in many countries may be a subculture of corruption and corrupt practices. Participate in the sub-cultural/ cultural life of the community of government servants may mean participation in corruption and corrupt practices. This is of foul smell and, therefore, should never be allowed or promoted. The Article in the UDHR-1948 is vague and needs to be altered and amended to stop injustices in the cultural life of the community.

48

Moral, Material and Non-Material Interests and Values

> "Everyone has the right to the protection of the moral and material interests resulting from any scientific, literary or artistic production of which he is the author".
>
> [*Article 27.2 of UDHR-1948*]

"Protection of the moral and material interests" may not be enough. The protection should be extended to the intellectual and non-material interests and values. The non-material culture consists of the traditional and customary values which society or community holds as secret or sacrosanct. If the people are not allowed to do so, then chaos and anomie will be resulted. Accordingly, the Article may be amended as :

> "Everyone has the right to the protection of the moral, intellectual, non-material and material interests and values resulting from any scientific, literary, artistic, intellectual and aesthetic production of which he is the author."

Article 27.2 and Justice

Material interests have an upper hand over moral interests. Though the saying goes: "If wealth is lost, nothing is lost", the fact remains that many things are lost when the wealth is lost. Again the saying goes on further: "If character is lost, everything is lost." This is nothing but the morality of a person or the moral character of an individual. The Declaration says that everyone has the right to the protection of the moral and material interests resulting from any scientific, literary or artistic production of which he is the author. What is seen today? As in the past, those who are affluent and capable to exploit the intelligence of the poor will exploit them and they may enjoy the material interests resulting from any scientific, literary or artistic production of theirs. This is what happens sometimes with scientists, with writers, with innovators and inventors. What interests can be protected by those who have no money to invest? Those who have money will be able to destroy the interests of others. Centuries old traditions, culture, buildings, architecture, art, literary works, libraries in Iraq were destroyed by the powerful and the affluent in the name of creating a better Iraq. Where is the right to protect the literary and artistic interest of the people of Iraq in the world of human rights? If this is what happens in a larger way, it is no less when it comes to the level of individuals. What is the moral right of the people? For example, publishing of books has become a kind of racketeering today. The authors are exploited and thus they are not allowed to protect their moral and material rights on their production. I am an author of more than 58 books in English and I see in the internet that DVDs of my books are available and they are sold by people whom I do not know. I see them in different languages and I need a lot of money to sue them and get my rights established. Copyright Act may be in force in many countries, but to get the rights established through a costly judiciary is indeed very difficult and expensive. There was a time when countries which ruled the world plundered the people in countries over which they had the control. They retain them still and the real owner-countries are denied of their right to get them back. If the governments in power violate the human rights, the people have no option but to suffer them. The injustice seen and done in this area may be visible, but not reacted upon in the way it should be.

49

Duties, Rights and Personality Development

> "Everyone has duties to the community in which alone the free and full development of his personality is possible."
>
> [*Article 29.1 of UDHR-1948*]

"Everyone has duties to the community"—this seems to me to be a sweeping statement meaning nothing much. Without specifying the duties, at least, in a general way or in some special areas, it seems to me, that the Article does not mean much to anyone.

The purpose of the above Article is to have a free and full development of one's personality. Personality is defined or described in many ways by psychologists, moralists and philosophers. If one goes by the meanings given in the Random House College Dictionary, it can be :

(1) The visible aspect of one's character as it impresses others.
(2) A person as an embodiment of a collection of qualities.
(3) Psychology: the sum total of the physical, mental, emotional and social characteristics of an individual.
(4) The organised pattern of behavioural characteristics of an individual.
(5) The quality of being a person; personal existence of identity, etc.

This word "personality means a lot" and the United Nations want, it seems to me, the human personality is to be developed in a human rights friendly way/manner. If that is the intention, then it must be made clearer to read :

"The free and full development of his personality in a human rights friendly way is possible." In the Universal Declaration of Human Rights, insistence on the development of one's personality in a human rights friendly way is quite understandable and is considered to be most needed too. Then the question is about the duties, their nature and areas, etc.

It has been proved by research studies that one's personality is developed by an interaction between heredity and environment. It means that one should give an appropriate environment for the proper development of one's personality. I have formulated a theory called Push-Pull-Ego Factor theory when I explained the criminal behaviour of a person. It is also proved by researchers that the most important period for the development of human personality is the early stages from the birth of a child (even earlier) till he/she reaches the age of 13-14 or a little less than that. Therefore, the duties to community for the free and full development of human personality centre around the development of children in the right direction with an upright conscience correctly formed. How to effect it? Hence I propose :

> "Everyone has the duties to the community towards bringing up children in the right direction in a human rights friendly way with an upright conscience rightly formed."

This may be the only Article which says something about one's duties to the community. The Universal Declaration of Human Rights says more or only about the RIGHTS and not about DUTIES. This has been an oft raised criticism against the said Declaration in the past and even today. Resultingly, many human rights activists speak only about the rights and nothing about the duties. Whatever that be, it is my honest view that the Article should have been made meaningful if the ideas and concepts are clearly communicated. I, further propose :

> "Everyone has the duties, obligations and responsibilities to the community in behaving in a human rights friendly manner so that the aspirations of the United Nations

stated in PREAMBLE of this Declaration are honestly actualised."

It may be remembered that one's duties, obligations and responsibilities to the society/community are the rights of others in the same society/ community.

Article 29.1 and Criminal Justice

What are the duties of everyone to the society? The duties are numerous, but to cite a few of them, I may go to the Constitution of India where it is written that everyone has a duty to secure to all her citizens (1) social, economic and political justice; (2) liberty of thought, expression, belief, faith and worship; (3) equality of status and of opportunity and to promote among the people all fraternity assuring the dignity of the individual, etc. I am one who may think that there is no better way to express the duties of everyone than what has been expressed in the Constitution of India. In the Preamble of the Universal Declaration of Human Rights, the same duties are expressed in the same or in a slightly different manner. Human Dignity, Equal and Inalienable Rights, Enjoyment of the Freedom of Speech and Belief, Freedom from Fear and Want, Protection of Human Rights by Law, Development of Friendly Relations between Nations, Worth of Human Person, Equal Rights of Men and Women, Promotion of Social Progress, Better Standards of Life in Larger Freedom, Universal Respect for and Observance of Human Rights and Fundamental Freedoms, a Common Understanding of Human Rights and Fundamental Freedoms are the lofty and sublime aim of the United Nations when the Universal Declaration of Human Rights was written. Do the people perform their duties to recognise and respect human dignity? What is happening in terrorism, insurgency, Naxalism, war, killing of the innocent, neglect of the old and infirm, capital punishment, etc.? 'Everything except the man has a value'–that is how I see around me. The victimisation of children, women, the poor, the members of the suppressed communities, etc., the communal riots and racial conflicts and mass-killings following them, exploitation of the weak and the needy, abuse of power, misuse of authority are the ways people show and express the wanton neglect of their duties to society. Adulteration of food, pollution of atmosphere, destruction of natural resources (the nature itself), are just of few examples to show how do the people avoid to observe their duties. There is threat to the freedom of speech and expression particularly in the areas of politics and religion. What do the fundamentalists do?- "salvation only through our religion, belief and politics" is their declared philosophy, approach and strategy. They see to it that everyone who objects to their belief and strategy is attacked or annihilated. What type of justice is it to deny the minority rights in a democracy? Small fishes are eaten by the big ones, small animals are attacked by big animals and likewise the small frogs in the human society are attacked, exploited, abused and done away with by the stronger ones. Yes, the survival of the fittest works here and the survival may be by neglecting the duties of man towards other human beings. There exist domestic violence, divorces, desertions, child abuses, sexual abuses of women and children, alcoholism, drug abuse and addiction, prostitution and immoral traffic on women and girls, slave-trade, abortions and mercy killing, etc. Are they the expressions of man's duties to society? No, never. Violence against human dignity, freedom and belief done to millions of people, especially children who are condemned to live in poverty, malnutrition and hunger (I see them in large numbers in the media and also around me) because of an unjust amassment of wealth by a few in the society is nothing but a refusal to perform one's duties to others. It is injustice indeed. I quote Pope John Paul II (from his encyclical Evangelium Vitae): "What of the spreading of death caused by reckless tampering with the world's ecological balance, by the criminal spread of drugs or by the promotion of certain kinds of sexual activity which, besides being morally unacceptable, also involve grave risk to life? It is impossible to catalogue completely the vast array of threats to human life, so many are the forms, whether explicit or hidden, in which they appear today !"

What is meant by "free and full development of personality"? What type of community/society do we see around us? What type of community/society do we see in the world? Take the daily newspapers and observe the T.V. news telecasts everyday. I have been doing them for the last few decades and I have a ready data-bank about what is happening in the community, society, world today. 40-70 per cent of the newspaper and almost the same per cent of the T.V. news-telecast time is devoted or spent for crime news. Criminal activities are exposed so much so that how does or can the free and full development of one's personality take place in the right way, to the right direction? Early morning when I wake up, I read the early news of crime in the newspapers and every hour, I see or hear the hourly news update almost in the same way or similar manner I see/read in the early morning. It continues till I see the day's night T.V. news telecast in which I see dead bodies and human faces with blood on the mini-screens. I used to have nightmares and honestly speaking I must confess that we are living in a world of crime where human rights are not respected—in a world where many people speak in loud voice and with a wide mouth about the sublimity of human rights, but simply refuse to follow what they preach or sermonize. What a tragedy indeed !

Democracy is the rule of the people. Politicians rule the people. Are the politicians upright in performing their duties to the community/society? Allegations are plenty that some of the politicians are real thugs, *goondas*, nexus criminals and unprincipled bandits of organised crime syndicates. In such a deplorable state of affairs, how can the people develop their personality? Many politicians are not always found to honour human rights so much so that, more often than not, there arise government sponsored human rights violations. The government (formed by the politicians and their vested interests) involve in mass-scale violations of human rights. Ultimately, the objectives of the Article in the Universal Declaration of Human Rights become a pious hope and an Utopean wish. Corruption and malpractices employed by the politicians in power, bureaucrats, businessmen, organised racketeers rule the people. In a world of corruption and corrupt practices, achievement of proper development of human personality becomes rather an impossibility.

The family all over the world is at disarray. The number of disorganised, broken, divorced, separated, deserted families is on the increase. Responsible parenthood may be lacking and it is roughly estimated by me that nearly 70 per cent of the crimes—social as well as legal—take place in or around the family. If family is lost, it means that the basic or fundamental unit of the society is shattered into pieces. What type of personality will be developed from such an environment? When a child is 3 years or above, the responsibility to develop his/her personality is the joint responsibility of the parents, teachers, home and the immediate surroundings. Do we have an enviable environment for the proper development of human personality? Do the people perform their duty in a responsible way? Children born and brought up in slums, crime-prone areas, overcrowded homes, unemployed families, indisciplined schools, values-lacking surroundings of children who are illegitimate, destitute, incorrigible, uncontrollable, neglected or who have problems with law or are members of the criminal gangs or belonging to gang cultures, or who experience culture conflicts, or who have inadequate formation of their superego, or suffering from excessive *id* impulses, or susceptible to corrupt practices or evil forces cannot and do not develop their personality in a desirable way. Do the people and agencies of socialisation and conscience–formation perform their duties as declared by the Article in the Universal Declaration of Human Rights? If they do not do the duties in the expected way, they are committing injustice to society and to the people.

Remember that everyone has a right to be protected from criminals and a duty to correct, reform, rehabilitate, resocialize and reintegrate a crime-doer so that he becomes a law-abiding citizen.

50

Social and International Order

> "Everyone is entitled to a social and international order in which the rights and freedoms set forth in this Declaration can be fully realised".
>
> [*Article 28 of UDHR-1948*]

It seems to me that the Article above does not mean anything as it is impossible to have a social and international order in which the rights and freedoms set forth in this Declaration can be fully realised. The world is so vast and the people living are different in many ways. Differences are found in the culture, economy, politics, race, colour, religion, etc., etc., so much so that a universal (social) order is just impossible. Human rights are many in number and to have them actualised requires a social and international order in all areas of human transactions and life. To think about a social and international order in all areas of human transactions is just another impossibility. One may be able to have such an order in few areas and not in all everywhere throughout the world. In my view, the entire Article 28 must be deleted from the Universal Declaration of Human Rights-1948.

To declare "everyone is entitled to a social and international order . . ." and to call it to be a human right means that the United Nations speak about something that does not exist at present or will not exist in future as well. When I say that there is a table in the other room, I mean that one can see it if he goes there. There, the existence is guaranteed whereas in Article 28 of UDHR-1948 there is nothing called a real social and international order. In all other articles in the UDHR-1948, one can see something in reality and the United Nations declare man's right to get that reality actualised. In this Article, no such reality ever exists and there is no chance to have the existence of such a reality ever. It is just like saying "a journey to Lilliput" and everyone knows that there is no place called Lilliput and no one can reach there. It is not even a wishful thinking! It is an illusion and the United Nations make it to be the *human rights* of the people and say that everyone is *entitled* to reach such an Utopian order which can never come into being. To say that everyone is entitled to have such an order (as a right) for realising the rights and freedoms set forth in this Declaration seems to be just empty utterances signifying nothing. Hence, I propose that the Article 28 of UDHR-1948 may be deleted from the Declaration itself.

51

Exercise of Rights and Performance of Duties

> "In the exercise of his rights and freedoms, everyone shall be subject only to such limitations as are determined by law solely for the purpose of securing the recognition and respect for the rights and freedoms of others and meeting the just requirements of morality, public order and the general welfare in a democratic society".
>
> [*Article 29.2 of UDHR-1948*]

"In a democratic society?"–What does it mean? It means that the general welfare in societies other than democratic societies does not come here? Does it mean that the human rights—being the birth rights of human beings—are not applicable in societies other than democratic societies? If human rights are the fundamental rights of people throughout the world, then "a democratic" in the Article above should be deleted and "society" alone is enough.

In Article 29.1 of the UDHR-1948, one reads the United Nations' declaration about one's duties to the community (in which alone the free and full development of his personality is possible) and the following clause (Article 29.2 UDHR-1948) confines only to the exercise of one's rights and freedoms. Why do the United Nations ignore the duties as well when limitations to the exercise of one's rights and freedom are declared? Is it not better to express: "In the exercise of his rights, freedoms and in the performance of his duties, everyone shall be subject to such limitations . . ."

"As are determined by law"—What does it mean? The laws are many, namely, the moral laws, the social laws, the cultural laws, the national laws, the international laws, etc. The very same Article 29.2 tells about the requirements of morality. Does it mean that the *laws* contemplated by the United Nations refer and relate to the moral laws?—or by the national laws?—by the international laws?—by the social laws?—by the cultural laws? Anyway, clarity is required. If I am to give my considered view, I may clearly specify the "national laws" along with equity and good conscience and will say :

". . . such limitations as are determined by the national laws, equity and good conscience . . ." Why do I say "national laws?" Every country makes its own laws and the Constitution of every country gives some fundamental rights for enjoyment by its citizens. The fundamental rights, so given, will be, as a rule, human rights friendly as well. Precisely, therefore, they will go in tune with the international law. Hence, my suggestion of "national laws" in the Article 29.2 of UDHR-1948 is found to be necessary. It is superb to add equity and good conscience to national laws.

"Solely for the purpose of securing the recognition and respect for the rights and freedom of others . . ." This is fine. Nevertheless, every nation will have to impose limitations which are not otherwise against the recognition and respect of the rights and freedoms of others. Such limitations may be in the areas of keeping the interests of sovereignty and integrity of the nation, the security of the state, friendly relations with foreign state, decency or in relation to contempt of court, defamation or incitement to an offence etc. Hence, I propose to delete "solely" from the Article 29.1 of UDHR-1948 to read : ". . . for the purpose of securing the recognition and respect for the human rights of others and meeting the just requirements of the interests of the sovereignty and integrity of the nations, the security of the states, friendly relations with foreign states, morality, public order, decency and the general welfare of the society, or in relation to contempt of court, defamation or incitement to an offence".

Thus the amended Article will read–

> "In the exercise of one's rights, freedoms and in the performance of his duties, everyone shall be subject to such limitations as are determined by the national laws along

> with equity and good conscience for the purpose of securing the recognition and respect for human rights of others and in meeting the just requirements of the interests of the sovereignty and integrity of the nations, the security of the States, friendly relations with the foreign States, morality, public order, decency and the general welfare of the society or in relation to contempt of court, defamation or incitement to an offence."

Article 29.2 and Criminal Justice

"Securing the recognition and respect for the rights and freedoms of others and meeting the just requirements of morality, public order and the general welfare in a democratic society"–this part of the Article creates a lot of problems. How? What is the meaning of the expression: "the just requirements of morality." There may be nothing called a universal morality and is there something called "the personal morality?" Objectivism and subjectivism in morality have been topic of discussion from time immemorial and the discussion is going on without reaching any consensus. The United Nations do not say what is morality, instead the Article makes a sweeping expression "the requirements of morality." I quote from the Evangelium vitae: "Whatever is opposed to life itself such as any type of murder, genocide, abortion, euthanasia or wilful self-destruction; whatever violates the integrity of human person such as mutilation, torments inflicted on body or mind, attempts to coerce the will itself; whatever insults human dignity such as sub-human living conditions, arbitrary imprisonment, deportation, slavery, prostitution, the selling of women and children, as well as disgraceful working conditions, where people are treated as mere instruments of gain rather than as free and responsible persons." It continues "All these things and others like them are infamies indeed. They poison human society, and they do more harm to those who practice them than to those who suffer from the injury. Moreover, they are a supreme dishonour to the Creator". Do the United Nations agree with the view of Pope John Paul II of the Catholic Church when they say the just *requirements* of morality? If they do not agree with it or have a different view, then what do they really say or declare in the Article? What is seen today? There exist licensed prostitutes in many parts of the world. Tender flesh trade, sex work, mobile prostitution, rent-a girl-system, five star brothels, pornography, blue films, sex-albums, obscene literature, crime-prone movies, perverted mass-media, gang culture, *nexus* transactions, organised criminality, Cosa Nostra, Mafia, mob, combination, crime syndicates, white collar criminality, terrorism, insurgency, murder of the innocent, enforcement crimes, corruption, bureaucratic hoarding of files, fake technicians, quack doctors, spurious drugs, NOC/Visa rackets, con-tricks, pipe-money, charity and religious frauds, false employment bureaus, paper organisations, revolving-chair enterprises, loan-sharking and *Blade* investments, *attimary* and other forms of coercions by unscrupulous people, political crimes, economic offences, alcoholism, goondaism and banditry, etc., are posing great threats to the morality of the society. Drugs kill the society and cause great havoc to the health of the people. Laws, laws and many laws are to be enacted to do justice to the people in society. Many nations do not enact laws and precisely, therefore, there exists a lot of human rights violations.

What is public order? Public order crimes are plenty and, more often than not, the politicians who rule the country or the politicians of the opposition create public order crimes. The police are made sterile to initiate action against the violators of public order. Many of the politicians have their followers and *goondas* with them. *Leaders* with a prefix "labour", "student", *religious*, *political* enjoy immunity from liability for the criminal acts which they commit during a public disorder situation. Cases registered against the political, communal, student, labour, etc. leaders are withdrawn by the governments themselves when a settlement is reached. This is injustice and an atrocious violation of the people's rights. The politicians who are otherwise known as the "gods on earth" encash on the strength of their followers/adherents of political party or they fish in troubled water. In both cases, the politicians are the winners or gainers. What does the expression "the just requirements of public order" mean? The public order in society is the political/ politician's will". If they are O.K., then most of the things are O.K. There may be other public order issues too.

What does the expression the general welfare in a democratic society mean? The term "general welfare" mentioned in the Article means the welfare of the public. The public are the people who vote in favour or against a government in power and not a faceless mass. General welfare means the welfare in relation to food, water, housing, clothing, health, transport, communication, peaceful coexistence, freedom, religious and communal harmony, racial tolerance and what not? A lot of injustice is going on and in the name of the general public many things are plundered by the so-called democratic leaders. It is here the injustice is committed. There is a school of thought which argues that the worst democracy is always better than the best bureaucracy, autocracy or military rule. Let them maintain their considered view on democracy. There is another school of thought and it believes that in autocracy or in a rule by a single king/emperor, there will be only one to live on the people, but in a democracy there are one thousand leaders–small, medium and high—to plunder the people. They commit dacoity and flourish in society. Like mosquitoes, they drink blood even on the udder of the cow. And the udder of the cow has pure milk. These 'mosquito-politicians' are more dangerous than the selfish autocrats. Let them too maintain their view. Between the two views, there will be the general public whose welfare must be taken into account by the human rights activists. Everyone has the human rights, but the enjoyment of the human rights is subject to some limitations. The limitations are such that they are determined by the laws. The laws may be social, cultural, moral, personal, religious over and above the laws enacted by the state. All laws need not necessarily be for the purpose of securing the recognition and respect for the rights and freedoms of others. For example, the social laws were sometimes human rights unfriendly just like the cultural laws have been. The caste system and untouchability in India were examples in point. Even today, I find untouchability or caste system even among the one time untouchables with respect to marriages and interactions. Certainly, the evils of casteism and untouchability prevail among the *one time high* and low castes. Whatever that be, the state laws should be to secure the rights and freedoms for all alike. Injustice is very intense in many areas of human transactions, but must be reduced to the minimum/ to zero point by the enactment of the state. Laws for the protection of human rights by imposing limitations, if that is required. Securing the recognition and respect for the rights and freedoms of others is of paramount importance in imposing limitations. Today, in a democracy, the allegation is that the law, however good it may be, is enforced against the enforceable. There are many people in a democracy and they are above the enforcement of law. No law can be enforced against them as they are above the laws. These greater "mortals" violate human rights and the general public are really afraid to tell them what the young, innocent child uttered: "The King is naked." In a democracy, there are people who are below the enforcement of laws. They are prepared to go to jails and suffer the sufferings. The law is helpless and the law enforcement officials too are helpless. They are like the members of *suicide squad* and they are prepared to die at any time. The law cannot deter them. They consider that greater injustice is done to them when the law is enforced; if not they become victims of injustice only. The Article, it seems to me, has not taken into account these and many other injustice done to people when the law is enforced, when the limitations are decided, when the rights and freedoms are exercised.

52

Exercise or Omission to Exercise Human Rights Violating the Purposes and Principles of United Nations

> "These rights and freedoms may in no case be exercised contrary to the purposes and principles of the United Nations"
>
> [*Article 29.3 of UDHR-1948*]

"In no case be exercised." —what does it mean? It means that the Universal Declaration of Human Rights-1948 speaks only about the positive actions, i.e., exercising. "Omissions to exercise" too is to be taken into account. Therefore, I propose—

"These rights may, in no case, be exercised or be omitted to be exercised contrary to the purposes and principles of the United Nations." The question is: "If one exercises or omits to exercise the rights contrary to the purposes and principles of the United Nations, will his act be considered as human rights?" No. why? If some act is to be considered as human rights friendly, then it must be in tune with the purposes and principles of the United Nations. If the act is in violation of the purposes and principles of the United Nations, then it becomes no longer a human right. Or, the United Nations cannot think of some human rights which can be exercised violating the purposes and principles of the United Nations. If there are any such human rights, then what are they? As such, human rights become human rights only if and if only they satisfy the purposes and principles of the United Nations. No one can exercise the right without respecting or honouring the purposes and principles of the United Nations. If any one exercises the rights violating the purposes or principles of the United Nations he may be exercising some "rights" which may not/cannot be the human rights. They may be other rights.

"Contrary to" means "opposite in nature or character; diametrically or mutually opposed, opposite in direction or position" etc. (The Random House College Dictionary). I may add (1) violating the purposes and principles of the United Nations; (2) diluting the purposes and principles of the United Nations; (3) deviating from the purposes and principles of the United Nations to 'contrary to'. Why? The reasons are :

(a) "Violating" means "to break, infringe or transgress (a law, agreement, etc.). It needs not be contrary to the purposes or principles of the United Nations.
(b) "Diluting" means to reduce the strength, force or efficiency of by admixture. This too needs not be contrary to the purposes or principles of the United Nations.
(c) "Deviate" means (1) to turn aside, as from a route, way or course; (2) to depart or swerve, as from a course of action or acceptable norm; (3) to disgress, etc.

Putting everything together, the new Article should be :

> "These rights and freedoms may in no case be exercised or be omitted to be exercised contrary to violating, diluting or deviating from the purposes and principles of the United Nations".

Article 29.3 and Criminal Justice

United Nations—it is a human organisation. It has many purposes and principles. Nevertheless, there is no infallibility for them. Infallibility means "exempt from liability to error." In other words, it means "immune from fallacy or error". The principles and purposes of United Nations need to undergo periodical changes—need to be amended from time to time when necessity arises—need to be updated. League of Nations with all the sublime and lofty purposes and principles perished in due course and thus the

United Nations came into existence. United Nations and their principles, policies and strategies become, sometimes, matters of dispute and discussion in the media. People talk in favour of or against the world organisation and the Universal Declaration of Human Rights (1948) remains as it is for more than 60 long years and the Article declares that "the rights and freedoms, may in no case, be exercised contrary to the purposes and principles of United Nations." This seems to be a difficult proposition so long as the principles and purposes do not undergo revisions. Whatever is accepted as lofty and sublime in 1948 when the Universal Declaration of Human Right was accepted need not necessarily be so during 2012 (presently) and afterwards. One of the basic truths is that the laws are dynamic and the purposes get changed as and when time passes. Take for example the principles and purposes behind the following, namely–

1. Universal Declaration of Human Rights (1948).
2. U.N. Bluebook for law enforcement officials.
3. Basic principles on the use of force and firearms by law enforcement officials (Eighth U.N. Congress on the Prevention of Crime and the Treatment of Offenders, Havana, 27th, August to 7th, September, 1990. U.N. Document A/ CONF. 144/28/ Rev.1 at 112 (1990).
4. Declaration of Basic Principles of Justice for Victims of Crime and Abuse of Power (G.A. 40/34, annex, 40 U.N. GAOR Supp. (No. 53) at 214, U.N. Doc. A/40/53 (1985).
5. Convention Against Torture and Other Cruel, Inhuman or Degrading Treatment or Punishment (G.A. res. 39/46, annex, 39 U.N. GAOR Supp. (No. 51) at 197, U.N. Doc. A/ 39/51 (1984).
6. Principles on the Effective Prevention and Investigation of Extra-legal, Arbitrary and Summary Executions (E.S.G. Res. 1989/65, annex, 1989 U.N. ESCOR Supp. (No. 1) at 52, U.N. Doc. E/1989/89 (1989).
7. Declaration on the Protection of All Persons from Enforced Disappearances (G.A. res. 47/133, 47 U.N. GAOR Supp. (No. 49) at 207, U.N. Doc. A/47/49 (1992). Adopted by the General Assembly Resolution 47/133 of 18, December, 1992.)

8. Body of Principles for the Protection of All Persons Under Any Form of Detention or Imprisonment (G.A. Res. 43/ 173, annex, 43 U.N. GAOR Supp. (No. 49) at 298, U.N. Doc. A/43/49 (1988).
9. Convention concerning the Prohibition and Immediate Action for the Elimination of the Worst Forms of Child Labour (ILO No. 182, 38 ILM 1207) (1999), entered into force on November 19, 2000).
10. International Covenant on Economic, Social and Cultural Rights (G.A. res. 2200 A (XXI) 21 U.N. GAOR Supp. (No. 16) at 49, U.N. Doc. A/6316 (1966), 1993 U.N.T. S.3)
11. International Covenant on Civil and Political Rights (G.A. Res. 2200 A (XXI), 21 U.N. GAOR Supp. (No. 16) at 52, U.N. Doc. A/6316 (1966), 999 U.N.T.S. 171).
12. Standard Minimum Rules for the Treatment of Prisoners (Adopted August 30, 1955 by the First United Nations Congress on the Prevention of Crime and Treatment offenders.)

Thus, the United Nations have many documents adopted, accepted, enacted from time to time and they are based on certain principles and purposes of the United Nations as they are approved then. Take, for example, the Standard Minimum Rules for the Treatment of Prisoners. Prisoners are no longer called prisoners by the international community. They are human beings sent to an institution for personality development for the purpose of correction, reformation, reintegration, resocialisation, rehabilitation, etc. The principle behind personality development is indeed divine and sublime. To call them prisoners still (They are prisoners in reality) is of bad taste as the purpose behind their imprisonment becomes nothing but a punishment of imprisonment or better imprisonment as punishment/for punishment. From Elmira movement (1878) the entire philosophy and outlook of imprisonment were changed into a positive outlook and approach so much so that the prisoners are no more called or labelled as prisoners. In or with all human dignity, they are called "the inmates of a Center for Personality Development" or "the residents of a Center for Personality Development". Hence, whatever may be the principle and purpose of United Nations to call the inmates of a Center for Personality Development "prisoners", I may emphatically say that the purpose has now become obsolete.

The Elmira Reformatory was established in 1878 and the reformatory ideas were gradually gaining acceptance everywhere in America and Europe. In India, the Elmira movement had its impact in the maiden legislation, i.e., the Prisons Act of 1894. I can understand the use of the expression prisons in 1894, but cannot understand the principles and purposes of naming the incarcerated as PRISONERS by the United Nations during 1955 when the Standard Minimum Rules were adopted and during 2012 when people all over the world look at the expression as human rights unfriendly in every sense. Precisely, therefore, the Article (29.3, UDHR-1948) cannot be accepted as it is. Accepting it as it is will be an injustice done to the inmates of a Center for Personality Development. The terms used by the United Nations should not condemn the inmates, should not put them down, should not be human rights unfriendly. That is the reason why I suggested a lot of changes in the Article.

53

Destruction or Dilution of Human Rights

> "Nothing in this Declaration may be interpreted as implying for any state, group or person any right to engage in any activity or to perform any act aimed at the destruction of any of the rights and freedoms set forth herein."
>
> [*Article 30 of UDHR-1948*]

"May be interpreted"—the expression is unnecessary. It is enough to say: "Nothing in this Declaration implies for any state, group or person . . ." Instead of "implies", I prefer to say "confers" to read: "Nothing in this Declaration confers to any state, group or person any right . . ." Why? If interpretation is good and strong, can a state, group or person enjoy the right to engage in any activity or to perform any act . . . ? "The Article 30 must be categoric and not based on some interpretations given by an individual, state or group with self-interests. No interpretation is final. Interpretation, counter-interpretation, further interpretation, etc., are possible in many cases and who is there to say that this interpretation is better than the other?—this interpretation is the correct one? History shows that interpretations have gone wrong or interpretations have no authority and, therefore, the Article must be written with clarity and certainty.

Why does the Declaration limit the operation of the Article 30 to only "engage in any activity or to perform any act". Human rights can be violated by "omissions" as well. Both commissions and omissions to engage in any activity or to perform any act should be taken into account. Accordingly, the Article 30, UDHR-1948 may be rewritten as :

> "Nothing in this Declaration confers to any state, group or person any right to engage in any activity, to perform any act, or omit to engage in any activity, to perform any act or to make any attempts or abetment to such commissions and/or omissions aimed at the destruction or diluting of any rights set forth herein."

In the amended Article, I have introduced attempts and abetments too. Why? I consider attempts and abetments as bad as engaging in any activity or performing any act or omitting to engage in any activity or to perform any act. I have noticed that the states, groups or persons making attempts and abetments—directly or indirectly—towards destruction or dilution of the human rights set forth in the Universal Declaration of Human Rights.

Article 30 and Criminal Justice

Destruction of the rights is a problem. Dilution of the right is another problem. For example, right to speedy trial in a criminal case may be a fundamental or human right. Nowhere, it is seen to have said something about how much is the delay to be called a human right violation. There was a situation of a person detained in judicial custody to remain there without trial for more than 7 years. Was it a delay? Some say that it is an undue delay while some others say that it is not. What exactly is the position? Hence, whenever an Article says something, it is necessary to say what exactly does the Article mean by it. For, dilution of the spirit of the Article is quite possible. Delay—undue delay—no delay: they mean a lot and anything can be said about each one of them at the will and pleasure of the one who interprets the law. Yes, the law is what the interpreter says or better is what the judge says.

What is victim justice? The law says that the victim should be compensated. But how? And who should compensate? In India, the law is that the victim may be compensated and the judge fixes the compensation. The amount is to be realised from the convicted. Normally the convicted do not pay the compensation and the victims of crime do not get it. Then the questions are: (1) Why should the compensation to be fixed for the convicted to ignore it? (2) How should the compensation be paid and (3) Who should pay the compensation. There will be dilution of the principles and spirit everywhere so much so that ultimately the compensation will not be paid by anyone or will not be received by anyone. The whole mountain was in labour and what came out was a little, ridiculous mouse—this is what happens now. It is an injustice done to the victim/s in every sense of the word.

Everybody is entitled to have a pollution-free environment. The environment is so polluted that everyone lives under unhealthy conditions. The governments are not concerned or if at all concerned, they do not do everything to make a pollution-free environment. They do something here and there and say that everything is done in perfect order. If somebody goes to a court of law, the courts do not take a decision speedily. Everything takes its own time and the court procedure is as per law and procedure established by law. Naturally, it is time consuming and by the time the verdict comes, the people in the affected area would have become victims of pollution. What to do? Whom to complain? How to go about? All these are dilutions or what not?

When one goes through the Articles in the Universal Declaration of Human Rights, I notice *dilutions* and *dilutions* everywhere by everybody. And, all of them say happily that All Is Well That Ends Well ! *Deo gratias* and a relief everywhere. Article 1 in the Universal Declaration of Human Rights is diluted as much as the other Articles in the same Declaration are diluted. They are diluted by the same people who are bound to protect them. And they say in one voice that everything is fine and GOOD NIGHT !

54

More Human Rights

When Adam and Eve violated God's commandments and eat the fruits of the forbidden tree in the Old Testament, the Almighty asked them: "have you been eating of the tree I forbade you to eat"?

The man replied: "It was the woman you put with me; she gave me the fruit, and I ate it". Then Yahweh God asked the woman: "What is this you have done"? The woman replied: "The serpent tempted me and I ate". Thus, the opportunity to explain one's position and give his version before the punishment is awarded is provided to anyone alleged to have violated a law—here the God's commandment—is seen from the creation of man. This is known as the Principle of Natural Justice. But the Universal Declaration of Human Rights does not speak specifically anything about man's right to Natural Justice which has been enjoyed by him from his creation. Hence, the new Article 46.

Article 46

> "Everyone has the right to have natural justice in all decisions taken in favour or against him by competent authorities or tribunals."

Why? I have seen that in many administrative and even in quasi-judicial decisions, the principles of natural justice are violated. Authorities who have little or no information about the principles of natural justice take decisions even in semi-judicial cases or quasi-judicial matters. Hence, the eligibility, suitability and competency of the authorities/tribunals must be ensured. For, it is a human right.

Again, in the beginning of creation, God said: 'let the earth produce vegetation: seed-bearing plants and fruit trees bearing fruit with their seed inside, on the earth". And so it was. The earth produced vegetation; plants bearing seeds in their several kinds, and trees bearing fruits with their inside their several kinds. God saw that it was good" (Gen: 1:11-13, *Old Testament*). All these vegetations were created before the creation of man. After the creation of man, God said: "See, I give you all the seed-bearing plants that are upon the whole earth, and all the trees with seed-bearing fruits; this shall be your food". Thus, the man got the right to have the full enjoyment of the environment with vegetation. He is not supposed to destroy it, but protect it so that he can have his food. It is seen that the environment is not protected although the protection of the environment is a human right. Hence, the Article.

Article: 47: (1), (2), (3)

(1) "Everyone has the right to have the environment protected against unreasonable and unjustifiable destruction.
(2) Everyone has the right to have the environment protected against pollution of all kinds.
(3) Everyone has the right to have healthy air, water, atmosphere, and pollution-free surroundings."

Man can be the masters of the fish of the sea, the birds of heaven, the cattle, all the wild beasts, and all the reptiles that crawl upon the earth (Gen-1 : 24-25, *Old Testament*). At the same time, he cannot be their destroyer or annihilator. Everyone has a right to have these fishes, cattle, wild beasts, birds, reptiles protected against unreasonable and unjustifiable destruction. Protection of them means the protection of their abode, environment and surroundings. Hence, the Article 48.

> "Everyone has the right to have the fishes, cattle, birds, wild animals, reptiles, insects and other living beings protected against unreasonable and unjustifiable destruction. Their protection includes the protection of their abode, environment and surroundings, by human activities and pollution."

The purpose of quoting from the *Old Testament* is just to show that these rights have been the rights of the people from the beginning of their creation. Similar or same rights have been given in other ancient books, mystical writings, intuitive visions, divine revelations and religious teachings and holy scriptures of all religions. And they show that their violation is not to be allowed.

I think that administration of criminal justice was a major concern of the United Nations when the Universal Declaration of Human Rights-1948 was accepted. But, in Indian mystical thinkings and in *Bhagvad Gita,* principles of victim justice could be seen. According to *Rig Veda* V, 85, 7, "if we have sinned against the man who loves us, have ever wronged friend or comrade, have ever done an injury to a neighbour whoever dwelt with us or even to a stranger, O Lord ! Free us from the guilt of this trespass." What does it mean? How can the Lord free people from the guilt of the trespass? Just a prayer cannot and will not free a person from the trespass. He has to compensate the loss sustained by his victim. The victimiser cannot become free from the guilt. Restitution and victim compensation—these concepts are as old as *Rig Veda.* A right accepted, honoured and respected from the Vedic period ought to have been there in the UDHR-1948 itself. Hence, the Article 49 :

> "Everyone, as a victim, has the right for restitution or compensation decided or fixed by a competent authority or tribunal and realisable by national laws. The victims include the victims of abuse of power, misuse of authority and all those who have become victims of miscarriage of justice from the courts of law/tribunals."

Why is it necessary to say "victims of miscarriage of justice from the courts of law/tribunals"? The reasons are many and various. Some of them are :

A number of people convicted by the courts and incarcerated to prison are found to be innocent. A conviction from a trial court becomes an acquittal from the appeal court. At the other end, there is a victim suffering the decisions of various courts which take decisions on the same facts in issue. Whatever that be, there are instances of wounded justice, less justice and injustice administration from the courts of law. Surprisingly enough, the courts of law which take decisions 'this way or that way' seem to have no accountability for the miscarriage of justice they commit. It is presumed that everything is fine in Rome when the facts are otherwise different. The victims should have their damages compensated.

In Bhagavad Gita, 1, 40 and 42, it is said: "In the destruction of family, immemorial family traditions perish; in the perishing of traditions, lawlessness overcomes the whole family. . . this confusion draggeth to hell the slayers of the family and the family". Human rights to protect the family is an honoured right ever since man and woman started to live together. But, today, this right is violated by many forces and pressures. Hence, every threat to family life and domestic harmony must necessarily be felt by the United Nations and must be declared in UDHR-Poverty, hunger, endemic diseases, violence, media, new values, divorces, desertions, new threats are emerging on an alarmingly unbelievable scale. Hence, whoever or whatever is opposed to a family life with harmony, peace, love and sharing; whatever or whoever violates the integrity of family life or insults the dignity of family life, treats the members of the family as mere instruments of self-interest, utility and gain, etc., all these and others like them are infamies and violations of human rights. Hence, the Article 50 :

Article : 50 :

> (1) "Everyone has the right to protect his family from the threats of destruction, disorganisation, divorces, desertions, domestic violence, subhuman living conditions, inhuman treatments, media invasions or any others like them."

Domestic justice is a concept widely recognised today. As the family is the basic and fundamental units of the society, as said earlier, the right to domestic justice is a human right. Hence, Article 50(2) :

> "Everyone has a right to domestic justice protected by law. This includes the right to live together peacefully and from domestic violence as well as the right to judicial separation and in deserving cases to divorce."

Justice has many dimensions today and gender justice is one

among them. Both genders—male and female—should get what is due to each one of them keeping the dignity of human sex and the person in the individual. Gender is cultural while sex is biological. It has been observed that the dignity of sex is not properly honoured. For example, in some countries and situations men are kept in nakedness or half nakedness in the custodial facility while women are given necessary clothings to cover their nakedness. In the Holy scripture, it is written about Adam and Eve that "So they sewed fig-leaves together to make themselves loin-cloths." Both sexes have gender dignity. Hence, the Article: Article 51(1) and (2)

Article 51(1 & 2) :

(1) Everyone has the right to have gender justice, due to each sex culturally honoured.
(2) Everyone has the right to have sex-identity biologically decided and is entitled to have special facilities and special needs due to the sex meted out.

What is equal justice? Is the right to claim equal justice a human right? People ask this justice to the criminal, to the victim, to the victim of abuse of power/misuse of authority, to the society and to the justice system itself. Everyone knows that they are the human rights in a criminal justice system and in a victim justice system. Justice to the society in an Equal Justice System means the justice to the tax-payers. In other words, does the output from the justice system satisfy the tax-payers who invest millions of rupees/dollars to sustain the system? If the output is negative or zero or below zero, then the system offers only miscarriage of justice. Precisely, therefore, the human rights of the people to live in dignity is violated.

Justice to the Justice System? What is this concept under an Equal Justice System? The justice system consists of the police (investigating sub-system), prosecutors (prosecuting sub-system), defence (the sub-system that pleads either guilty or not guilty and thereby defending the accused), the court (the sub-system that adjudicates), the public and media (the subsystems that aids the administration of justice), the institutions for personality development (the sub-system that corrects, reforms and rehabilitates the convicted crime-doers) including after-care services. Every sub-system is expected to perform its duties and fulfil its obligations in the best way possible for realisation of its objectives in a human rights friendly way. Every individual in the society has a right to expect and demand such services under an equal justice system. As such he is entitled to go for public litigations, approach the State and National Human Rights Commissions, make media demands, etc., for public interest. Today organisations including NGOs do so. I, for one, feel that such a right ought to be enjoyed by every individual as he is a part of the society. He must enjoy it as his human right. Hence, the Article 52 :

Article 52

> "Everyone has the right to claim equal justice under law. He is entitled to go for public litigations, to approach any tribunals, etc., for actualisation and protection of rights of the public subject to the condition that everything is done *bona fide* for public interest."

Today, there are countries where accusatorial system is in vogue. There are countries where inquisitorial system is in existence. Both are prejudiced against either to the prosecution (accusatorial)/accused (inquisitorial) or in favour of the accused (accusatorial)/prosecution (inquisitorial). As such, there is an allegation that the approach is not with a clean slate. The mindset is defective and it is the human rights of every individual to claim or demand for an approach with a 'Tabula Rasa" for administration of justice. Otherwise, miscarriage of justice will be resulted. In order to overcome this defect, there are people who want a "Noquisitorial system" with its procedures and evidence laws. Hence the Article 53.

Article 53

> Everyone has the right to get justice under a noquisitorial system of justice.

The immediate question that follows is "what is this noquisitorial system of justice?" According to me, the noquisitorial system of justice is one in which the presumption formed will be "either or". In other words, the system presumes—

(1) The accused is either guilty or innocent. The burden of proof is on his shoulders.
(2) The prosecution is either true or false. The burden of proof is on the shoulders of the prosecution.

In such a system of justice, there is no prejudice, bias or presumption either *in favour* or *against* anyone before a court of law. The greatest disadvantage of the accusatorial system is that a good many of the accused leave the court without being punished. The acquittal rate goes up and correspondingly, the conviction rate comes down. This is nothing but miscarriage of justice. In order to avoid such demerits, the 'Noquisitorial system of Justice' is considered as the human rights of people who seeks justice.

Terrorism, insurgency and terror causing "isms" rule many nations and resultingly, the innocent people are injured, killed, maimed for life, etc. They create public order crimes and disturb the mental peace of the society in general and innocent individuals in particular. Today one sees governments sponsored terrorism as well as countries sponsored terrorism. Many suffer as a consequence. Insurgency is another problem. Terror causing 'isms' are expressed and exhibited by *goondas*, mafias, liquor lobbies, organised criminals, drug traffickers, tender flesh-traders, politicians of ill-repute, 50-named *religious men*, loan sharks, etc. It is the human rights of people to get protection from these bandits. Hence, the Article.

Articles 54: (1) and (2)

(1) Everyone has the right to protection from terrorism, insurgency and terror-causing 'isms', communal, racial, ethnic riots and atrocities.
(2) Every victim of terrorism, insurgency, terror causing 'isms', communal, racial, ethnic riots and atrocities has the right to get victim-compensation decided by a competent tribunal.

Today, some countries give some *petty compensations* in a ritualistic way. That is not enough. The compensation must be fixed on merit by a competent tribunal in a judicious way or manner.

There are countries which administer justice on the basis of centuries old penal, procedural and evidence laws. They were enacted at a time when the concept of human rights was not known to many. Hence, it is the right of the people to enact laws afresh so that the miscarriage of justice or the injustice administered by the old, dilapidated and museum piece legislations of the foregone days do not rule them. Hence, the Article 55.

Article 55

> "Everyone has the right to get new legislations timely enacted to get proper and fair justice to the best interest of the accused and to the national and international community."

The legislations should take into account the best interests by incorporating the new ideas found out from research studies.

Right to information is and should be made a fundamental and basic right of the people. There is excessive secrecy and clandestine ways of administration. Right to information is a human right recognised and respected from time immemorial. Again, go to Genesis (3:1-4) of the *Old Testament*. Immediately after the creation of man, the narration goes as under :

"The serpent was the most subtle of all the wild beasts that Yahweh God had made. It asked the woman, did God really say you were not to eat from any of the trees in the garden?" The woman answered the serpent. "We may eat the fruit of the trees in the garden". But of the fruit of the tree in the middle of the garden, God said. "You must not eat it, nor touch it, under pain of death." The woman was not bound to answer the question the serpent asked. The serpent was not seek information from Eve about what God told her. Yet, the serpent sought answer to its question and Eve gave information. Hence, the right to information is accepted as a human right.

Article 56(1) and (2)

(1) "Except in those cases exempted by law, everyone has a right to information and the administration—legislative, executive

and judiciary—is bound to provide such information requested for in a speedier way within the time stipulated by law.

(2) Everyone has a right to get the official services within a stipulated time/fixed time by the national laws failing which the sufferer has a right for compensation.

> "This right extends to all who seek information for public interests."

What I have suggested above are my considered recommendations to be taken into account when a new UDHR is prepared by the international community. Such a right is a human right of the individuals. There is no meaning in dealing with people with legislations enacted in 1860, 1861, 1872 or 1960 or 2005 as it is done in the former British ruled colonies, territories or countries.

United Nations which enthusiastically brought the Universal Declaration of Human Rights, somehow or other, did not think about a Universal Declaration of Duties which ought to be the other side of the human rights. In my view, they should be put "side by side" and on the "other side" of the UDHR-1948. No one should enjoy a right without doing the duty. For example, one cannot claim human rights if he, himself, is not prepared to respect the human rights of others. Some people ask: "What human rights do the terrorists have when they, themselves, are not prepared to respect the human rights of others?" The same question is asked by policemen. "What human rights do the people have when they, themselves, are not prepared to respect the right to life of the policemen?" Yes, 600 policemen are attacked in a small State like Kerala in India. One observes State sponsored terrorism and human rights violations. After all, what or who constitutes the State? No doubt, some prominent people—a minority—in politics, administration or society–have many things to do and while doing something, they violate human rights. For example, in police human rights are violated by individual police officers who refuse to understand that their duty is to protect human rights and not to violate them. Hence, it is absolutely essential and inevitable to have the duties enumerated by the United Nations side by side to the rights accepted by them. Yes—everyone must endeavour to—

(1) Promote regional, national, international peace and security.
(2) Maintain just, fair and honourable relations between individuals, institutions, States and nations every time.
(3) Foster respect for regional, national and international laws on human rights and fundamental duties of men.

55

(The New) Universal Declaration of Human Rights

The Universal Declaration of Human Rights given below is drafted by me and it does not have any acceptance, recognition or approval by anyone including the United Nations. Nevertheless, I think that my research and revision of the existing Universal Declaration of Human Rights (1948) by the United Nations will be a help for anyone who thinks with me or like me. More than 60 long years from 1948 to this day (2011) is indeed a long period and most of those who drafted, finalised and approved the said Universal Declaration may be no more today to revise the Articles. The founding fathers of the Universal Declaration of Human Rights certainly have entrusted us to do the work, if needed. Many Constitutions which came into existence during the said point of time (1948) have made many amendments [for example, the Constitution of India (1950)] ever since their inception. But, similar revisions or amendments are not seen in the case of the Universal Declaration of Human Rights. Certainly, the Universal Declaration of Human Rights was an inevitable, necessary and absolutely essential need of the period. But today, their revisions/amendments have become the urgently warranted need of the hour. The international community cannot ignore or overlook their obligation and responsibility.

I have worked in a department for nearly long 30 years. I have seen protection of human rights, violation of human rights, promotion of human rights, annihilation of human rights, propagation of human rights and degrading of human rights, etc.

The interesting and the most unfortunate aspect is that one and the same people do all these things and I have noticed that many of them are not clear about the very concept of human rights. They read the existing Universal Declaration of Human Rights, but it seems to me that many do not understand clearly what the concepts really are. Yes, some Articles and some expressions in the Articles are not couched in clarity. I have taken it to be a challenge to make a total revision of all Articles in the existing Universal Declaration of Human Rights 1948 and thus this revised edition.

I have great pleasure to place the amended/revised version of the existing Universal Declaration of Human Rights 1948 for the discussions and deliberations by the international community.

(The New)

Universal Declaration of Human Rights

PREAMBLE

Whereas recognition of the inherent dignity and of equal and inalienable rights of all members of the human society is an absolute condition for establishing total and equal justice; visible acceptance and positive acting upon it are essential for ensuring human happiness, coexistence and social welfare in the world.

Whereas a failure or refusal to recognise and respect human rights or disregard shown to them are found to have been instrumental to result in human unhappiness, difficulties for harmonious coexistence and social welfare disabling the people to enjoy their rights to life, equality, liberty and dignity with freedom from fear and want which are proclaimed as very genuine and legitimate aspirations of the people of the world and humanity.

Whereas, it is essential if man is not to be compelled to have recourse, as an inevitable and necessary strategy, to rebellion against tyranny and oppression by a despotic ruler or by administrators under a ruler who has commitment to respect human rights, the human rights should be protected by the rule of law and justice.

Whereas it is essential to establish and/or promote positively human rights oriented and centred relations between nations.

Whereas the people of the United Nations have in the Charter reaffirmed their trust in human rights to life, liberty, equality and dignity; have determined to establish and promote human happiness, freedom and social welfare.

Whereas the Member-States have agreed themselves to achieve and actualise in cooperation with the United Nations the universalisation of the recognition, acceptance and promotion of respect for and observance of human rights.

Whereas a common and universal understanding and realisation of these rights are an absolutely necessary condition for the wholistic actualisation of this agreement.

Now, therefore, we, the people of the Member-States of the United Nations and territories thereunder have solemnly resolved to proclaim this new Universal Declaration of Human Rights as a necessary standard of achievement for all people and all nations to the end that every individual and every institution of the society keeping this Declaration constantly alive in mind shall strive positively and constructively by teaching and educating and acting upon to establish accept and promote respect for those rights and by progressive measures and strategies, national and international to secure and cement their universal and meaningfully effective recognition, observance and operating upon, both among the people of the Member-States themselves and among the peoples of the territories under their jurisdiction.

Article 1

All human beings are born equal in rights endowed with a potency to develop an upright conscience rightly formed and should act in toward one another in brotherhood.

[*Chapter 10*]

Article 2

Everyone has the right without distinction of any kind in status, either inherited or acquired as the case may be.

Provided that those who are involved in the commission of an offence will be entitled to enjoy only those rights sanctioned by the criminal laws which are human rights friendly.

Provided further that the infliction of death penalty is

considered to be human rights unfriendly as it violates the right to life.

No distinction shall be made on the basis of the political, jurisdictional or international status of the country or territory to which a person belongs, whether it be independent, trust, non-self-governing or under any other limitation of sovereignty.

[*Chapter 11*]

Article 3

Everyone has the right to life, liberty, equality and dignity.

[*Chapter 12*]

Article 4

No one shall be held in slavery and the slave trade shall be prohibited in all their forms.

[*Chapter 12*]

Article 5

No one shall be made a victim of organised crimes, crime syndicates, *mafia*, nexus criminality, enforcement crimes, terrorism, terror causing 'isms' and insurgency. They must be prohibited by laws and made punishable under the criminal laws.

[*Chapter 12*]

Article 6

(1) No one shall be subjected to torture—physical, mental or both.
(2) No one shall be subjected to cruel, inhumane or degrading treatment.

Provided that the criterion to decide the nature of cruel, inhumane or degrading treatment shall be the cultural/sub-cultural laws and majority views of the people put together.

[*Chapter 13*]

Article 7

(1) No one shall be subjected to a punishment which is not

intended for the personality development of the punished in nature and content.

(2) Every punishment shall have its ultimate objective to be personality development through correction, reformation, resocialisation, rehabilitation and reintegration of the crime-doers to society back.

[*Chapter 13*]

Article 8

(1) Everyone has the right to recognition everywhere as a person before law and has the duties which follow from the enjoyment of such rights.

(2) Every person entitled to have right shall—

(i) abide by human rights laws in letter and spirit;

(ii) recognise and respect the ideals enshrined in this Declaration, International Covenants and Conventions and national laws on human rights;

(iii) uphold and protect the human rights of all residing in any part of the world irrespective of any considerations;

(iv) defend the human rights of others wherever necessary and to protect their interest in the enjoyment of human rights;

(v) render service for the promotion of human rights when called upon or even otherwise;

(vi) promote human rights consciousness among the people so that they live in harmony and human co-existence;

(vii) maintain common brotherhood amongst all people of the world transcending religious, ethnic, linguistic, caste, sub-caste, regional, racial, sectional diversities;

(viii) renounce practices derogatory to the dignity of man, woman, children, the old and the infirm, the handicapped—socially, economically, politically and culturally;

(ix) value and preserve the rich heritage of world's pursuit to the enjoyment of human rights; and

(x) strive towards excellence in all spheres of human rights activities so that the peoples of the United Nations/world will rise to the highest levels of social progress, better living and enjoyment of larger freedom in letter and spirit.

[*Chapter 14*]

Everyone has the right to demand the performance of each one's duties stated above.

Article 9

(1) The laws are the same for all in theory and in practice.
(2) All are equal before the law and are ensured without discrimination and distinction to equal protection under the law.

[*Chapter 15*]

Article 10

(1) Everyone has the right to all effective remedies by the competent national tribunal for acts violating the human rights declared to be so by this Declaration and the laws applicable to the country to which he belongs.
(2) Everyone has the right for victimological compensation/ restitution through a competent tribunal for acts and omissions violating the human rights declared to be so by this Declaration or by other laws applicable to the country to which he belongs.
(3) Everyone has a right to set the law into motion for the punishment of the violators of human rights by a competent human rights court.

[*Chapter 16*]

Article 10

(1) No arrest or taking into custody shall be made but upon probable cause supported by evidence.
(2) No one shall be detained in a non-transparent, secret or clandestine way.
(3) The detainee has the right to be released on bail in all bailable offences without causing undue delay.
(4) No one shall be detained in custody without trial for a longer

period than the period of imprisonment prescribed under the law for the offence/s alleged to have been committed.

[*Chapter 17*]

Article 11

Everyone has a right for a public trial in fairness, equity and good conscience.

Provided that (1) in a trial for any offence against the womanhood or in cases related to terrorist/ insurgency activities, it may be done in-camera,

(2) The trial shall be conducted by an independent, impartial and competent tribunal,

In determination of his rights and obligations and of any criminal charge against him.

[*Chapter 18*]

Article 12

Everyone charged with an offence has the right to be considered and treated as 'either or' status until proved innocent or guilty, as the case may be, according to law and procedure established by law in a public trial in all cases except in those which are exempted from such a trial for in-camera at which he has all the rights necessary for his defence.

[*Chapter 19*]

Article 13

(1) No person shall be guilty of any offence for violation of the law—national or international—in force at the time of commission or omission of the act charged as an offence, nor be subjected to a penalty more severe than that which has been inflicted under the law in force at the time of the commission/omission of the act.

(2) No person shall be prosecuted and punished for the same offence more than once.

(3) No person charged with an offence shall be compelled to be a witness against himself.

[*Chapter 20*]

Article 14

Everyone has the right for protection against any interference by any method—electronic or otherwise—without probable cause supported by evidence to the privacy, family, home or correspondence, or to attacks upon one's honour, reputation, character, esteem, status, personality, individuality and good name he has.

[*Chapter 21*]

Article 15

Everyone has the right to freedom of movement and mobility (physical, vertical and lateral) and residence (owned, possessed, rented, mortgaged or leased out) within the borders of each state.

[*Chapter 22*]

Article 16

(1) Everyone has the right to a nationality and citizenship.
(2) Everyone has the right to voluntarily acquire the nationality and citizenship of another country, if he so desires.
(3) No person shall be either deprived of his nationality and/or citizenship or denied the right to acquire the same of another country except according to procedure established by law and on legal grounds supported by evidence.
(4) Everyone has the right to leave any country lawfully including his own and lawfully return to his country.

[*Chapter 23*]

Article 17

(1) Everyone who is not a minor as per law has the right for a monogamous marriage with a person of complementary sex and found a family just like everyone has the right not to marry and found a family.
(2) The husband and wife have equal rights as to marriage and during marriage.

[*Chapter 24*]

Article 18

Marriage shall be with the free will and full consent of the aspiring parties.

[*Chapter 25*]

Article 19

Family is the inevitable, necessary and fundamental group unit of society and it has the right to be protected by the State.

[*Chapter 26*]

Article 20

Everyone has the right to lawfully enjoy property as owner, mortgagee, lessee, possessor, licensee, etc. either alone or along with others.

[*Chapter 27*]

Article 21

No one shall be deprived of his property of all kinds and descriptions save by authority of law.

No property shall be compulsorily acquired or requisitioned save for a public purpose and save by authority of a law which provides for acquisition or requisitioning of the property for an amount or compensations which may be fixed by such law or which may be determined in accordance with principles and given in such manner as may be specified in such law.

[*Chapter 28*]

Article 22

(1) Everyone has the right to freedom to or not to accept, profess, teach, practise, promote, worship and in a lawful way propagate his religion;
(2) The above right includes freedom to change from one religion or faith to another as well as to remain irreligious or non-religious.
(3) Everyone has the right to freedom to manifest his religion

or faith in worship and observance either alone or in community with others in public or private or both taking due care and caution to maintain religious tolerance and harmony.

[*Chapter 29*]

Article 23

(1) Everyone has the right to freedom of opinion and expression subject to the condition that the said freedom should not be exercised in violation of any reasonable restrictions imposed by the national and international laws on the exercise of the right conferred by this Article in the interest of the sovereignty and integrity of the nation, the security of the state, friendly relations with foreign states, public order, decency, morality, public interest or in relation to contempt of court, defamation or incitement to an offence or in contravention of the principles of human rights of the people.

(2) This freedom stated above includes the right to hold opinion and to seek, receive, enrich and impart information and ideas through any media or otherwise and regardless of frontiers of any kind.

[*Chapter 30*]

Article 24

Everyone has the right to freedom of peaceful assembly, association and union for any objective which is not against the sovereignty and integrity of the state or which may affect adversely or likely to affect adversely the maintenance of public order or morality.

[*Chapter 31*]

Article 25

No one shall be compelled by inciting, persuading, provoking, exhorting or forcing to belong to an association, assembly or union.

No person who is not a willing member of such an association, assembly or union shall be necessitated to support, offer help, contribute, patronise or aid, etc., of the said association, assembly or union and their activities without his free will and full consent.

[*Chapter* 32]

Article 26

Everyone including those in an institution of personality development of a state has the right to vote and take part in the government of his country, directly or indirectly through freely elected representatives.

[*Chapter* 33]

Article 27

There shall be the right to equality of opportunity for all in matters relating to employment or appointment to any office under country.

No one shall, only on grounds of race, colour, sex, language, caste, political or other opinion, social or ethnic origin, property, birth, residence, decent or any of them be ineligible for or discriminated against in respect of any employment or office under the state. People belonging to the backward classes of citizens and who are not adequately represented in the services under the state have a right to reservation of appointments or posts in favour of them.

No one other than a person professing a particular religion, faith or belonging to a particular denomination has any right to claim appointments or post in connection with the affairs of any religious or denominational institutions or to become a member of the governing body thereof.

[*Chapter* 34]

Article 28

The will of the people shall be the basis and source of power for the authority of government. This will shall be exercised in periodic and genuine elections which shall be by universal and equal suffrage and shall be held by secret vote by ballot or by equivalent free voting procedure.

This will shall be exercised by expressing the right to call back the representative held by secret vote by ballot or other equivalent free voting procedure; this will shall also be exercised by casting one's vote to none in the ballot sheet or calling back the representative already elected.

[*Chapter 35*]

Article 29

Everyone, as a responsible member of the society, has a right to social security along with his sincerity to fulfil his obligations and duties for claiming the social security. He is entitled to realisation through national effort and international cooperation and in accordance with the organisation and resources of each state, of the economic, social and cultural rights indispensable for his dignity and the development of his personality in the right direction and with an upright conscience with acceptable values and morality.

[*Chapter 36*]

Article 30

Everyone has the right to work and an equal right not to work with its consequences, to free choice of employment, to just and favourable conditions of work decided by the national and international laws and protection against unemployment and underemployment.

[*Chapter 37*]

Article 31

(1) Everyone, without any discrimination, has the right to minimum wages for a work. The minimum wages will be fixed by the national laws and standards made from time to time.
(2) Everyone, without any discrimination, has the right to equal pay for equal work throughout the territory of a state.
(3) The convicted in any institution for personality

development have a right to get a pay equal to what is given for the same or similar type of work outside the institution.

[*Chapter 38*]

Article 32

(1) Everyone who works has the right to just and favourable remuneration fixed by the national laws respecting international standards. The remuneration so fixed for the work will be considered sufficient to ensure for himself and his family an existence worthy of human dignity.
(2) The just and favourable remuneration is applicable equally to all convicted inmates working in an institution for personality development.

[*Chapter 39*]

Article 33

(1) Everyone has the right to form and to join trade unions for the protection of his interest and for the promotion of harmony between himself and the management.
(2) The right shall be exercised for the mutual benefits of the employers and employees and for the development of the nation as a whole in an atmosphere ensuring cooperation and unity of purpose for betterment.
(3) The right to form and to join trade unions for the protection of one's interest shall be subject to reasonable restrictions imposed by law and shall not be against public interest and nation's development.

[*Chapter 40*]

Article 34

(1) Everyone has the right to rest and leisure for eight hours a day and the right shall be exercised depending upon the nature of the work and subject to reasonable restrictions.
(2) Everyone who works beyond eight hours has a right to get overtime pay or allowances.

[*Chapter 41*]

Article 35

Everyone has the right to a standard of living adequate for health, protection of human rights and the well-being of himself and of his family including, food, clothing, proper socialisation, housing and medical care and necessary social services and the right to security in the event of unemployment, sickness, disability, widowhood, old age, accident, natural calamities, attacks—military or otherwise, abuse of power, misuse of authority, terrorism, insurgency or other lack of livelihood in the circumstances beyond his control.

[*Chapter* 42]

Article 36

(1) Womanhood, virginity and motherhood are entitled to special care, assistance and protection.
(2) Infancy and childhood are entitled to have special care, protection and assistance.
(3) The old, the young old, the old old, the older old and the oldest old and their oldness are entitled to have special care, assistance and protection depending upon the nature and age of different categories of the aged.
(4) All children will enjoy the same care, social protection and assistance.

[*Chapter* 43]

Article 37

(1) Everyone has the right to education—academic, social, cultural and moral—in formal, informal or non-formal ways. Education on human rights and their utility, applicability and relevance ought to be compulsory and free at least in the elementary and fundamental stages.
(2) Education on human rights should be compulsory for teacher training courses—both induction and inservice—and they shall be included in the course contents of teacher-education programmes, training of police, prison and other law enforcement officials, degree/diploma

courses of universities, secondary and higher secondary courses, law colleges and judicial academies as well as in special training programmes organised for judicial functionaries by other institutions or agencies.

(3) Technical and professional education shall be generally available. Researches shall be promoted and the findings of researches shall be acted upon. Researches on human rights shall be encouraged in government departments, universities and other centres of education, training and higher learning.

(4) Higher education shall be equally accessible to all, on the basis of merits decided by entrance tests or other objectively valid assessment scales.

Provided that nothing stated above will prevent a member state from making any provision for the reservation of seats in educational institutions in favour of any classes of citizens which need special care and protection in the field of education.

[*Chapter* 44]

Article 38

Education shall be directed to the full development of human personality in the right direction with an upright conscience rightly formed and to the strengthening of respect for human rights and the person in the other. It shall establish and promote understanding, tolerance, harmonious human co-existence and genuine friendship among all nations, racial and religious groups and shall further the vision, commitment and activities of the United Nations for the establishment and maintenance of peace.

[*Chapter* 45]

Article 39

(1) Parents have a joint responsibility toward their children and a prior right to choose the kind of education that shall be given to their children.

(2) The children have a joint responsibility with their parents and a right to choose the kind of education that shall be received by them.

(3) The children have the right to change the kind of education they have chosen with their parents, if that is found necessary.

[*Chapter 46*]

Article 40

(1) Everyone has the right freely to participate in the dominant as well as in the special cultural life (which is not criminal or violative of the norms) of the society and the community to which he belongs.
(2) Everyone has the right freely to enjoy the arts, to enrich by its literature, to keep up the moral traditions, to follow the customs and to share in scientific advancement and its benefits.

[*Chapter 47*]

Article 41

Everyone has the right to the protection of the moral, intellectual, non-material and material interests and values resulting from any scientific, literary, artistic, intellectual and aesthetic production of which he is the author.

[*Chapter 48*]

Article 42

(1) Everyone has the duties to the community towards bringing up children in the right direction in a human rights friendly way with an upright conscience rightly formed.
(2) Everyone has the duties, obligations and responsibilities to the community/society in behaving in a human rights friendly manner so that the aspirations of the United Nations stated in the Preamble of this Declaration are actualised.

[*Chapter 49*]

Article 43

In the exercise of one's rights, freedoms and in the performance of his duties, everyone shall be subject to such limitations as are determined by the national laws along with equity and good conscience for the purpose of securing the recognition and respect for human rights of others and in meeting the just requirements of the interests of the sovereignty and integrity of the nations, the security of the States, friendly relations with the foreign States, morality, public order, decency and the general welfare of the society or in relation to contempt of court, defamation or incitement to an offence.

[*Chapter 51*]

Article 44

These rights and freedoms may in no case be exercised or be omitted to be exercised contrary to violating, diluting or deviating from the purpose and principles of the United Nations.

[*Chapter 52*]

Article 45

Nothing in this Declaration confers to any state, group or person any right to engage in any activity to perform any act or omit to engage in any activity, to perform any act or to make any attempts or abetment to such commissions and/or omissions aimed at the destruction or diluting of any rights set forth herein.

[*Chapter 53*]

Article 46

Everyone has the right to have natural justice in all decisions taken in favour or against him by competent authorities and tribunals.

[*Chapter 54*]

Article 47

(1) Everyone has the right to have the environment protected against unreasonable and unjustifiable destruction.
(2) Everyone has the right to have the environment protected against pollution of all kinds.

(3) Everyone has the right to have healthy air, water, atmosphere and pollution free surroundings.

[*Chapter 54*]

Article 48

(1) Everyone has the right to have fishes, cattle, birds, wild animals, reptiles, insects and other living beings protected against unreasonable and unjustifiable destruction.
(2) The protection includes the protection of their abode, environment and surroundings from being contaminated by human activities or polluted.

[*Chapter 54*]

Article 49

Everybody, as a victim, has the right for restitution or compensation decided or fixed by a competent authority or tribunal and realisable by national laws. The victims include the victims of abuse of power, misuse of authority and all those who have become the victims of miscarriage of justice from the courts of law/tribunals.

[*Chapter 54*]

Article 50

(1) "Everyone has the right to protect his family from threats of destruction, disorganisation, divorces, desertions, domestic violence, subhuman living conditions and inhuman atmosphere.
(2) Everyone has a right to domestic justice protected by law. This includes the right to live together peacefully and free from domestic violence as well as the right to judicial separation and in deserving cases to divorce.

[*Chapter 54*]

Article 51

(1) Everyone has the right to have everywhere gender justice due to each sex culturally honoured.
(2) Everyone has the right to have sex-identity biologically

decided and is entitled to have special facilities and special needs due to sex meted out.

[*Chapter 54*]

Article 52

Everyone has the right to claim equal justice under law. He is entitled to go for public litigations, to approach any tribunals for actualisation and protection of the rights of the public subject to the condition that everything is done *bona fide* for public interest.

[*Chapter 54*]

Article 53

Everyone has the right to get justice under a noquisitorial system of justice.

[Chapter 54]

Article 54

(1) Everyone has the right to protection from terrorism, insurgency and terror-causing 'isms', communal, racial, ethnic riots and atrocities.
(2) Every victim of terrorism, insurgency, terror-causing 'isms', communal, racial, ethnic riots and atrocities has the right to get victim-compensation decided by a competent tribunal.

[*Chapter 54*]

Article 55

Everyone has the right to get new legislations timely enacted to get proper and fair justice to the best interest of the accused and to the national and international community.

[*Chapter 54*]

Article 56

(1) Except in those cases exempted by law, everyone has a right to information and the administration—legislative,

> executive and judicial—is bound to provide such information requested for in a speedier way within the time stipulated by law.

This right extends to all who seek information, in good faith, for public interest.

[*Chapter* 54]

(2) Everyone has a right to get the official services within a stipulated time/fixed time by the national laws failing which the sufferer has a right for compensation

The laws are dynamic and likewise, the human rights laws ought to be dynamic. Being a criminologist, I may even go to the extent of saying that the *man has a right to misbehave in certain situations* and the misbehaviour should be taken as a normal behaviour and the expression of a human right. When many people starve, a group of people enjoy life in 5 star or 7 star hotels. I could see such hard and thought provoking situations. Though I will not say that *it is the right of the poor man to misbehave,* yet I may say that the wealth of the world is for all human beings and everyone has an equal right to enjoy it. Some people are exploited by some others who are powerful and affluent. Hence, should we make "Right to be protected against exploitation" a human right? The richer becomes richer by exploitation and the poor becomes poorer by suffering or becoming victims of exploitation. The ignorant, the weak, the handicapped, the poor, the disabled, the tribals and so on are exploited. There should be an end to such exploitations. The right to be protected from exploitation, therefore, must be a human right.

Transparency and accountability may be lacking in administration. People, therefore, are kept in darkness. There may not be transparency. The "birth" in a millionaire's house and the "death" in a hut are not known. The "birth" means illegitimate birth and "death" means a natural death. Why? Many things happening at the higher or highest levels of administration are not transparent to the ordinary man on the street. Should we not declare that the right to transparency is a human right?—i.e., everyone has a right to have an administration transparent to all". The non-transparent, clandestine, secretive administration is suspicious and an insult to human dignity.

Accountability in administration is lacking today and I may say that everybody is accountable to what he does. This is the basic theory on which the entire human rights justice rests. If so, people have a human right to have accountability in administration. The legislators, the executives, the judicial functionaries ought to be accountable to the ordinary people who are the tax-payers. Hence, why not we think of right to accountability a human right?—i.e., everyone has the right to demand accountability from administration—legislative, executive and judicial. Accountability to the people is a guarantee against maladministration, misuse of authority, abuse of power, administration of wounded justice, less justice, injustice or miscarriage of justice. Though *accountability* is getting more and more acceptance and recognition as a human right, the administration seems to have an unfavourable attitude towards such an approach. They want to enjoy power and authority without any accountability. Hindu Mysticism, inspired writings, biblical teachings, Islamic beliefs, ancient literature, antique culture and civilisation, etc., did accept and recognise accountability as sacred or sacrosanct. It is essential now to make it a human right in the new Universal Declaration of Human Rights by the United Nations.

To wind up, in my view, it is high time that the United Nations think about a Universal Declaration of Human Duties. For, duties are as important as rights. What is seen today is that people who are very conscious about their rights are not so conscious about their duties. The rights and duties to be written on the same side of the coin although some people say that they should be inscribed on both sides of the coin. In my view, the rights and duties must be written side by side so that one who becomes aware about his rights will become equally aware of his duties as well.

APPENDIX

The Universal Declaration of Human Rights

PREAMBLE

Whereas recognition of the inherent dignity and of equal and inalienable right of all members of the human family is the foundation of freedom, justice and peace in the world.

Whereas disregard and contempt for human rights have resulted in barbarous acts which have outraged the conscience of mankind, and the advent of a world in which human beings shall enjoy freedom of speech and belief and freedom from fear and want has been proclaimed as the highest aspiration of the common people.

Whereas it is essential, if man is not to be compelled to have recourse, as a last resort, to rebellion against tyranny and oppression, the human rights should be protected by the rule of law.

Whereas it is essential to promote the development of friendly relations between nations.

Whereas the peoples of the United Nations have in the charter reaffirmed their faith in fundamental human rights, in the dignity and worth of the human person and in the equal rights of men and women and have determined to promote social progress and better standards of life in larger freedom.

Whereas Member-States have pledged themselves to achieve, in cooperation with the United Nations, the promotion of universal respect for and observance of human rights and fundamental freedoms:

Whereas a common understanding of these rights and freedoms is of the greatest importance for the full realization of this pledge.

Now therefore,

The General Assembly

Proclaims this Universal Declaration of Human Rights as a common standard of achievement for all peoples and all nations, to the end that every individual and every organ of society, keeping this Declaration constantly in mind, shall strive by teaching and education to promote respect for these rights and freedoms and by progressive measures, national and international, to secure their universal and effective recognition and observance, both among the people of Member-States themselves and among the Peoples of territories under their jurisdiction.

Article 1 : All human beings are born free and equal in dignity and rights. They are endowed with reason and conscience and should act in towards one another in a spirit of brotherhood.

Article 2 : Everyone is entitled to all the rights and freedoms set forth in this Declaration, without distinction of any kind, such as race, colour, sex, language, religion, political or other opinion, national or social origin, property, birth or other status. Furthermore, no distinction shall be made on the basis of the political, jurisdictional for international status of the country or territory to which a person belongs, whether it be independent, trust, non self-governing or under any other limitation of sovereignty.

Article 3 : Everyone has the right to life, liberty and the security of person.

Article 4 : No one shall be held in slavery or servitude; slavery and the slave trade shall be prohibited in all their forms.

Article 5 : No one shall be subjected to torture or to cruel, inhuman or degrading treatment or punishment.

Article 6 : Everyone has the right to recognition everywhere as a person before the law.

Article 7 : All are equal before the law and are entitled without any discrimination to equal protection of the law. All are entitled to equal protection against any discrimination in violation of this Declaration and against any incitement to such discrimination.

Article 8 : Everyone has the right to an effective remedy by competent national tribunals for acts violating the fundamental rights granted to him by the Constitution or by law.

Article 9 : No one shall be subjected to arbitrary arrest, detention or exile.

Article 10 : Everyone is entitled in full equality to a fair and public hearing by an independent and impartial tribunal, in the determination of his rights and obligations and of any criminal charge against him.

Article 11 : (1) Everyone charged with a penal offence has the right to be presumed innocent until proved guilty according to law in a public trial at which he has had all the guarantees necessary for his defence.

(2) No one shall be held guilty of an penal offence on account of any act or omission which do not constitute a penal offence, under national or international law, at the time when it was committed. Nor shall a heavier penalty be imposed than the one was applicable at the time the penal offence was committed.

Article 12 : No one shall be subjected to arbitrary interference with his privacy, family, home or correspondence nor to attacks upon his honour and reputation. Everyone has the right to the protection of the law against such interference or attacks.

Article 13 : (1) Everyone has the right to freedom of movement and residence within the borders of each state.

(2) Everyone has the right to leave any country including his own and return to his country.

Article 14 : (1) Everyone has the right to seek and to enjoy in other countries asylum and protection.

(2) This right may not be invoked in the case of prosecutions genuinely arising from non- political crimes or from acts contrary to the purposes and principles of the United Nations.

Article 15 : (1) Everyone has the right to a nationality.

(2) No one shall be arbitrarily deprived of his nationality nor denied the right to change his nationality.

Article 16 : (1) Men and women of full age, without any limitation due to race, nationality or religion, have the right to marry and to found a family. They are entitled to equal rights as to marriage, during marriage and at its dissolution.

(2) Marriage shall be entered into only with the free and full consent of the intending spouses.

Article 17 : Everyone has the right to own property alone as well as in association with others. No one shall be arbitrarily deprived of his property.

Article 18 : Everyone has the right to freedom of thought conscience and religion; this right includes freedom to change his with others and in public or private, to manifest his religion or belief in teaching, practice, worship and observance.

Article 19 : Everyone has the right to freedom of opinion and expression; this right includes freedom to hold opinions without interference and to seek, receive and impart information and ideas through any media and regardless of frontiers.

Article 20 : (1) Everyone has the right to freedom of peaceful assembly and association.

(2) No one may be compelled to belong to an association.

Article 21 : (1) Everyone has the right to take part in the government of his country directly or through freely chosen representatives.

(2) Everyone has the right of equal access to public service in his country.

(3) The will of the people shall be the basis of the authority of government; this will shall be expressed in periodic and genuine elections which shall be by universal and equal suffrage and shall be held by secret vote or by equivalent free voting procedures.

Article 22 : Everyone, as a member of society, has the right to social security and is entitled to realisation, through national effort and international co-operation and in accordance with the organisation and resources of each state, of the economic, social and cultural rights indispensable for his dignity and the free development of his personality.

Article 23 : (1) Everyone has the right to work, to free choice of employment, to just and favourable conditions of work and to protection against unemployment.

(2) Everyone, without any discrimination, has the right to equal pay for equal work.

(3) Everyone who works has the rights to just and favourable remuneration ensuring for himself and his family an existence worthy of human dignity and supplemented, if necessary, by other means of social protection.

(4) Everyone has the right to form and to join trade unions for the protection of his interests.

Article 24 : Everyone has the right to rest and leisure, including reasonable limitation of working hours and periodic holidays with pay.

Article 25 : (1) Everyone has the right to a standard of living adequate for the health and well-being of himself and of his family, including food, clothing, housing and medical care and necessary social services, and the right to security in the event of unemployment, sickness, disability, widowhood, old age or other lack of livelihood in circumstances beyond his control.

(2) Motherhood and childhood are entitled to special care and assistance. All children whether born in or out of wedlock, shall enjoy the same social protection.

Article 26 : (1) Everyone has the right to education. Education shall be free, at least in the elementary and fundamental stages. Elementary education shall be compulsory. Technical and professional education shall be made generally available and higher education shall be equally accessible to all on the basis of merit.

(2) Education shall be directed to the full development of the human personality and to the strengthening of respect for human rights and fundamental freedoms. It shall promote understanding, tolerance and friendship among all nations, racial or religious groups and shall further the activities of the United Nations for the maintenance of peace.

(3) Parents have a prior right to choose the kind of education that shall be given to their children.

Article 27 : (1) Everyone has the right freely to participate in the cultural life of the community, to enjoy the arts and to share in scientific advancement and its benefits.

(2) Everyone has the right to the protection of the moral and material interests result from any scientific, literary or artistic production of which he is the author.

Article 28 : Everyone is entitled to a social and international order in which the rights and freedoms set forth in this Declaration can be fully realised.

Article 29 :

(1) Everyone has duties to the community in which alone the free and full development of his personality is possible.

(2) In the exercise of his rights and freedoms, everyone shall be subject only to such limitations as are determined by law solely for the purpose of securing the recognition and respect for the rights and freedoms of others and meeting the just requirements of morality, public order and the general welfare in a democratic society.

(3) These rights and freedoms may in no case be exercised contrary to the purposes and principles of the United Nations.

Article 30 : Nothing in this Declaration may be interpreted as implying for any state, group or person any right to engage in any activity or to perform any act aimed at the destruction of any of the rights and freedoms set forth herein.

BIBLIOGRAPHY

Authoritative and authentic books authored by Dr. James Vadackumchery

Acquittals in Administration of Justice, Ph.D. Thesis, Kerala University, (mimeo), Thiruvananthapuram, 1983.

Activism, Accountability and Justice (ISBN: 81-7341-4324-X), Indian Publishers' Distributors, Delhi, 2004.

Arkansayile Kuruvikal (Akasaparavakalude Kuttavicharana) [Malayalam], H & C. Publishing House, Thrissur, 2012.

Bankers' Safety: Methods and Techniques, (ISBN: 81-7022-937-5), (Second edition), Concept Publishing Company, Delhi, 2002.

Child Labour (Malayalam), State Literacy Mission, Thiruvananthapuram, 2000.

Crime and Society: Current Issues and Trends, (ISBN: 81-7648-024-X), A.P.H. Publishing Corporation, Delhi, 1999.

Crime, Law and Police Science, (ISBN: 81-7022-995-2), (Second edition), Concept Publishing Company, Delhi, 2003.

Crime, Police and Correction, (ISBN: 81-7024-939-2), A.P.H. Publishing Corporation, Delhi, 1998.

Criminology and Penology, Kairali Books International, Trivandrum, 1983.

Departmental Inquiries and Injustice, (ISBN: 81-7024-899-X), A.P.H. Publishing Corporation, Delhi, 1997.

Goodbye Police: Memoirs of a Criminologist, (ISBN: 81-7341-390-8), Indian Publishers' Distributors, Delhi, 2005.

Human Behaviour and Law Enforcement, (ISBN: 81-7024-688-1), Ashish Publishing House, Delhi, 1995.

Human Relations in Banking: How to get along better with people?, Santha Publishing House, Cochin, 1988.

Human Rights and the Police in India, (ISBN: 81-7024-722-5), A.P.H. Publishing Corporation, Delhi, 1996.

Human Rights Friendly Police: A Myth or Reality?, (ISBN: 81-7648-150-5), A.P.H. Publishing Corporation, Delhi, 2000.

Human Values and Police Behaviour, Bureau of Police Research and Development, Ministry of Home Affairs, Government of India, 2000.

India's Supreme Court and Police: Consensus and Conflicts, (ISBN: 81-7341-301-0), Indian Publishers' Distributors, Delhi, 2003.

Indian Police 2001: What Went Wrong Here? (ISBN: 81-7024-967-8), A.P.H. Publishing Corporation, Delhi, 1998.

Indian Police and Equal Justice Under Law, (ISBN: 81-7648-066-5), A.P.H. Publishing Corporation, Delhi, 1999.

Indian Police and Miscarriage of Justice, (ISBN: 81-7024-792-6), A.P.H. Publishing Corporation, Delhi, 1997.

Indian Police and Nexus Crime, (ISBN: 81-7835-037-8), Kalpaz Publications, Delhi, 2002.

Judiciary and Juvenile Justice, (ISBN: 81-7341-389-4), Indian Publishers' Distributors, Delhi, 2005.

Juvenile Delinquency (Malayalam), State Literacy Mission, Thiruvananthapuram, 2000.

Kuttakrithyangalude Kanapurangal [Malayalam], H & C. Publishing House, Thrissur, 2009.

Management Thoughts on Police Administration, (ISBN: 81-7024-914-7), A.P.H. Publishing Corporation, Delhi, 1998.

Management Thoughts on Justice Administration, Logos Press, Delhi, 2012 (in press)

Mavelinattile Kazhukanmar (Savamtheeni Kalkkethireyulla Kuttapathram) [Malayalam], D.C. Books, Kottayam, 2012 (in press)

Misguiding Philosophies and Millennium Police, (ISBN: 81-7341-278-2), Indian Publishers' Distributors, Delhi, 2003.

National Police Commission: Issues for Rethinking, (ISBN: 81-7024-826-4), A.P.H. Publishing Corporation, Delhi, 1998.

Police and Human Rights,(ed.), Kerala Police Officers' Association, Thiruvananthapuram, 1994.

Police and the People (Translation of the title: Public Relations at the Cutting Edge Level: Case Study materials by Prof. C.K.

Muhammed Ummer), The State Institute of Language, Kerala, Thiruvananthapuram, 2000.

Police and the Society, Kairali Books International, Trivandrum, 1985.

Police Criminology and Crimes, (ISBN: 81-7835-094-7) Kalpaz Publications, Delhi, 2002.

Police Enforcement Crimes and Injustice, (ISBN: 81-212-0471-5), Gyan Publishing House, Delhi, 2001.

Police Interrogation: DOs which the Police do not do, (ISBN: 81-7024-974-0), A.P.H. Publishing Corporation, Delhi, 1998.

Police Leadership: The Inside Story, (ISBN: 81-7648-120-3), A.P.H. Publishing Corporation, Delhi, 1999.

Police Morality, (ISBN: 81-7835-038-6), Kalpaz Publications, Delhi, 2001.

Police, Victim and Victim Justice, (ISBN: 81-7479-043-8), Kaveri Books. Delhi, 2001.

Police, Women and Gender Justice, (ISBN: 81-7648-137-8), A.P.H. Publishing Corporation, Delhi, 2000.

Policing the Largest Democracy: 50 Years and After, (ISBN: 81-7024-979-1), A.P.H. Publishing Corporation, Delhi, 1998.

Policing the Police: A Nation's Cry, (ISBN:81-7479-060-81), Kaveri Books, Delhi, 2003.

Professional Police Witness Interviewing, (ISBN: 81-7648-061-4), A.P.H. Publishing Corporation, Delhi, 1999.

Public Relations at the Cutting Edge Level: Case Study Materials, National, Delhi, 1985.

Road Users' Guide (Malayalam), Assistant Motor Vehicle Inspectors' Association, Ernakulam, 1997.

Sahiyadrithazhvarayile Baliyadukal, (Kuttakrithyangalkku lrayavunna-varude Dhenarodhanam) [Malayalam], D.C. Books, Kottayam, 2012 (in press)

Society, Police and Crimes: Tasks and Challenges, (ISBN: 81-7341-266-0), Indian Publishers' Distributors, Delhi, 2002.

Sociology of Policing India: 2000 and Beyond, (ISBN: 81-7341-279-0), Indian Publishers' Distributors, Delhi, 2003.

The Complete Reference Methodology of Research in Criminology Law Justice and Correction (Vol. I), *(ISBN: 81-7341-414-8),* Indian Publishers' Distributors, Delhi, 2007.

The Complete Reference Methodology of Research in Criminology Law Justice and Correction (Vol. II), (ISBN: 81-7341-448-0), Indian Publishers' Distributors, Delhi, 2010.

The Complete Reference Methodology of Research in Criminology Law Justice and Correction (Vol. III), (ISBN: 81-7341-449-7), Indian Publishers' Distributors, Delhi, 2010.

The Justice Less Administered, (ISBN: 81-7341-380-0), Indian Publishers' Distributors, Delhi, 2005.

The Police and Delinquency in India, (ISBN: 81-7024-725-X), A.P.H. Publishing Corporation, Delhi, 1996.

The Police, The Accused and Criminal Injustice, (ISBN: 91-7024-806-X), A.P.H. Publishing Corporation, Delhi, 1997.

The Police, the Court and Injustice, (ISBN: 81-7024-806-X), A.P.H. Publishing Corporation, Delhi, 1997.

The Police, The People and Criminal Justice, (ISBN: 81-7024-862-9), A.P.H. Publishing Corporation, Delhi, 1999.

The Unseen Phases of Crimes, (Malayalam), (ISBN: 81-909360-1-8), H&C Publishing House, Trissur, 2009.

Third Millennium Police: Take off Trends in India, (ISBN: 81-7648-062-2), A.P.H. Publishing Corporation, Delhi, 1999.

United Nations and Indian Mysticism: Parallels on Human Rights and Police, (ISBN: 81-7022-664-2), Concept Publishing Company, Delhi, 2002.

Values and God's Commandments, (Malayalam) Catechetical Centre, Thalassery, 1995.

Vishafambukalude Vasathi (Ezhaganthukkal Viharikkunna Keralam) [Malayalam], D.C. Books, Kottayam (in press), 2012.

Why I Am Not A Policeman, (ISBN: 81-7479-042-X), Kaveri Books, Delhi, 2001.

Wounded Justice and the Story of Indian Police, (ISBN: 81-7479-045-4), Kaveri Books, Delhi, 2001.

Index